Information Systems Research in Vietnam

Nguyen Hoang Thuan · Duy Dang-Pham ·
Hoanh-Su Le · Tuan Q. Phan
Editors

Information Systems Research in Vietnam

A Shared Vision and New Frontiers

Editors
Nguyen Hoang Thuan ⓘ
School of Business and Management
RMIT Vietnam
Ho Chi Minh, Vietnam

Duy Dang-Pham ⓘ
School of Business and Management
RMIT Vietnam
Ho Chi Minh, Vietnam

Hoanh-Su Le
Faculty of Information Systems
University of Economics and Law
Vietnam National University Ho Chi
Minh City
Ho Chi Minh, Vietnam

Tuan Q. Phan
Business School
University of Hong Kong
Hong Kong, Hong Kong

ISBN 978-981-19-3806-1   ISBN 978-981-19-3804-7 (eBook)
https://doi.org/10.1007/978-981-19-3804-7

This Springer imprint is published by the registered company Springer Nature Singapore Pte Ltd.
The registered company address is: 152 Beach Road, #21-01/04 Gateway East, Singapore 189721,
Singapore

Preface

The rise of Vietnam's economy and the digital world in recent years has increased interest in information systems within the country. Yet, there was little literature and information on the Vietnamese context. Practitioners and researchers needed to refer to outside sources and adapt and apply them to the country's social–economic environment, ecosystem, and culture. There was a lack of systematic, centralized, and definitive source of peer-reviewed, quality, and curated research on information systems to provide guidance on the application of technology and digitization in Vietnam.

As a result, the aim of this book was to create a Vietnam-oriented body of research on information systems to meet the needs of managers, researchers, and policy-makers to make a positive impact on Vietnam. The book aims to highlight not only successful cases, but also factors which are relevant to Vietnam, advance theoretical contributions, and provide insights.

To encourage diversity and collaboration, the editorial team consists of academics and researchers from RMIT Vietnam, University of Economics and Law (UEL), and The University of Hong Kong. The book received 22 submissions with authors from Vietnam, Japan, Ireland, Finland, Australia, and Canada across a variety of topics including COVID-19 readiness and adoption, blockchains, education, consumer behavior, digitization, and start-up ecosystems. While the methodologies heavily leaned toward quantitative research using surveys, there are plenty of opportunities to conduct empirical and applied research using machine learning approach and design science research.

The editorial team recruited expert reviewers within Vietnam as well as expert academics and researchers from Hong Kong, Singapore, China, Japan, the Republic of Korea, Italy, and Sri Lanka. The international panel of reviewers was satisfied with the quality of the submissions and recommended some for publication. The authors also worked hard to revise the papers and took constructive feedback to improve the manuscripts. Overall, the review process produced positive outcomes to improve the quality of research which merits publication.

In addition to the book, the Vietnamese academic community has recently formed the Vietnam Association of Information Systems (VAIS) to support academic research, organize conferences and events, and create a collaborative research community. Through conferences, invited overseas researchers, and editors, VAIS and this book can act in conjunction to encourage quality research on information systems with a Vietnamese orientation. VAIS has generously supported this book through their time, commitment, and network. In going forward, VAIS hopes to continue support of the book and other forms of publications to support quality research and publish impactful projects. Based on the success of this first book, there are plans for a second book and possibly an annual publication.

While this book has turned out exceeding our expectations, there are also opportunities to increase the quality of research. While the current methodology has been dominated by survey and qualitative research methods, researchers can adapt more modern methodologies including empirical and economic approaches including the use of econometrics and causal inference on high-quality primary historical datasets through collaborations with companies. Econometrics can also be used on publicly available datasets to analyze the causal impact of policies. Secondly, there are also opportunities to collaborate with industry partners to conduct field experiments and randomized controlled trials (RCT) to better isolate causal factors. For example, an RCT conducted on an educational digital platform can test psychological and causal mechanisms on students' learning to guide policies. Third, Vietnam information systems communities can benefit from design science research to create machine learning and artificial intelligence methods which have a Vietnamese orientation. For example, how can deep learning be adapted for natural language processing (NLP) on Vietnamese text? How can this be used for different business outcomes? Can image analysis on Vietnamese social media be used for better marketing and targeting, identify Vietnamese food dishes, and find local fashion trends? Can optical character recognition (OCR) be used to recognize Vietnamese handwritten medical notes from doctors which can save lives, increase efficiency, and build resilience in the healthcare system? While the information systems literature discusses use of big data and artificial intelligence, Vietnam researchers can take the lead by innovating on methodologies, demonstrating its applications, and quantifying its impact.

Overall, this book has shown a tremendous potential in the Vietnam information systems research community. Readers can sample a wide variety of topics related to the Vietnam context. This book can have a wide appeal for other researchers to find inspiration for new research, policy-makers can use it to guide decisions, managers and practitioners can find the chapters to guide strategy, and students can learn how to do research in the Vietnam context. I hope you will find the book useful and interesting.

Ho Chi Minh, Vietnam   Nguyen Hoang Thuan
Ho Chi Minh, Vietnam   Duy Dang-Pham
Ho Chi Minh, Vietnam   Hoanh-Su Le
Hong Kong   Tuan Q. Phan

Editorial Review Board

Contents

About the Editors

Nguyen Hoang Thuan is Senior Lecturer and Senior Program Manager for the digital business program in the School of Business and Management. He has been Research Committee Member. Before joining RMIT University in Vietnam, he worked as Head of Software Engineering Department (Faculty of Information Technology) and Deputy Head of Department of Scientific Affairs at Can Tho University of Technology, Vietnam. He has a Ph.D. in Information systems from Victoria University of Wellington, New Zealand. He has published +30 papers, including journal articles in *Communications of the Association for Information Systems, Information Systems Frontiers, Australasian Journal of Information Systems, Group Decision and Negotiation, Journal of Retailing and Consumer Services, The International Review of Retail, Distribution and Consumer Research, Scandinavian Journal of Information Systems*, and several international refereed conferences, such as the Pacific Asia Conference on Information Systems, Australasian Conference on Information Systems, and other international conferences. He can be contacted via Thuan. NguyenHoang@rmit.edu.vn

Duy Dang-Pham is Senior Lecturer of Business Innovation and HDR Coordinator in the School of Business and Management (SBM), RMIT Vietnam. Prior to joining SBM, he was Lecturer of IT and Senior Program Manager (IT and Software Engineering) in the School of Science, Engineering and Technology (SSET). In 2016, he received the RMIT Prize for Research Impact (Enterprise), which recognized his active engagement with the industry through conducting impactful research. Since 2018, he has received various research and teaching awards from RMIT University, including the "Living RMIT's Values" award in 2021 which recognized his contributions to growing the programs while maintaining excellence in research and teaching. His teaching and research focus on information security management, technology management, digital transformation, and applied analytics for business and learning. He has more than 40 publications, including chapters and research articles in highly ranked journals and international conference proceedings.

Hoanh-Su Le is Lecturer and Dean of School of Information Systems of University of Economics and Law, Vietnam National University Ho Chi Minh City. He is Associate Editor of the *Journal of Information Processing Systems* and in editor committee of several international journals in E-commerce and Information Systems. He is Co-organizer of several international conferences such as SCECR 2017, MITA 2019, and ICSME 2020 and Co-founder of Vietnam Chapter of the Association of Information Systems (AIS Vietnam). He received the Bachelor of Engineering, M.Sc. in Management Information Systems, and MBA degrees from Vietnam National University Ho Chi Minh City, and Ph.D. degree in Management Information Systems from Pukyong National University, South Korea. He has experience as Senior Engineer, Project Team Leader at Global CyberSoft, and R&D Director at Apax Leaders of E-Group. His research interests are in the areas of data analytics, big data, and artificial intelligence. He can be contacted via sulh@uel.edu.vn

Tuan Q. Phan is Associate Professor at the University of Hong Kong (HKU), Faculty of Business and Economics, and director of the Representative Office of HKU in Vietnam. His research uses large and population-size datasets and spans multiple disciplines including economics, marketing, consumer behavior, computer science, and statistics. His expertise covers various industries including FinTech, retail and e-commerce, logistics and transportation, social media, news and video media, technology and consumer products, and education. His research has been published in leading scientific and management journals including the *Proceedings of the National Academy of Science* (PNAS), *Marketing Science, Journal of Marketing Research* (JMR), *and Information Systems Research* (ISR). He was previously tenured at the National University of Singapore (NUS) in the Department of Information Systems and Analytics (School of Computing), and the Department of Analytics and Operations (Business School). He received his doctorate from Harvard Business School and an undergraduate from MIT. He is also Entrepreneur and frequently consults industry leaders.

Introduction to Information Systems Research in Vietnam: A Shared Vision

Nguyen Hoang Thuan, Duy Dang-Pham, Hoanh-Su Le,
Prasanta Bhattacharya, and Tuan Q. Phan

Abstract Information Systems (IS) have been widely applied in Vietnam, and the IS advent has received much attention from Vietnamese practitioners and researchers. However, a shared account of IS knowledge in Vietnam is still lacking. Addressing this gap, we need a shared understanding of what we know and what we are doing, which can help coordinate our future actions. This introductory chapter sets a background for this shared understanding by reviewing the main themes of IS research in Vietnam. The chapter then updates the progress of the field by introducing nine current IS studies that are based in Vietnam. As a result, it contributes a contemporary reference and outlines future research directions for IS research in Vietnam.

Keywords Introduction · Information systems · Literature review · Vietnam

1 Introduction

Information Systems (IS) has received much attention over the years from Vietnamese practitioners and researchers. Since the early times, Vietnamese researchers

N. H. Thuan (✉) · D. Dang-Pham
School of Business and Management, RMIT University, Ho Chi Minh City, Vietnam
e-mail: Thuan.NguyenHoang@rmit.edu.vn

D. Dang-Pham
e-mail: duy.dangphamthien@rmit.edu.vn

H.-S. Le
University of Economics and Law, Ho Chi Minh City, Vietnam
e-mail: sulh@uel.edu.vn

Vietnam National University, Ho Chi Minh City, Vietnam

P. Bhattacharya
Institute of High Performance Computing (IHPC), A*STAR, Singapore, Singapore
e-mail: prasanta_bhattacharya@ihpc.a-star.edu.sg

T. Q. Phan
The University of Hong Kong, Pok Fu Lam, Hong Kong
e-mail: tphan@hku.hk

© The Author(s), under exclusive license to Springer Nature Singapore Pte Ltd. 2023
N. H. Thuan et al. (eds.), *Information Systems Research in Vietnam*,
https://doi.org/10.1007/978-981-19-3804-7_1

1

have studied diverse IS topics, including user acceptance model, ontology, information processes, informatics, and system analysis [1, 2]. Recently, the IS field in Vietnam has continued to progress in diverse and emerging research topics, including artificial intelligence, learning analytics, collective intelligence [3, 4]. Aligning to this progress, the Vietnam Association for Information Systems (VAIS) has recently been launched,[1] offering more opportunities for Vietnamese researchers to collaborate, research and promote their work. All of these indicate the key role of IS research in Vietnam.

The IS development in Vietnam can also be seen from a practical perspective where multiple Vietnamese companies have made significant advances in the development and adoption of information systems to support their business success. For instance, most banks in Vietnam have achieved digital transformation [5]. The uptake of IS innovations by Vietnamese companies is also fast catching up with others in the region. For instance, AhaMove has successfully leveraged its mobile application to become the largest last-mile delivery provider in Vietnam [6]. Further, Vietnam has steadily emerged as a massive market for developing, applying, testing, and expanding different information system applications, including mobile payment, blockchain, and digital transformation [6, 7]. It is now more than ever that companies in Vietnam feel the need for further IS innovations, digitalization strategies, and guidance on value creation using IS applications.

While IS research and practice is an increasingly vibrant community in Vietnam, a shared account of IS knowledge in Vietnam is still lacking. As of this writing, we are not aware of any study or book that describes the structure of the IS field in Vietnam. We can only find a few studies that have analyzed Vietnamese research in general [8, 9], without an in-depth investigation of the IS field. Consequently, a comprehensive picture of the state of art in IS research is still missing.

Addressing this gap, the current chapter aims to develop a shared understanding of what we know and what we are doing, as part of the IS community in Vietnam. This shared understanding will provide us with a solid background for coordinating our future actions. As so, the chapter objectives are twofold. First, it sets a background for developing a shared understanding by reviewing the main themes of IS research in Vietnam. Second, it presents the current progress by introducing nine contributed chapters on current IS studies in Vietnam. The contributed chapters can be grouped into two categories: IS value creation, and IS in the time of Covid-19. As a result, it contributes a contemporary reference and outlines future outlook for the IS field in Vietnam.

The remainder of this chapter is structured as follows: Sect. 2 sets up the background of the IS research. Section 3 briefly reviews some key studies to illustrate the development of IS Research in Vietnam from 2011 to 2021. Section 4 introduces the nine chapters on new IS studies based in Vietnam. Finally, Sect. 5 provides some concluding remarks on future outlook and opportunities.

---

[1] https://vn-ais.org/.

2 Background

IS research studies the use of information technology (IT) within a socio-technical system that comprises individuals and organisations. The primary questions addressed by IS research include those that inquire how IS can affect and generate value in our personal lives, businesses, and societies. Given its broad focus and the fast-changing nature of technologies and social phenomena, IS research has been attracting important contributions from both scholars and practitioners in multiple disciplines, including computer science and engineering, behavioural and psychological sciences, management science, to name only a few.

First appeared in the 1960s, the field of IS research has made significant progress and achieved maturity as an applied discipline. According to the most recent statistics from the Association for Information Systems (AIS), more than 54,000 research papers have been published and archived in the eLibrary of AIS, which received close to a total of 10 million downloads. Within the IS community, there exists multiple leading conferences including the International Conference on Information Systems (ICIS), Americas Conference on Information Systems (AMCIS), Pacific Asia Conference on Information Systems (PACIS), and European Conference on Information Systems (ECIS). In terms of journals, notable venues include the Senior Scholars' Basket of Eight which comprises eight top tier journals in the IS field, namely: MIS Quarterly (MISQ), Information Systems Research (ISR), European Journal of Information Systems (EJIS), Information Systems Journal (ISJ), Information Systems Research, Journal of AIS (JAIS), Journal of Information Technology (JIT), Journal of MIS (JMIS), and Journal of Strategic Information Systems.

To understand the diversity of research topics within the IS field, studies have performed text mining on bibliographic data about IS publications. For instance, Jeyaraj and Zadeh [10] identified the following 13 prevalent topics from 2962 articles retrieved from the Basket of Eight journals: IS implementation, IT adoption, IS development, business value of IT, research methodology, e-commerce, social media, IS usage, online trust, IT capability, knowledge management, IT outsourcing, and IS security. Similarly, Dang-Pham and Kautz [11] analyzed 2528 publications that appeared in the Australasian Conferences on Information Systems (ACIS) between 1990 and 2016, from which they identified 84 topics that were categorized into the following 16 themes: IS management, mixed topics, IT, public IS, IS development, method and theory, IS security, other topics, education, IS process, e-commerce, healthcare, people and IS, data management, knowledge management, informatics, and sustainability.

By examining publication trends, Jeyaraj and Zadeh [10] found that topics such as business value of IT, IS security, IS usage, online trust, and social media had gained attention over the years, whereas the number of publications in the areas of e-commerce, IT adoption, knowledge management, IS implementation, and IS development had observed a downward trend. Indeed, as new data-driven technologies such as artificial intelligence and fintech become more popular and accessible to users, it is expected that IS research on the characteristics and usage of these technologies will likely attract greater interests. Likewise, research on other trending topics such as sustainable IS e.g., implementation of green IT, digital transformation, and social media will generate important implications as well.

As seen from the above studies, the IS discipline is dynamic and diverse by nature. At the local level, we expect to find a similar dynamic and diverse set of IS-related phenomena in Vietnam. To further understand this dynamic, the next section will review recent IS research in Vietnam.

3 An Overview of IS Research in Vietnam

This section aims to explore what we know about IS research in Vietnam. To do so, we conduct a brief review of recent IS studies that are based in Vietnam, and published between 2011 and 2021. Adopting a scoping literature review [12], the review process is elaborated below.

Literature search. In order to facilitate this review, we extracted research papers published in proceedings of leading IS conferences (e.g., ICIS, PACIS, AMCIS, ACIS etc.), leading AIS journals (e.g., MIS Quarterly, Journal of AIS) as well as related journals from INFORMS (e.g., Management Science, Organization Science etc.). We used a keyword search to identify papers with the terms "Vietnam" and "Information Systems" in either their title, subject, author affiliations, abstract or keywords. Our initial search gave us multiple papers across 33 journals and conferences.

Literature refinement. We filtered the papers to focus specifically on those that met the following inclusion criteria: (i) papers that specifically focus on the development or application of an IS in Vietnam, (ii) papers that specifically discuss an IS-relevant theme with an explicit reference to its application in Vietnam, and (iii) IS research on a broader topic but using Vietnamese companies or users as an empirical context. We did not include papers by Vietnamese authors on research topics that do not explicitly concern Vietnam-based companies or research themes critical to Vietnam. Similarly, we did not include papers that do not specifically focus on Vietnam, but include it as part of a large cross-country analysis. As a result, our final review dataset consisted of 39 papers (see Appendix).

Analyze of selected papers. We analyzed the selected papers based on their key themes, which provided us with an overview of the IS field in Vietnam. The analysis consisted of three steps. First, we extracted main themes and sub-themes relevant to IS research in Vietnam. Second, we synthesized duplicated themes, such as information security and security awareness. Third, we mapped the sub-themes into their main themes. In addition to analyzing themes, we also analyzed and synthesized the related theories and methods. The results of this analysis are presented next.

3.1 Main Themes of IS Research in Vietnam from the Reviewed Dataset

We now report the review results, starting with the most popular research themes. Our analyses show that IS research in Vietnam has focused on a number of critical organizational contexts, spanning traditional industry sectors (e.g., shipbuilding or supply chain) as well as emerging internet-enabled industries (e.g., cloud computing and e-commerce). The results identify six themes and 18 sub-themes, as extracted from the review dataset. Table 1 shows the main research (sub) themes of IS research in Vietnam.

As in clear from Table 1, IS and IT usage is the dominant theme in the reviewed papers. A growing number of studies have investigated the use of IS and IT in different contents in Vietnamese companies. In this theme, Enterprise system (ES) and enterprise architecture (EA) have received considerable attention [13, 14]. For instance, in their study, Trinh and Tran look at how customer agility is perceived by managers in Vietnam, and the relationship between enterprise systems and customer agility in ten organizations [14]. The authors found that while most organizations use some form of EA for customer data storage, very few effectively exploit it to improve customer agility. Recent studies have also investigated more emerging themes concerning mobile technologies, information security, cloud-computing

Table 1 Overview of reviewed studies (refer to appendix for the illustrative papers)

Theme	Sub-theme	Illustrative papers
IS and IT usage	Enterprise systems	[6, 7, 8, 38]
	Mobile technologies	[5, 28, 36]
	Information security	[9, 31]
	Cloud computing	[14, 37]
	Knowledge management	[18, 19]
	IS adoption	[6, 21]
	Business intelligence	[17]
	Dynamic capability	[11]
	Green IS	[20]
Supply chain	Supply chain management	[25]
IS outsourcing	Outsourcing in Vietnam	[34]
IS education	Knowledge resources, sharing & management	[33]
	Online learning	[1]
IS application in economics	Retail	[28]
	E-commerce	[5]
	Travel	[10]
	Microcredit	[14]
IS in health care	Health record digitalization	[32]

and software-as-a-service (SaaS) platforms, business intelligence and analytics, IS adoption, and green IT.

Given Vietnam's strategic location as a manufacturing hub, two other key themes are supply chain management and outsourcing. In a study on customer collaborative practices, the authors have tried to study the information exchange and collaborative patterns between a ship-building company and its customers, focusing particularly on the degree, context and nature of information exchange [15]. Similarly, a summary paper of a panel discussion on outsourcing in the Asia–Pacific region have highlighted the "importance of the Asia–Pacific region as an important contributor to the outsourcing world", and the challenges, opportunities and innovations that would be important to consider for outsourcing success in countries like Vietnam [16]. For a country like Vietnam, building successful and sustaining collaboration models with global partners is critical for not just logistics and trade, but also in promoting multi-country initiatives in areas like fintech and microcredit [17].

There have also been a number of studies looking at important questions in the fields of education and health. The ongoing disruptions to education systems in light of the Covid-19 pandemic, as well as increasing demands on our healthcare systems, have increased the need and criticality for research in this space. Studies on education in Vietnam have focused on creation of online teaching and learning frameworks to ensure seamless transition to online education during Covid-19 [18, 19]. Within healthcare, researchers have studied the design and development of a gamified system to improve treatment adherence as well as well-being for tuberculosis patients in Vietnam [20]. In other work, Phung et al. have developed a neural network-based approach to recognizing medical records written in Vietnamese handwriting [21].

3.2 Key Theories and Research Methodologies

In our review, we discover that researchers have leveraged a wide collection of individual-level and organizational-level theories. Regarding the former, a number of studies have used, adapted or extended IS adoption and success theories such as the Technology Acceptance Model [22], the IS Success Model and the Expectation-Confirmation Model [23]. Interestingly, we also find evidence for wide use of cognitive and behavioral theories, such as the classic Theory of Planned Behavior [24], Cognitive Evaluation Theory [20], as well as Bandura's Social Cognitive Theory [25], to name a few.

Regarding organizational-level theories, a number of reviewed studies have drawn on the resource-based view of firm to discuss the competitive advantage of developing IS/IT resources, and if these can be considered to be rare and inimitable for organizations [26]. Other studies have looked at organization-level adoption theories such as Diffusion of Innovation Theory and Technology-Organization-Environment Framework that look at the processes as well as the contextual factors affecting adoption of technological innovations within organizations [27]. A few studies have also used new institutional theories to study IS/IT adaptation, development and change [13].

In terms of methodology, the reviewed studies have adopted both qualitative and quantitative approaches. Among the qualitative approaches, the reviewed studies used multiple methods, including single case studies, multi-case studies, focus groups, and in-depth interviews [13, 15, 28, 29]. For quantitative studies, surveys were the most commonly reported research method [22, 24, 25]. In addition, a few studies also reported big-data or machine learning [21, 30] based methods. Lastly, a small number of studies focused on the IS development and discussion at a conceptual level, without any associated empirical studies.

Overall, the above review shows that IS research in Vietnam has addressed diverse research themes, and used different theories and research methods. The review, to some extent, presents what we know about the emergence of IS research in Vietnam. Yet, it also raises a question of what is the current state of the field? This question will be addressed in the next section.

4 Introduction to Book Chapters

This section aims to address the question of what the current state of the IS field in Vietnam is. We believe that no individual study can potentially answer this question in isolation. With this in mind, we issued a call for chapters on IS research in Vietnam, with a specific aim of compiling and synthesizing current IS research in Vietnam. The call for chapters resulted in 22 manuscript submissions. Following two rounds of peer-review and revisions, we selected a total of nine chapters for the current edited book.

As the call for chapters coincided with the peak of the Covid-19 pandemic, the contributed chapters focused largely on two categories: IS value creation and IS in the time of COVID-19. The first group considers the usage, application, and expansion of IS to create value for different Vietnamese industries. The second group concerns how IS research continues to play a role in dealing with the COVID-19 pandemic. In both groups, the chapters cover relevant and timely research themes that are pertinent for Vietnamese companies, as well as the wider IS community. Table 2 offers an overview of the themes, methodological approaches and key contributions from these chapters.

As seen via Table 2, the chapters in this book have researched important and contemporary themes of IS research in Vietnam. Following the current introduction chapter, Chapter "Optimising Business Process by Multi-method Modelling: A Case Study of Customer Support Centre for Fashion Omnichannel e-Retailing" studies omnichannel e-retailing, referring to the integrated and simultaneous use of multiple online and offline customer touchpoints to sell products, and interact with customers. The chapter specifically focuses on the problem of optimizing customer support efficiency and effectiveness for such omnichannel retailers. This comprises a rather complex business process involving the allocation of customer support representatives, managing multiple channels, and performing time sharing of key personnel. The chapter uses the context of the customer support team at "G fashion", a large fashion retailer in Vietnam, who are faced with a high call rate, and an increasing rate of call loss. Using a combination of discrete event and agent-based models,

Table 2 Overview of the book chapters (refer to the book for the detailed chapter)

Chapter number	Theme/sub-theme	Methodology	Main contributions
IS value creation			
2	E-retailing, Omnichannel retailing, business process optimization	Multi-method analysis involving discrete event modeling, agent based modeling, and qualitative interviews	The chapter offers a modeling strategy to optimize the related customer service allocation during normal and promotional periods with increased demand
3	Entrepreneurship, digital innovation	Critical case study involving secondary data analysis and informal interviews	The chapter uncovers main ways by which Quang Trung Software City can support high-tech startups
4	Enterprise architecture (EA)	Qualitative case study involving interview, participant observation, informal discussions	The chapter documents a case study of how EA adoption changed the process and style in a Vietnamese public sector
5	Blockchain enabled traceability (BET), blockchain adoption	Qualitative case study involving literature analysis and interviews	The chapter identifies a list of important challenges in the implementation of BETs in the food supply chain industry in Vietnam
Information systems in the time of Covid-19			
6	Information security behavior, remote work practices	In-depth interviews	The chapter identifies a number of important factors that can affect employees' protection of organizational information security while working from home
7	Digital transformation, remote work practices	Self-administered surveys and informal interviews	The chapter investigates the factors associated with working-from-home productivity in the aftermath of Covid-19

(continued)

Table 2 (continued)

Chapter number	Theme/sub-theme	Methodology	Main contributions
8	Mobile commerce	Online survey	The chapter finds that Gen X consumers' buying intentions via mobile commerce are positively associated with mobile shopping efficiency, effort expectancy, and the perceived severity of Covid-19
9	Mobile app adoption, food delivery applications	Survey	The chapter finds that the intention to use the Go Food app in Vietnam was positively associated with the perceived ease of use, perceived usefulness, subjective norm, service performance, and perceived price fairness
10	e-Learning, digital transformation	Analysis of secondary survey	The chapter explores the students' readiness for digital transformation in the aftermath of Covid-19

the chapter provides prescriptive suggestions to G fashion on how to maintain high utilization rates and low call loss rates.

Chapter "High-Tech Start-Up Ecosystems in Vietnam: The Case of Quang Trung Software City (QTSC)" analyzes the emergence and growth dynamics of high-tech start-up ecosystems in Vietnam, by using the case of the popular Quang Trung Software City (QTSC). High-tech start-ups constitute a rapidly emerging and high-value digital innovation ecosystem in not just Vietnam, but many other countries in South East Asia. This chapter seeks to expand our understanding of what factors are important for the survival and continued success of such innovation ecosystems. Based on interview data collected from managers in QTSC and its constituent start-ups, the chapter theorizes four key affordances that QTSC provides for its constituent organizations: (i) Management capabilities and expertise, (ii) Knowledge management, sharing, and protection, (iii) Measurement of key performance indicators, and (iv) Increased collaboration and networking opportunities.

Chapter "Organizational Change and Enterprise Architecture Adoption: A Case Study in the Public Sector seeks to understand the factors and organizational change outcomes associated with the EA adoption in public sector organizations in Vietnam. The chapter points out that while EA offers the Vietnamese public sector an opportunity to improve their administrative effectiveness and transparency, the lack of explicit guidance on how to adopt and apply EA has led local agencies to develop their own usage patterns. The chapter uses a qualitative case study to illustrate how the successful adoption of EA led to a sustained improvement in how the organization provided services and communicated with its customers. The successful adoption also created an increased impetus for other organizations to adopt such technologies in reforming their administrative processes.

Chapter "Blockchain-Enabled Traceability in Sustainable Food Supply Chains: A Case study of the Pork Industry in Vietnam" presents a study of a blockchain-enabled food supply chain system that is being used in the pork industry to improve traceability, monitoring, ingredient tracking, payments and compliance. The chapter argues that the application of blockchain technologies in developing countries, such as Vietnam, remain understudied, even though the potential benefits from its adoption remain high. The chapter lists four key application areas for blockchain adoption that might be relevant to organizations in Vietnam: (i) digital registration of assets, (ii) digital identification of people and personal records, (iii) supply chain transactions that are automated and fully traceable, and (iv) secure solutions for data exchange.

Chapter "Protecting Organizational Information Security at Home During the COVID-19 Pandemic in Vietnam: Exploratory Findings from Technology-Organization-Environment Framework" revisits the context of employee productivity during COVID-19, but focuses on the organizational information security concerns, which have become salient with the increased popularity of remote working arrangements. The chapter highlights the growing information security challenges and threats aimed at home-based workers, in the aftermath of the pandemic. Through in-depth online interviews with a group of professional workers, the chapter uncovers a number of factors such as (i) use of secure remote working software, (ii) flexible work arrangement at home, (iii) lack of social interactions with colleagues, and (iv) organizational culture, which exert considerable influence on employees' information security behavior.

Similar to the previous chapter, Chapter "Technology Readiness and Digital Transformation: A Case Study of Telework During COVID-19 Pandemic and Future Work in Vietnam" focuses on the impacts of Covid-19 on the telecommuting or teleworking behavior of employees in Vietnam. While existing surveys show that a majority of employees prefer to work from home, the chapter notes that indirect estimates suggest that only about a third of all jobs in Vietnam can be feasibly done remotely. This creates an organizational dilemma for decision makers in balancing business needs with employee expectations. By combining data from a self-administered survey spanning employees from 52 companies based in Vietnam, and informal interviews with mid-level managers and senior executives, the authors show that the employees' technology readiness, as well as the availability of suitable equipment and training are important drivers of remote productivity.

Chapter "Generation X's Shopping Behavior in the Electronic Marketplace Through Mobile Applications During the Covid-19 Pandemic" investigates the factors that associate with Gen-X users' adoption of mobile commerce. Using the Theory of Acceptance and Use of Technology model (UTAUT), and the Task-technology fit model (TTF) as a theoretical foundation, the chapter performs a survey to elicit mobile shopping behavior and preferences for users during Covid-19. Their results show that the Gen X consumers' mobile shopping intentions were positively associated with mobile shopping efficiency, effort expectancy, and the perceived severity of the pandemic.

Chapter "Factors Influencing the Intention to Use Food Delivery Application (FDA): The Case Study of GoFood During Covid 19 Pandemic in Vietnam" looks at the fast growing and hypercompetitive market for food delivery apps in Vietnam, which features well known organizations like Now (Foody), GoJek, and Grab Food. Particularly, in light of Covid-19 induced movement restrictions, food delivery apps have witnessed a surge in popularity and sustained use. In particular, this chapter investigates the factors that affect customers' intention to use food delivery apps (FDA). Drawing on the popular Technology Acceptance Model (TAM) and the Theory of Planned Behaviour (TPB), the authors show that subjective norms (SN) constituted the most significant factor affecting customers' intention to use Go Food, a popular FDA, while perceived price fairness was found to be the least important factor.

Finally, Chapter "Digitization of Education in Vietnam in the Crisis of Covid-19 Pandemic" discusses the critical importance of digital transformation of educational institutions in Vietnam during Covid-19. The chapter contends that in dealing with the pandemic, crisis management in educational institutions has remained an under-studied area, when compared to other organizational contexts. In the backdrop of a steadily digitalizing education sector, the pandemic has served to catalyze the transition to online platforms and processes. The chapter further analyzes students' readiness for digital transformation on six dimensions, and show that their readiness is positively associated with COVID-19, their self-study ability, perceived ease of use, perceived usefulness and attitude. The chapter will likely help educators and policy makers better understand and predict the impact of Covid-induced digitalization policies among Vietnamese students.

5   Conclusion and Future Outlook

Information systems as a scholarly discipline has witnessed growing interest from several researchers in Vietnam, who are currently studying its adoption and application within Vietnamese organizations and society. There is a strong consensus on the critical role of IS research and applications among both academics and practitioners in Vietnam. Given this backdrop, we believe that it is important to have a shared understanding of what we know so far, and what we hope to achieve as a community.

This chapter looks back of what we know by reviewing published papers in the IS field in Vietnam (Sect. 3). The review shows that the IS field in Vietnam has studied diverse topics, ranging from the essential themes of information systems to the interdisciplinary applications of emerging technologies. While the review is by no means comprehensive, it begins to paint an overall picture of the IS field in

Vietnam. Over time, with the growing maturity and popularity of the field, we will develop more structured and systematic reviews.

To understand what the IS community in Vietnam is doing, we called for chapters to collect and synthesize current IS research in Vietnam. Through a rigorous blind review process, we have selected nine chapters that reflect contemporary topics covering the IS field in Vietnam (Sect. 4). These chapters have shown how IS implementations create values in business, and how IS has helped in our response to Covid-19. This also shows the timeliness of the field in reacting to the pandemic. As such, these chapters provide theoretical and practical implications that reflect unique characteristics of IS research in Vietnamese business and society. These included chapters will serve to provide a resource for those who plan to research, educate and learn about IS in Vietnam.

Regarding future directions, we will continue to witness and track the dynamic evolution of IS research and practices in Vietnam. While the detailed directions can be found in each chapter, we wish to highlight two important research directions. First, multiple chapters in this book have presented accounts of how IS research can help with dealing with the Covid-19 pandemic. We expect that this line of research will continue post Covid-19, with IS staying at the forefront of the recovery in Vietnamese businesses and society. Second, while the IS discipline draws on two complementary paradigms: behavioral science and design science [31, 32], the IS community in Vietnam has mainly adopted behavioral science approaches. With the increasing importance of design science [33, 34], we expect to see more design science research being used for building innovative artifacts by the IS community in Vietnam.

Appendix: Selected Reviewed Papers

#	Reference
1	Au, B., Nkhoma, C., & Nkhoma, M. (2020). Online learning framework - Rapid framework development as a response to the Covid-19 pandemic. Proceedings of the 2020 AIS SIGED International Conference on Information Systems Education and Research, 165–175
2	Avgerou, C. (2008). Information systems in developing countries: a critical research review. *Journal of Information Technology*, *23*(3), 133–146. https://doi.org/10.1057/palgrave.jit.2000136
3	Bui, N. (2018). BIM technology implementation in Vietnam: an institutional perspective on a bridge project. *Proceedings of PACIS 2018*, Paper 152
4	Bulte, E., Lensink, R., & Vu, N. (2017). Do gender and business trainings affect business outcomes? Experimental evidence from Vietnam. *Management Science*, *63*(9), 2885–2902
5	Chau, N.T., & Deng, H. (2018). Critical determinants for mobile commerce adoption in Vietnamese SMEs: A preliminary study. *Proceedings of ACIS 2018*, 1–11

(continued)

(continued)

#	Reference
6	Dang, D., & Pekkola, S. (2020). Institutional perspectives on the process of enterprise architecture adoption. *Information Systems Frontiers*, 22(6), 1433–1445
7	Dang, D.D., & Pekkola, S. (2017). Enterprise architecture and organizational reform: A project debrief. *Proceedings of PACIS 2017*, Paper 71
8	Dang, D.D., & Pekkola, S. (2016). Institutionalising enterprise architecture in the public sector in Vietnam. *Proceedings of ECIS 2016*, Paper 139
9	Dang-Pham, D., Pittayachawan, S., & Bruno, V. (2016) Who influences information security behaviours of young home computer users in Vietnam? An ego-centric network analysis approach. *Proceedings of ACIS 2016*, 1–11
10	Dao, K.T., Nguyen, T.T.H., Tapanainen, T., Nguyen, H.T., & Nguyen, N.D. (2017). Information safety, corporate image, and intention to use online services: Evidence from travel industry in Vietnam. *Proceeding of AMCIS 2017*, 1–10
11	Dao, K.T., Tapanainen, T.J., Hai, N.T.T., & Tuyen, B.Q. (2016). Dynamic capability link with firm performance: Evidence from a Vietnamese IT company. *Proceedings of AMCIS 2016*, 1–10
12	Dell, M., Lane, N., & Querubin, P. (2018). The historical state, local collective action, and economic development in Vietnam. *Econometrica*, 86(6), 2083–2121
13	Dieu, P., & Le, N. (1995). Vietnam's IT -2000 Program: The Challenges Ahead. *Proceedings of PACIS 1995*, Paper 65
14	Eder, L., Nguyen, T.N., Pham, T.N., & Lo, J. (2012). Collaborative microcredit project moves to the cloud. *Proceedings of PACIS 2012*. Paper 141
15	He, E.J., & Goh, J. (2021). Profit or Growth? Dynamic Order Allocation in a Hybrid Workforce. *Management Science, online first*. https://doi.org/10.1287/mnsc.2021.4177
16	Thuan, N. H. (2019). Business Process Crowdsourcing: Concept, Ontology and Decision Support. Springer. https://doi.org/10.1007/978-3-319-91391-9
17	Kulkarni, U.R., & Robles-Flores, J.A. (2013). Development and Validation of a BI Success Model. *Proceedings of AMCIS 2013*, Paper 1
18	Le Dinh, T., Rinfret, L., Raymond, L., & Dong Thi, B.T. (2012). Reconciling knowledge management and e-collaboration systems: The information-driven knowledge management framework. *Proceedings of ECIS 2012*, Paper 126
19	Leung, N.K.Y., Lau, S.K., Fan, J., Kang, S.H., & Tsang, N. (2011) An Ontology-Based Collaborative Interorganizational Knowledge Management Network. *Proceedings of ICEB 2011*, 381–389
20	Leung, N. K., Lau, S., & Lau, S. Y. (2019). A Study of Factors Influencing Green IT Practices, Buying and Subscription Behaviours of Computer and Mobile Devices, and Streaming Services. *Pacific Asia Journal of the Association for Information Systems*, 11(1), 4. https://doi.org/10.17705/1pais.11104
21	Lin, F. T., Wu, H. Y., & Tran, T. N. N. (2015). Internet banking adoption in a developing country: an empirical study in Vietnam. *Information Systems and e-Business Management*, 13(2), 267–287
22	Malesky, E., & Taussig, M. (2019). How do firms feel about participation by their peers in the regulatory design process? An online survey experiment testing the substantive change and spillover mechanisms. *Strategy Science*, 4(2), 129–150. https://doi.org/10.1287/stsc.2019.0084

(continued)

#	Reference
23	Manh, H. D. (2015). Scientific publications in Vietnam as seen from Scopus during 1996–2013. *Scientometrics*, *105*(1), 83–95. https://doi.org/10.1007/s11192-015-1655-x
24	McMillan, J., & Woodruff, C. (1999). Interfirm relationships and informal credit in Vietnam. *The Quarterly Journal of Economics*, *114*(4), 1285–1320. https://doi.org/10.1162/003355399556278
25	Molka-Danielsen, J., Le, B.T.N., & Engelseth, P. (2017). The role of information exchange in supply chain collaboration: A case study of a Vietnam ship parts supplier. *Proceedings of the Annual Hawaii International Conference on System Sciences,* 657–666
26	Nguyen, Q., Tate, M., Calvert, P., & Aubert, B. (2017). Intellectual capital, organizational learning capability, and ERP implementation for strategic benefit. *Proceedings of ECIS 2017*, Paper 21
27	Nguyen, T. V., Ho-Le, T. P., & Le, U. V. (2017). International collaboration in scientific research in Vietnam: an analysis of patterns and impact. *Scientometrics*, *110*(2), 1035–1051. https://doi.org/10.1007/s11192-016-2201-1
28	Nguyen, V.T., Le, T.N., Bui, Q.M., Tran, M.T., & Duong, A.D. (2012) Smart shopping assistant: A multimedia and social media augmented system with mobile devices to enhance customers' experience and interaction. *Proceedings of PACIS 2012*, Paper 95
29	Nguyen-Trinh, H. A., & Rizopoulos, Y. (2017). Market conditions and change for low-carbon electricity transition in Vietnam. *The Journal of Energy and Development*, *43*(1/2), 1–26
30	Ostern, N.K., Perscheid, G., & Moormann, J. (2021) Designing a gamified adherence system for tuberculosis treatment support in urban Vietnam. *Proceedings of the Annual Hawaii International Conference on System Sciences 2021*. 3466–3473
31	Pham, H.C., Ulhaq, I., Nkhoma, M., Nguyen, M.N., & Brennan, L. (2018) Exploring knowledge sharing practices for raising security awareness. *Proceedings of ACIS 2018*, Paper 85
32	Phung, T.M., Dinh, M.N., Dang-Pham, D., Van, H.M.T., & Thwaites, L. (2020) A Machine Learning-based Approach to Vietnamese Handwritten Medical Record Recognition. *Proceedings of ACIS2020*, Paper 22
33	Phung, V.D., Hawryszkiewycz, I., Chandran, D., & Ha, B.M. (2017) Knowledge sharing and innovative work behaviour: A case study from Vietnam. *Proceedings of ACIS2017*, Paper 91
34	Sedera, D., Lokuge, S., Krcmar, H., & Srivastava, S. C. (2014). The future of outsourcing in the Asia–Pacific Region: Implications for research and practice—panel report from PACIS 2014. *Communications of the Association for Information Systems*, *35*(1), 17. https://doi.org/10.17705/1cais.03517
35	Stafford, T.F., & Syler, R.A. (2016) Geopolitical factors impacting ICT4D: Comparing Singapore with Vietnam. *Proceedings of AMCIS 2016*, Paper 5
36	Tang, N.H., & Lee, Y.C. (2016). Korean and Vietnamese user loyalty: KakaoTalk case. *Proceedings of AMCIS 2016*, Paper 8
37	Trinh, T.P., Pham, C.H., & Tran, D. (2015). An adoption model of software as a service (SaaS) in SMEs. *Proceedings of PACIS 2015*, Paper 18
38	Trinh, T.P., & Tran, D. (2015). Enterprise systems and customer agility exploratory study in Vietnam. *Proceedings of PACIS 2015*, Paper 4

(continued)

(continued)

#	Reference
39	Winkler, M., Huber, T., & Dibbern, J. (2014). The software prototype as digital boundary object-A revelatory longitudinal innovation case. *Proceedings of ICIS 2014*, Paper 12

References

1. Vo, B., Hong, T.-P., & Le, B. (2013). A lattice-based approach for mining most generalization association rules. *Knowledge-Based Systems, 45*, 20–30.
2. Thuan, N.H. (2019). *Business process crowdsourcing: Concept, ontology and decision support.* Progress in IS. Springer.
3. Nguyen, A., et al. (2021). Design principles for learning analytics information systems in higher education. *European Journal of Information Systems, 30*(5), 541–568.
4. Pham, P., et al. (2022). Bot2Vec: A general approach of intra-community oriented representation learning for bot detection in different types of social networks. *Information Systems, 103*, 101771.
5. Le, T. L. V., & Pham, D. K. (2022). The ICT impact on bank performance: The case of Vietnam. *Advances in Computational Intelligence and Communication Technology* (pp. 165–174). Springer.
6. Kautz, K. (2021). Editorial for the Australasian journal of information systems 2021. *Australasian Journal of Information Systems, 25*.
7. Bui, M. L. (2021). A journey of digital transformation of small and medium-sized enterprises in Vietnam: Insights from multiple cases. *The Journal of Asian Finance, Economics and Business, 8*(10), 77–85.
8. Manh, H. D. (2015). Scientific publications in Vietnam as seen from Scopus during 1996–2013. *Scientometrics, 105*(1), 83–95.
9. Nguyen, T. V., Ho-Le, T. P., & Le, U. V. (2017). International collaboration in scientific research in Vietnam: An analysis of patterns and impact. *Scientometrics, 110*(2), 1035–1051.
10. Jeyaraj, A., & Zadeh, A. H. (2020). Evolution of information systems research: Insights from topic modeling. *Information & Management, 57*(4), 103207.
11. Dang-Pham, D., & Kautz, K. (2018). A *social network analysis of co-authorship at the Australasian conference on information systems (Acis)*, 2018.
12. Paré, G., et al. (2015). Synthesizing information systems knowledge: A typology of literature reviews. *Information & Management, 52*, 183–199.
13. Dang, D. D. & Pekkola, S. (2016). Institutionalising enterprise architecture in the public sector in Vietnam. In *ECIS 2016 Proceedings*, 2016.
14. Trinh, T. P., & Tran, D. (2015). *Enterprise systems and customer agility exploratory study in Vietnam.*
15. Molka-Danielsen, J., Thi Ngoc Le, B., & Engelseth, P. (2017). The role of information exchange in supply chain collaboration: a case study of a Vietnam ship parts supplier. In *HICSS 50 Proceedings, 2017: Paper 7.*
16. Sedera, D., et al. (2014). The future of outsourcing in the Asia-Pacific Region: Implications for research and practice—Panel report from PACIS 2014. *Communications of the Association for Information Systems, 35*(1), 17.
17. Eder, L., et al. (2012). Collaborative microcredit project moves to the cloud. In *PACIS 2012 Proceedings, 2012: Paper 141.*
18. Pham, H. C., et al. (2021). *Classrooms going digital-evaluating online presence through students' perception using community of inquiry framework.* In *Covid-19 and education: Learning and teaching in a pandemicconstrained environment* (pp. 29–49).

19. Au, B., Nkhoma, C., & Nkhoma, M. (2020). Online learning framework-rapid framework development as a response to the Covid-19 pandemic. *Online Learning, 12*, 21–2020.
20. Ostern, N., Perscheid, G., & Moormann, J. (2021). Designing a gamified adherence system for tuberculosis treatment support in urban Vietnam. In *HICSS 54 Proceedings, 2021: Paper 2.*
21. Phung, T. M., et al. (2020). A machine learning-based approach to Vietnamese handwritten medical record recognition. In *ACIS 2020 Proceedings, 2020: Paper 22.*
22. Dao, T. K., et al. (2017). *Information safety, corporate image, and intention to use online services: Evidence from travel industry in Vietnam.*
23. Tang, N. H., & Lee, Y.-C. (2016). Korean and Vietnamese user loyalty: kakaotalk case. In *Twenty-second Americas Conference on Information Systems, 2016* (pp. 1–10).
24. Leung, N. K., Lau, S., & Lau, S. Y. (2019). A study of factors influencing green IT practices, buying and subscription behaviours of computer and mobile devices, and streaming services. *Pacific Asia Journal of the Association for Information Systems, 11*(1), 4.
25. Phung, V. D., et al. (2017). *Knowledge sharing and innovative work behaviour: A case study from Vietnam.*
26. Nguyen, Q., et al. (2017). Intellectual capital, organizational learning capability, and ERP implementation for strategic benefit. In *Proceedings of the 25th European Conference on Information Systems, 2017.* Association for Information Systems.
27. Chau, N. T., & Deng, H. (2018). Critical determinants for mobile commerce adoption in Vietnamese SMEs: A preliminary study. In *29th Australasian Conference on Information Systems, Sydney, Australia, 2018.*
28. Bui, N. (2018). BIM technology implementation in Vietnam: an institutional perspective on a bridge project. In *PACIS 2018 Proceedings, 2018: Paper 152.*
29. Dao, T. K., et al. (2016). Dynamic capability link with firm performance: Evidence from a Vietnamese IT Company. In *Americas Conference on Information Systems (AMCIS), 2016.*
30. Nguyen, V.-T., et al. (2012). *Smart shopping assistant: A multimedia and social media augmented system with mobile devices to enhance customers' experience and interaction.*
31. Hevner, A., et al. (2004). Design science in information systems research. *MIS Quarterly, 28*(1), 75–105.
32. Thuan, N. H., Drechsler, A., & Antunes, P. (2019). Construction of design science research questions. *Communications of the Association for Information Systems, 44*(1), 332–363.
33. Antunes, P., Thuan, N. H., & Johnstone, D. (2021). Nature and purpose of conceptual frameworks in design science. *Scandinavian Journal of Information Systems, 32*(2), 3–40.
34. Gregor, S., & Hevner, A. (2013). Positioning and presenting design science research for maximum impact. *MIS Quarterly, 37*(2), 337–355.

Optimising Business Process by Multi-method Modelling: A Case Study of Customer Support Centre for Fashion Omnichannel e-Retailing

Tram T. B. Nguyen and **Huy Quang Truong**

Abstract Optimising business processes (BP) is the essential task of any business organisation. However, it is not easy for managers to adjust limited organisational resources to achieve a specific business goal with the desired level of efficiency and effectiveness. Multi-method modelling, combined between discrete event and agent-based modelling, is used to illustrate how it helps simulate real situations emphasising limitations in resources to optimise business processes for the fashion e-retailing to satisfy their customers through omnichannel. Customer support centre (CSC) plays a crucial role in serving e-consumers by high volumes of service and support requests, common questions related to products, fulfilment, and returns with fast response to different communication channels (e.g., phone, email, live-chat, social media) (Ilk et al in Decis Support Syst 105:13–23, 2018, [1]). Allocating and assigning service workforces across channels with different skill requirements (e.g., talking over the phone, text-based messaging, social media monitoring) is a complex task to optimise human resources. In this study, multi-method modelling is applied to design and optimise a customer support centre for a fashion omnichannel e-retailing to deal with customer requests. Several scenarios are established to adjust the number of workers as organisational resources and analyse the efficiency and effectiveness based on lost calls and utilisation in fulfilling customers' requests. Multiple scenarios are analysed for normal conditions and promotional events using the software AnyLogic. The results of these scenarios are discussed, compared, and contrasted to identify the model's outcomes in each scenario and to suggest many practical recommendations for managers in designing and optimising business processes. BP can contribute to overall business performance by satisfying and attracting customers while maintaining efficient and effective organisational resources. Also, the role of CSC in fashion omnichannel e-retailing is highlighted in fulfilling customer requests.

T. T. B. Nguyen (✉)
Ho Chi Minh City Open University, 35-37 Ho Hao Hon Street, District 1, Ho Chi Minh City, Vietnam
e-mail: tram.ntb@ou.edu.vn

H. Q. Truong
School of Business and Management, RMIT University, 702 Nguyen Van Linh Street, District 7, Ho Chi Minh City, Vietnam

© The Author(s), under exclusive license to Springer Nature Singapore Pte Ltd. 2023
N. H. Thuan et al. (eds.), *Information Systems Research in Vietnam*,
https://doi.org/10.1007/978-981-19-3804-7_2

Finally, through the study, multi-method modelling shows its strengths and limitations in facilitating managers in designing business processes and optimising the company resources to maximise efficiency and effectiveness in the dynamic fashion business environment.

Keywords Designing business process · Omnichannel · Customer support centre · Multi-method modelling · e-retailing · Optimising resources

1 Introduction

Business process (BP) is the combination of several initiatives and approaches, namely systems thinking, operations research, data processing, socio-technical systems, systems modelling, process reengineering, TQM, Lean and Six Sigma systems and so on [2]. The ultimate purpose of BP is to innovate and continuously transform businesses and entire cross-organisational value chains besides productivity gains [3]. Hence, cross-functional business processes are usually core to the organisation, including a significant number of nonmanufacturing-related activities. Designing BP is a complicated and cross-functioned task involving multi-levels to create goods or services of value to a market.

According to Laguna and Marklund [4], there are two main requirements for BP design. Designing BP is to establish how to do things in a good way, reflecting process efficiency and effectiveness. BP design is all about satisfying customers' requirements [4]. In other words, a well-designed BP does the right things in the right way to deliver customer value; otherwise, it is useless. For this purpose, coordination and suboptimisation across the functional or departmental lines of the organisation are considered the most valuable in dealing with complex horizontal processes to reach the end customer.

In addition, a poorly designed BP might be the main reason for long response times, low service levels, unbalanced resource utilisation, unhappy customers, backlog, damage claims, and loss of goodwill. To this end, BP design can contribute to overall business performance through the fundamental need for any business, profit maximising through satisfying and attracting customers while maintaining efficient use of organisational resources.

Omnichannel retailing refers to the integrated use of multiple buying and delivery channels to fulfil customer demands and provide a seamless experience [5]. Customer support centre plays a crucial role in selling clothes to consumers by high volumes of service and support requests, common questions related to products purchase, fulfilment, and returns with fast response to different communication ways (e.g., phone, email, live chat on social media) [1]. Allocating and assigning service workforces across channels with different skill requirements (e.g., talking over the phone, text-based messaging, social media monitoring) can be a complex task to optimise their efforts and time. Therefore, optimising a process for the customer support centre is essential to increase the efficiency and effectiveness in fulfilling customers' requests for different events of e-commerce businesses.

Taking this research objective, discrete event modelling combined with agent-based—a multi-method modelling is used to model the lowest level—task level for omnichannel fashion e-retailing to support their customers and generate turnover. For the reason that multi-method modelling is able to represent a complex system behaviour. Also, low efforts and expenses for designing and optimising BP is the main reason for using simulation software as the primary tool to optimise the organisational resources [6]. In other words, this chapter uses a pragmatism approach to identify how multi-method modelling enhances business performance in optimising their resources to find the best solution for the current problems instead of analysing in-depth the technical aspect of process modelling. The chapter is constructed as follow. The following section is a relevant literature review on designing and optimising BP, omnichannel e-retailing in the fashion industry. Next, the research method-ology is introduced, containing problem formulation, concept model and experiment configurations. After that, the findings emerging from the analysis are presented and discussed along with their implications. Finally, the conclusions, including the iden-tification of limitations and possible further developments of the study, are stated in the final section.

2   Theoretical Backgrounds and Research Context

2.1   Designing Business Process

According to Bastenie et al. [3], the top-level is the entire organisation as a system. The second level depicts the organisation's Value Creation System (VCS), which is how the organisation creates, sells, and delivers products/services. The three lower levels include processing sub-systems level, process level and subpro-cess/task/subtask level, from separated organisation functions to specific tasks. Ordi-narily, the process architecture or structure is formed based on five main elements: the inputs and outputs, the flow units, the network of activities and buffers, the resources, and the information [4]. First, inputs and outputs can be tangible or intangible within an organisation. Second, the flow unit can be a unit of input (a customer or raw mate-rial) or output (e.g., a serviced customer or finished product) or intermediate products or components. Third, a process is a network of activities and buffers through which the flow units or jobs have to pass to be transformed from inputs to outputs. Fourth, resources are necessary tangible assets to perform activities within a process. The last element is the information structure specifying which information is required and available to make the decisions necessary for performing the activities in a process.

2.2 Omnichannel e-Retailing in Vietnam

In Vietnam, e-commerce is one of the most developed markets. According to e-Conomy SEA 2020 report, Vietnam e-commerce in 2020 increased by 16% and reached over 14 billion USD. In detail, online retail sales increased by 46%, ride-hailing and food delivery increased by 34%, online marketing, entertainment, and online games went up by 18%. In comparison, online travel services declined by 28% due to the Covid-19 pandemic [7]. It is predicted that the average growth rate throughout 2020–2025 will be 29%, and the e-commerce scale will reach 52 billion USD by 2025. Along with e-commerce development, online-offline channel integration leads to channel synergies rather than channel cannibalisation [8]. Omnichannel e-retailing is the synergetic management of the numerous available channels and customer touchpoints to optimise the customer experience and the performance across channels [9]. This has revolutionised the way retailers operate to gain a competitive advantage by integrating and optimising different channels.

2.3 Challenges in Fashion Omnichannel e-Retailing Industry

Concerning the study background, this paper focuses on the fashion industry, which is one of the most critical sectors of the world economy, a key element in the international financial markets, and a unique tool of contemporary cultural movements [10]. In this industry, fashion brands usually face several challenges to provide a seamless experience for customers [11, 12]. First, the relationship between online and offline is more complex for businesses to create pathways of physical and digital as a customer may switch between digital and bricks-and-mortar several times [13]. Second, using data to create a personalised customer experience based on their preferences and buying history is critical for offers and suggestions. Additionally, creating a luxury experience on digital is challenging, especially for high-end brands [14]. Usually, fashion companies use 24/7 hotlines and live chat available to online shoppers, along with social media, like Facebook, Twitter, and Instagram for responsive and personalised customer service. Fourth, controlling the consistent brand message and style across all channels ensures that the customer knows what to expect and is never left disappointed. Lastly, giving customers more ways to shop is required to approach and encourage more buying. Subsequently, a customer support centre (CSC) is inevitable for the fashion industry in assisting, supporting, encouraging more buying personalised products as well as gaining more satisfying experiences.

3 Research Methodology

3.1 Problem Formulation

In order to investigate BP design from a practical view, a fashion brand company is used as the focal case study for this research. The company information is provided by an anonymous manager in charge of operating its CSC. Established in 2015, G fashion brand has been firmly positioned in the market and has become the fastest growing fashion brand in Vietnam, with nearly 90 showrooms nationwide. G fashion is the best-seller brand on the most popular e-marketplaces in the country, such as Tiki, Lazada, Shopee, Sendo, and goes global on Amazon shortly. It establishes the business model grounded on a fashion supermarket for everyone, every family in Vietnam. G fashion aims to provide customers with high-quality products in a homelike shopping space. Although nearly 100 stores are temporarily closed due to the impact of Covid-19, the company is still doing well thanks to e-retailing about 6000 up to 10,000 orders per day in the second quarter of 2021.

Currently, its website records the most significant number of customers, with an average of 1.2 million monthly visits across the country. The number of customer inquiries related to purchase, return and refund at the CSC each day is enormous. Consequently, according to the focused interview with the manager at G fashion, there are several critical issues in customer service. The first challenge is slow response time because no customer wants to wait on hold. They also do not want to spend time being rolled among departments or agents for searching solutions. Second, incompetent CSC staff might lead to wrong offer/support to customers as well as fail to meet their expectations. Thus, the company applies omnichannel CSC, a synchronised operating model of aligned communications channels to deliver consistent CSC. It expects that CSC effectively operates as a single channel, delivering high-value customer experiences across all the touchpoints no matter how a customer reaches out to the company.

Among all factors, human resource is the centric element of any CSC. At G fashion, a team of ten employees working in CSC are overloaded due to the number of inquiries and the high rate of lost calls. G fashion determines to solve these problems to optimise the number of employees at CSC with the lowest cost solution identification. Discrete event modelling is a method to model process—a sequence of operations being performed across entities, including delays, usage of resources, and waiting in queues [15]. It is familiar to the business world and has become the most successful method in penetrating the business community. At the same time, agent-based is used to model the behaviours of adaptive actors who make up a social system and who influence one another through their interactions [16]. This combination is created to get a deeper insight into systems that are not well-captured by a single modelling method. The model is established based on AnyLogic modelling, version 8 PLE and Java programming language with the real inputs from G fashion to run the experiment in the model.

3.2 Tasks Specification

To describe the work of the CSC at G fashion, requests from customers come to the centre based on three popular methods via calls (hotline), chat messages (Facebook, Zalo), and emails. Each request has different tasks with diverse complexity levels related to G product categories: male products (MP) and female products (FP). Calls get the highest priority among the inquiries since customers cannot wait too long. Waiting time is required to be short; otherwise, customers will hang up. It also depends on the maximum task complexity in the request. Chat has higher priority than emails, but both can wait, and employees can answer any time. They queue at the next level if they are not fulfilled depending on its prevailed product category (Fig. 1). Arrival rate requests during the daytime are usually higher than the night shift.

At G fashion, task complexity is divided into three levels: 1—entry levels for all requests, 2—easy (e.g., checking order status, size consultation) and 3—complicated (e.g., return, refund, and complaints). The mean processing time for each task is based on this complexity. Also, each employee has a specialisation for only one product category and is assigned to one level of task complexity. There are four processing tiers following task complexity. In detail, tier 0 is for trainees; tier 1 is the entry-level in charge of redirecting requests to a suitable tier. Tier 2 processes basic inquiries, and tier 3 handle complex requirements from customers.

Among different communication methods, calls via hotline can be redirected to employees at the next Tier only if there are any free employees. If not, the employees from the last Tier keep customers busy until an employee from the next Tier is free. Chats and emails will work similarly to call requests and go to queue at the next Tier if not fulfilled, depending on their prevailed product categories. If there are several free employees, chats go to the one with the corresponding specialisation. In case the request requires employee speciality in different product categories, there is an additive multiplier (m) for time processing tasks $T_P = (1 + m) * normal\_time$, which is longer than usual. To this end, working employees are at various skill levels. After a while, they will get promoted to a higher Tier when they can deal with more complex requests. Employees have different states: at work, on vacation and retire (or quit) following the national labour law through agent-based statecharts in AnyLogic

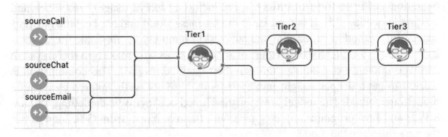

Fig. 1 Processing tiers

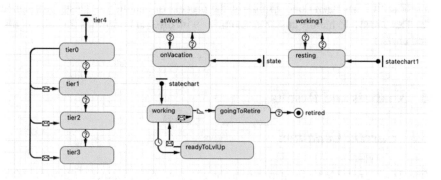

Fig. 2 Employee's statechart

(Fig. 2). Four shifts of employees ensure that at least one is working while three resting shifts. There are different turnover rates associated with different tiers.

3.3 Designing Processing Flowcharts

Discrete models to process all inquiries are divided into two separate ones. The first one is to handle all customer requests no matter which method. The process of handling requests is illustrated in Fig. 3 for Tier 1, which is the entry-level for all inquiries. Inquiries are agents, while employees and their supervisors are resources. Calls get the top priority along with delay and expire if there is no response from employees. Then inquiries are processed by getting supervisors' approval and then providing employees' decisions. There are several decisions related to further requests from customers, which can be done, or the process starts over if the customers request again. The output data is generated, and statistics are collected at the blocks, as well as by the agents while they move through the process flowchart. Each inquiry measures time spent in the process by making a timestamp when employees handle

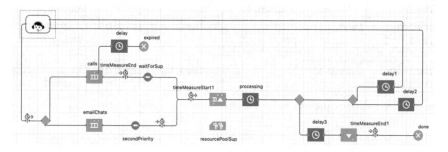

Fig. 3 Tier 1

a task until it has been done. Similarly, the process of handling requests is designed for Tier 2 and 3 to handle customer inquiries with different priorities for calls, chats, and emails.

4 Analysis and Results

4.1 Current Condition

Based on the provided information from the manager, each month, G fashion has 6000 to 12,000 orders. In normal conditions (no promotion or big events), inquiries are stable as demands, which are about 6000–8000 orders per month generating approximately 100–150 requests per day (nightshift arrival rate equals 20% of dayshift). Each week they have new employees for CSC, processing inputs are average numbers, as seen in Table 1. The formula for utilisation rate is the number of actual working hours divided by the total number of available hours. Customers usually hang up after five minutes of waiting at Tier 1 and 2, 10 minutes at Tier 3. Currently, G fashion has twelve employees, including four at Tier 1, four at each other tier and two trainees working at CSC. The current condition has been run and analysed in AnyLogic within one month (30 days). The results show that the team could process 8947 inquiries per month; however, it is ineffective since only 12% of inquiries were finished while losing 45% inquiries (3987 calls) and 44% inquiries in waiting. Tier 2 is overloaded with over 90% utilisation while Tier 1 is 78%, and the rest only reach from 12 to 43% utilisation.

Table 1 Model input of the current condition

Number of employee (person)	Mean of processing time (minutes)	Arrival rate (per hour)	Time to tier up (days)	Monthly turnover	Other inputs
Tier 0 (trainee): 2 Tier 1: 4	Level 1: 10	• Calls: 4 • Chats: 3 • Email: 1	To Tier 1: 15	Tier 1: 0.5	Max task quantity at request: 5
Tier 2 MP: 2 Tier 2 FP: 2	Level 2: 15		To Tier 2: 60	Tier 2: 0.3	Additive multiplier m = 0.5
Tier 3 MP: 2 Tier 3 FP: 2	Level 3: 20		To Tier 3: 90	Tier 3: 0.2	Request routine time = 2 (mins)

4.2   Experiment Configurations

There are two specific scenarios for running experiments in AnyLogic. First, in normal condition, there is a need to improve the current situation by identifying how many employees are optimal at each Tier. Second, when there are promoting events, demands increase sharply in a concise time, how many employees are suitable to handle excessive inquiries. G fashion concerns how many employees at each Tier are suitable to maximise utilisation rate and reduce lost calls and customer waiting time. Several scenarios with different employees have been run and analysed in AnyLogic within 1 month (30 days) following inputs of current condition except for the number of employees and arrival rate for promotion events. According to G fashion, the arrival rate will be doubled during promotional events. The number of employees at each Tier has been increased from the number of the current condition to identify the optimal number of employees for each Tier during normal and promotional conditions.

Normal condition

The number of employees at all tiers is needed to increase significantly since they cannot handle all inquiries. The experiments have been run with the number of each Tier increasing limited from 2 to 15 due to the difficulties in human resource management. In detail, the constraint in human resource poses many challenges for G fashion regarding time and cost for hiring and training new employees. Therefore, the company does not want to increase the number of employees too quickly in a short time. The experimental results show that lost calls decrease significantly when each Tier reaches 10 and 14 employees for Tier 1. Raising the employees of Tier 1 over 14 is not efficient as lost calls increase and the employees of other tiers are the same as utilisation rates decrease Table 2.

In detail, in scenarios N2, N3, and N4, lost calls increase; even more employees are added to each Tier, which is ineffective in using human resources. Other experiments generating inefficient results are not fully presented in the paper. Concerning the effectiveness of the solution, turnover generating scores are calculated as monthly turnover multiplied by finished inquiries at each Tier. As seen in Fig. 4, scenario N1 has the highest turnover generating score, which is the most effective for doing business.

Promotion events

Similarly, the arrival rate will be doubled during the promotional period. Keeping the optimal number of employees from the above subsection is inefficient since the team will lose 5202 calls, as seen in scenario P1 in Table 3.

The number of employees at all tiers is needed to increase accordingly. The experiments have started with doubled employees of each Tier following the increasing arrival rate of inquiries. Scenario P2 shows that lost calls decrease significantly with 96% finished inquiries. P3 represents increasing more employees for female products instead of increasing employees for Tier 1. Lost calls drop significantly even though only two more employees are needed compared to P2. However, there is about 70 in

Table 2 Experiments of normal conditions

Scenario	Number of employees (person)	Total inquiries	Inquires status	Lost calls	Utilisation rate	Finished inquiries
N1	Tier 1: 14 Tier 2 MP: 5 Tier 2 FP: 5 Tier 3 MP: 5 Tier 3 FP: 5	8.953	Finished: 82% Lost: 18% Waiting: 0%	881	Tier 1: 52% Tier 2 MP: 68% Tier 2 FP: 84% Tier 3 MP: 60% Tier 3 FP: 71%	Tier 1: 2016 Tier 2: 2665 Tier 3: 3421
N2	Tier 1: 15 Tier 2 MP: 5 Tier 2 FP: 5 Tier 3 MP: 5 Tier 3 FP: 5	8.953	Finished: 82% Lost: 18% Waiting: 0%	1611	Tier 1: 67% Tier 2 MP: 53% Tier 2 FP: 94% Tier 3 MP: 51% Tier 3 FP: 64%	Tier 1: 1770 Tier 2: 2438 Tier 3: 3130
N3	Tier 1: 14 Tier 2 MP: 6 Tier 2 FP: 6 Tier 3 MP: 6 Tier 3 FP: 6	8.868	Finished: 86% Lost: 12% Waiting: 2%	1056	Tier 1: 75% Tier 2 MP: 64% Tier 2 FP: 79% Tier 3 MP: 68% Tier 3 FP: 75%	Tier 1: 1951 Tier 2: 2474 Tier 3: 3227
N4	Tier 1: 15 Tier 2 MP: 6 Tier 2 FP: 6 Tier 3 MP: 6 Tier 3 FP: 6	8.916	Finished: 88% Lost: 10% Waiting: 1%	914	Tier 1: 65% Tier 2 MP: 70% Tier 2 FP: 78% Tier 3 MP: 52% Tier 3 FP: 48%	Tier 1: 1960 Tier 2: 2523 Tier 3: 3393

total inquiries decreasing compared to P2. Other scenarios have been run; the results show they are inefficient as lost calls increase and the employees of other tiers are the same as utilisation rates decrease. Hence, turnover generating scores are calculated as seen in Fig. 5, and scenario P2 has the highest turnover generating score, which is the most effective for doing business.

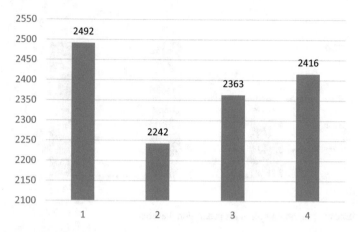

Fig. 4 Turnover generating score for normal condition

Table 3 Promotional experiment running

Scenario	Number of employees (person)	Total inquiries	Inquires status	Lost calls	Utilisation rate	Finished inquiries
P1	Tier 1: 14 Tier 2 MP: 5 Tier 2 FP: 5 Tier 3 MP: 5 Tier 3 FP: 5	17,795	Finished: 42% Lost: 29% Waiting: 29%	5202	Tier 1: 87% Tier 2 MP: 51% Tier 2 FP: 92% Tier 3 MP: 81% Tier 3 FP: 64%	Tier 1: 1967 Tier 2: 1767 Tier 3: 3768
P2	Tier 1: 28 Tier 2 MP: 10 Tier 2 FP: 10 Tier 3 MP: 10 Tier 3 FP: 10	17,909	Finished: 96% Lost: 4% Waiting: 0%	706	Tier 1: 67% Tier 2 MP: 78% Tier 2 FP: 92% Tier 3 MP: 71% Tier 3 FP: 84%	Tier 1: 4277 Tier 2: 5517 Tier 3: 7392
P3	Tier 1: 25 Tier 2 MP: 10 Tier 2 FP: 11 Tier 3 MP: 10 Tier 3 FP: 11	17,830	Finished: 95% Lost: 3% Waiting: 2%	549	Tier 1: 52% Tier 2 MP: 79% Tier 2 FP: 85% Tier 3 MP: 63% Tier 3 FP: 71%	Tier 1: 4283 Tier 2: 5504 Tier 3: 7209

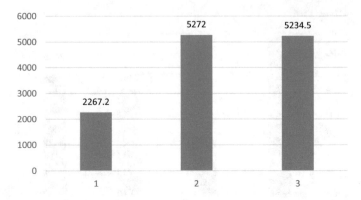

Fig. 5 Turnover generating scores for promotional events

5 Discussion

Implementing an omnichannel strategy helps fashion e-retailing businesses better understand customer needs and wants based on their buying history and behaviour to deliver personalised support by integrating the reactive channels with the digital channels. Hence, CSC plays a critical role in supporting and generating revenues for the company as it becomes the helpful touchpoint for customers via hotline (calls), live chats and emails. With the multi-modelling method, the study uses a pragmatic approach to optimise CSC's business process at a Vietnamese fashion e-retailing business. In particular, the company's process was simulated and run several experiments to find the optimal number of employees for each Tier to handle customers' inquiries during both the normal condition and promotional events. To increase the effectiveness and efficiency of CSC and contribute to overall business performance, several scenarios have been analysed to compare measurable assessment criteria of the BP, in this case, lost calls, utilisation rates, the number of finished inquiries, and their revenue-generating scores.

In the following, the findings highlight the role of BP design using multi-method modelling in satisfying customers while optimising the efficient use of organisational resources. Although multi-method modelling is not a new method in designing and optimising BP, the findings highlight the paper's novelty aspects in identifying optimal solutions for G fashion's CSC with several input variables. The multi-method modelling showed that the employee number of the current CSC team is not efficient since there are 45% lost calls based on the inputs from the company in the simulation experiment. The simulation suggests that G fashion should hire more employees for each Tier accordingly, especially for Tier 1, to increase finished inquiries up to 82%. Also, when there are promotional events, G fashion also prepares new employees to deal with the excessive demand by keeping the same employees as the optimal normal condition associated with 29% lost calls. G fashion also does not need to double the employee number of CSC team regardless of the doubled inquiries, only increasing 56% employees at Tier 1 and doubling employees at Tier 2 and 3.

In the literature, omnichannel retailers need to efficiently manage both direct distribution and reverse channels to ensure success in their logistics operations and customer satisfaction [17]. In this study, the case was conducted in the context of Vietnamese fashion industry. It is also illustrated that among all consumers' requests, return and refund—the main dealing tasks for Tier 3 of G fashion—is the most difficult working level but generates lower revenue compared to others. The processing times for these tasks are usually longer and more complex than other requests. However, these activities will improve customers' perception of the buying process and increase their confidence in the company [18]. In addition, designing and optimising BP for CSC of G fashion plays a vital role in providing this e-retailer more opportunities to understand customers' needs better, improve post-sales services, and handle product returns. Last but not least, the most desirable outcome of CSC is to generate more sales while assisting customers.

Through the case study, it is evident that multi-method modelling brings a lot of advantages for businesses to design their BP and optimise the organisational resources. First, the combination between agent-based and discrete event simulation creates the opportunities for G fashion to observe and determine how small changes in the number of employees at each Tier may influence revenue generation and utilisation. Whereas discrete event simulation in the model takes account of variability in the time taken to process consumer inquires and changes of all inputs. In line with other research, this study illustrates that multi-method modelling is able to represent a complex system behaviour where its different parts can be better captured by two or more simulation methods [19, 20]. Second, considering efforts and expenses for designing and optimising BP, this study showcases how to design BP with minimum effort by AnyLogic software as the primary tool and considerable time for interviews to collect data from G fashion to run the model. Third, the modelling for BP is highly flexible when the business needs to change. The model can be changed quickly by adjusting the existing conceptual model under-taken by a modeller, such as the objectives, inputs, outputs, and model content.

Finally, the study contributes to the literature of business process, simulation, and e-commerce by the use of multi-method modelling in solving practical issues of designing business processes for e-commerce companies, which could be applied for cases similar to G fashion. In particular, the study illustrates a business process of CSC for fashion e-retailing in optimising human resources to increase customer satisfaction. The role of the effective simulation method is explored and applied to solve the challenges that fashion omnichannel e-retailing is dealing with. Furthermore, some of the issues emerging from the study's findings relate specifically to practitioners in the fashion business. First, the complex mixture between physical and digital touch-points for customer require responsiveness in e-retailing service. Consequently, a CSC is vital to support and encourage more buying and gaining more satisfying experiences. Second, human resource is a critical element of any business process when customers try to reach the company regardless digital business environment of e-retailing. Frequent training activities and flexible replacements are indispensable for meeting customers' expectations and gaining a competitive advantage by integrating and optimising different channels.

6   Concluding Remarks

With the increase of e-commerce and the growing trend for omnichannel in the retailing industry, it is crucial that companies pay attention to designing BP for CSC as the seamless touchpoint to process all customer requests via hotline, live chats, and emails. This case study illustrates applying multi-method simulation with the aim of optimising human resources for the fashion e-retailing fulfilling customers' inquiries. Hence, the findings of this research provide insightful implications for fashion e-retailers and researchers in designing BP.

First, the study contributes to our understanding of BP design and optimisation through multi-method modelling and specific issues of the business limitations. It can contribute to overall business performance by satisfying and attracting customers while maintaining efficient organisational resources. Second, these findings highlight the role of CSC in fashion omnichannel e-retailing. It is expected to assist customers and enhance their confidence in buying as well as post-sale processes. Finally, this study strengthens the idea of what simulations are and how it contributes to business analysis to identify the best solution for specific business problems. This study is an illustrated experiment in fashion e-retailing, in which simulation modelling is flexible, easy to use, low cost and suitable for running different scenarios to optimise the company resources while enhancing effectiveness and efficiency for CSC.

The generalisability of these findings is subject to certain limitations, which has thrown up several questions in need of further investigation. The main limitation of this study is the use of the focal case. Future studies can extend the current study by investigating other industries or e-commerce marketplaces with more diverse customer requirements. They can also explore further how to design BP and optimise other organisational resources, such as cost, space, revenue, profit and so on. Furthermore, this study combines discrete and agent-based modelling to design the process using AnyLogic software. There are a few drawbacks in interpreting the results due to the assumptions and simplifications of the model. In this study, assumptions are made based on the focal case. Also, simplifications in the unit of analysis are incorporated in the model for rapid model development, ease usage, and improved transparency. Future research could use different methods and approaches to anticipate these limitations and elaborate the model.

References

1. Ilk, N., Brusco, M., & Goes, P. (2018). Workforce management in omnichannel service centers with heterogeneous channel response urgencies. *Decision Support Systems, 105*, 13–23. https://doi.org/10.1016/j.dss.2017.10.008
2. Seethamraju, R. (2012). Business process management: A missing link in business education. *Business Process Management Journal, 18*, 532–547. https://doi.org/10.1108/146371512112 32696
3. Bastenie, P. A., Franckson, J. R., De Meutter, R., & Conard, V. (2015). *Handbook on business process management 1.* Springer.

4. Laguna, M., & Marklund, J. (2013). Process management and process-oriented improvement programs. In *Business process modeling, simulation and design* (pp. 41–88). Chapman and Hall/CRC
5. Chopra, S. (2018). The evolution of omni-channel retailing and its impact on supply chains. *Transportation Research Procedia, 30*, 4–13. https://doi.org/10.1016/j.trpro.2018.09.002
6. Tram, N. T. B. (2022). Simulation modeling—An effective method in doing business and management research. *Ho Chi Minh City Open University Journal of Science-Economics and Business Administration, 12*, 108–124. https://doi.org/10.46223/HCMCOUJS.econ.en.12.1.1916.2022
7. Google, Temasek, B. (2020). *e-Conomy Southeast Asia*
8. Herhausen, D., Binder, J., Schoegel, M., & Herrmann, A. (2015). Integrating bricks with clicks: Retailer-level and channel-level outcomes of online-offline channel integration. *Journal of Retailing, 91*, 309–325. https://doi.org/10.1016/j.jretai.2014.12.009
9. Verhoef, P. C., Kannan, P. K., & Inman, J. J. (2015). From multi-channel retailing to omni-channel retailing. *Journal of Retailing, 91*, 174–181. https://doi.org/10.1016/j.jretai.2015.02.005
10. Lorenzo-Romero, C., Andrés-Martínez, M.-E., & Mondéjar-Jiménez, J.-A. (2020). Omnichannel in the fashion industry: A qualitative analysis from a supply-side perspective. *Heliyon, 6*, e04198. https://doi.org/10.1016/j.heliyon.2020.e04198
11. Aiolfi, S., & Sabbadin, E. (2019). Fashion and new luxury digital disruption: The new challenges of fashion between omnichannel and traditional retailing. *International Journal of Business and Management, 14*, 41. https://doi.org/10.5539/ijbm.v14n8p41
12. Lynch, S., & Barnes, L. (2020). Omnichannel fashion retailing: Examining the customer decision-making journey. *Journal of Fashion Marketing and Management: An International Journal, 24*, 471–493. https://doi.org/10.1108/JFMM-09-2019-0192
13. Van, N. A. T., McClelland, R., & Thuan, N. H. (2022). Exploring customer experience during channel switching in omnichannel retailing context: A qualitative assessment. *Journal of Retailing and Consumer Services, 64*, 102803. https://doi.org/10.1016/j.jretconser.2021.102803
14. KHOA, B. T. (2020). The antecedents of relationship marketing and customer loyalty: A case of the designed fashion product. *The Journal of Asian Finance, Economics and Business, 7*, 195–204. https://doi.org/10.13106/jafeb.2020.vol7.no2.195
15. Borshchev, A. (2013). The big book of simulation modeling—AnyLogic simulation software. *Anylogic North America*, 1–614.
16. Harrison, J. R., Lin, Z., Carroll, G. R., & Carley, K. M. (2007). Simulation modeling in organizational and management research. *Academy of Management Review, 32*, 1229–1245. https://doi.org/10.5465/amr.2007.26586485
17. de Borba, J. L. G., de Magalhães, M. R., Filgueiras, R. S., & Bouzon, M. (2020). Barriers in omnichannel retailing returns: A conceptual framework. *International Journal of Retail & Distribution Management, 49*, 121–143. https://doi.org/10.1108/IJRDM-04-2020-0140
18. Xu, X., & Jackson, J. E. (2019). Investigating the influential factors of return channel loyalty in omni-channel retailing. *International Journal of Production Economics, 216*, 118–132. https://doi.org/10.1016/j.ijpe.2019.03.011
19. Currie, C. S. M., Fowler, J. W., Kotiadis, K., et al. (2020). fv6v How simulation modelling can help reduce the impact of COVID-19. *Journal of Simulation, 14*, 83–97. https://doi.org/10.1080/17477778.2020.1751570
20. Cigolini, R., Pero, M., Rossi, T., & Sianesi, A. (2014). Linking supply chain configuration to supply chain perfrmance: A discrete event simulation model. *Simulation Modelling Practice and Theory, 40*, 1–11. https://doi.org/10.1016/j.simpat.2013.08.002

High-Tech Start-Up Ecosystems in Vietnam: The Case of Quang Trung Software City (QTSC)

Long Hai Nguyen Lam, Thinh Gia Hoang⦿, Dat Anh Le, and Nam Hai Vu⦿

Abstract The start-up ecosystems have emerged in different countries and areas all over the world since the 2000s, including key facilitators and essential capabilities that gravitate toward growth ventures. These ecosystems focus on particular disciplines, present a variety of features and dynamics, and have their own variety of evolution over time. Since Vietnam has pushed strategies and incentives to take advantage of digital technology in order for the country's start-up sector and supporting technical adaptation to grow, the high-tech sector has been dominating the start-up ecosystem in Vietnam. This chapter sheds light on the dynamics of the high-tech start-up ecosystem in Vietnam by taking the Quang Trung Software City (QTSC) as a critical case. By adopting a qualitative research inquiry based on interview data collected from managers in QTSC, and start-ups operating and located in QTSC, this chapter highlights several facilitators that QTSC has delivered to digital start-ups. Our chapter contributes to the emerging literature on the development of the high-tech start-up ecosystem and our case ecosystem also contributes highly to improving the maturity of Vietnam tech start-ups.

Keywords Start-ups · Start-up ecosystem · High-tech start-ups · Software city

L. H. N. Lam
International University, Vietnam National University, Ho Chi Minh City, Vietnam

T. G. Hoang (✉)
Department of Business Innovation, School of Business and Management, RMIT University, Ho Chi Minh City, Vietnam
e-mail: thinh.hoanggia@rmit.edu.vn

D. A. Le
Institute of Economics and Strategic Management, Hanoi, Vietnam

School of Science and Technology, RMIT University, Ho Chi Minh City, Vietnam

N. H. Vu
Faculty of International Trade and Logistics, Hoa Sen University, Ho Chi Minh City, Vietnam

© The Author(s), under exclusive license to Springer Nature Singapore Pte Ltd. 2023
N. H. Thuan et al. (eds.), *Information Systems Research in Vietnam*,
https://doi.org/10.1007/978-981-19-3804-7_3

33

1 Introduction

Although the past decade has seen the rapid development of innovation in many business areas, innovation is actually reported as usually taking place outside the organization's boundary through collaboration and engagement with a wide range of different parties, thereby overcoming the limitations of capability and resources of a single company [19, 25]. In addition, the innovation is embedded and developed in the extent of an ecosystem which enables the accumulation of available resources including both tangible and intangible resources such as intellectual or policies and incentives [20, 28]. In fact, high-tech entrepreneurship ecosystems have been reported as being able to accelerate ventures based on their technology-enabled advantages. Some examples of high-tech ecosystems include Silicon Valley in California, US, Cambridge Science Park, Cambridge, UK; and Medicon Valley, Sweden. Other developing countries around the world, especially Asia, have also seriously started to develop technological and high-tech entrepreneurship ecosystems to leverage the national economy, industrial and information technology (IT) capabilities such as Zhangjiang Hi-Tech Park in Shanghai, Zhongguancun Science & Technology Zone in Beijing, China; Technopark, Trivandrum, India.

Existing research high-tech entrepreneurship ecosystems create a significant contribution to the development of the economy as well as accelerating the development of digital start-ups [26, 27]. Nonetheless, existing research on innovation and technology management favors the research in the level of organization (for instance, see [4, 19] and disregards innovation and technological advancement at the ecosystem level [9]. The traditional thoughts of innovation or R&D development in an organization were that the boundaries in the organization may reduce the transaction costs required for innovation and R&D activities. However, the transaction costs can in fact only be reduced when there are clear distributions of resources, labor, and efforts following a clear action agenda [10, 24]. In the context of the entrepreneurship ecosystem, the involvement of a variety of parties inside an ecosystem is clearly recognized, although a comprehensive investigation of how technological entrepreneurship ecosystems manage such involvements and support the development of digital start-ups, requires further examination. In other words, unlike the organizational structure, a start-up ecosystem lacks the managerial authority for management and supervision, thus, how a startup ecosystem can perform division of labor and task allocation may need further investigation. In addition, start-up ecosystems may include a variety of startups that do not share the same goal and free decision-making depending on their interests, which may result in potential conflicts rather than cooperation [16]. Thus, the insights into how tech startup ecosystems facilitate and manage coordination and collaboration among participating startups may need further investigation.

As a result, this chapter intends to explore how a digital entrepreneurship ecosystem is able to support the development of digital start-ups. To fulfil this purpose, a critical case study of Quang Trung Software City (QTSC), a successful business and technological park, and a number of digital start-ups located and operated inside QTSC, were approached. The aim of this research is twofold; first, we explore the current difficulties and challenges that digital start-ups have faced. Second, we also examine how QTSC is able to support the digital start-ups to overcome these challenges, which therefore facilitates development of digital start-ups. Our chapter extends the digital entrepreneurship literature by investigating digital entrepreneurship at the ecosystem level, which highlights that a digital entrepreneurship ecosystem is able to accumulate support and available resources to facilitate the development of digital start-ups.

This paper is organized as follows: in the next section, this chapter reviews relevant literature on digital entrepreneurship and the digital entrepreneurship ecosystem. The research methodology of this paper is introduced next. In Sect. 4, the research background of the case study is discussed. Section 5 presents research findings. Finally, a brief conclusion is provided in Sect. 6.

2 Literature Background

2.1 Digital Entrepreneurship

Digital entrepreneurship can be understood to be an entrepreneurial venture that takes place digitally through technology-enabled applications and platforms rather than original direct forms [18]. Given that digital entrepreneurship, products, services, distribution channels, business activities, interaction and communication, or even the workplace and operations could be enabled or facilitated by digital or technological advancement [11, 13], these digital ventures have developed or adopted different business models, suffered from different challenges, and faced different opportunities. However, the current interest in digital entrepreneurship mainly focuses on the marketing operation in the digital environment (e.g., also known as digital marketing), although in most of the aspects of digital ventures, entrepreneurs can face new business opportunities and unexpected advantage competitiveness associated to management, branding, and resources, which directly influence the overall performance of their businesses [12, 15, 26, 27].

Market orientation is at the heart of any digital enterprise, it is the higher extreme digital feature of a business and also the most vital component of market orientation [14]. This can be explained by adding that digital enterprise may focus on advancing the digital features, products or services, forgetting the fact that consumers are more interested in the applicable aspect of those features, products, and services [18]. In addition, given the recent increase in competitive and rapid expansion of digital businesses and marketplaces, the focus on market orientation on customers' demands is a fundamental characteristic to define whether a new digital venture can survive and continue growing [21].

Given the emergence of this popular use of technology, and the technology-enabled applications, platforms, and social media among global citizens, any digital venture can be accessed by a wide range of customers [12]. However, the negative implications of technology-enabled platforms and applications can also deliver negative effects to businesses, and continue to reshape all aspects and features of digital enterprises or start-ups. More research is needed to explore how new digital ventures develop as well as how the surrounding support and facilitators challenge the development of digital start-ups.

2.2   Innovation and Digital Entrepreneurship Ecosystem

Digital Innovation involves the integration of digital capability and available resources, including physical resources, human capital, and intellectual capital to develop evolutionary products, services, and operation processes. Due to the limitations of resources, management, and intellectual capital from a single organization, it is challenge for a single firm to generate a significant innovation [19, 26, 27]. Instead, collaboration and participation work from a number of organizations enables us to expand boundaries and overcome limitations of resources and capabilities from a single firm, which results in a huge leap in innovation [5]. As a result, an ecosystem consisting of available resources, network, and collaboration can be seen as a nest for digital innovation activities. The nexus between innovation and entrepreneurship came from digital businesses or start-ups, which are grounded by the unique digital innovation [13].

According to Allen [1], digital entrepreneurship can be defined as a multi-dimensional phenomenon, which contains three intertwined aspects, including the business aspect, the knowledge aspect, and the institutional aspect. The first dimension, the business aspect, involves the establishment of a new business, which is a typical type of entrepreneurship. Second, the knowledge aspect involves the construction of a new venture based on creative knowledge or an innovative idea, in which a unique competitive advantage of a business is maintained. Innovators and inventors are typical examples of knowledge entrepreneurs [18]. Finally, the institutional aspect enables the transformation of a traditional business model into a new one through leveraging available resources or technological tools, for instance, a number of companies such as eBay, Amazon, or Airbnb have developed new types of business based on the traditional retail sector. A number of scholars suggest that digital ventures need to integrate these three aspects of a business in order to construct a successful digital enterprise, which is firstly based on a typical business form, with additional creative technological features products, services, or features and then transforms the regular business form into a new and innovative one, embracing institutional implications.

The digital entrepreneurship ecosystem can be defined as an ecosystem nurturing and facilitating the establishment and development of new digital ventures. As an ecosystem integrates sufficient resources, facilitators, and supporting factors beyond the organizational boundary, a digital entrepreneurship ecosystem is thus vital for the success of digital enterprises as well as new ventures [15]. Similarly, Elia et al. [7] argue that a digital entrepreneurship ecosystem comprises a technology-enabled infrastructure and available support that enables the utilization of technologies and digital platforms to support knowledge transfer and opportunities generation to stimulate the digital business ecosystem. Finally, Steininger [22] distinguished the digital entrepreneurship ecosystem from other entrepreneurship ecosystems as the digital entrepreneurship ecosystem enables digital enterprise chasing opportunities based on the advancement of innovative technologies and digital species rather than other regular business and institutional aspects, enabled by the regular entrepreneurship ecosystem. Nonetheless, extant researches on digital entrepreneurship have focused on organizational innovation, in which business processes, internal and external institutional contexts are the critical aspects [9, 11], and there is a scarcity of research focusing on digital entrepreneurship in the ecosystem level. Besides, ecosystem-enabled innovation capabilities to support new digital ventures should be given more attention to shed light on the innovation supporting capabilities offered by the entrepreneurship ecosystem in Vietnam.

Early research attempts of the digital entrepreneurship ecosystem classified the implications of digital entrepreneurship ecosystem for startups into three main aspects: "task allocation", "task division" and "information flow" (Puranam et al., 2014) [16, p. 2].

"Task division" relates to the managerial tasks that divide the primary goal of an organization into detailed tasks for each part of an organization. Put differently, this process results in a list of duties that all parts of an organization need to fulfill. Researchers in this research stream highlight a number of aspects that directly relate to "task division", such as "excluding members that do not fit the system goal"; "no essential tasks remaining incomplete", and "little redundancy among subtasks" (Puranam et al., 2014) [16, p. 2], maintaining the co-specialization and effective collaboration between members [23], and transparency of task division [2].

"Task allocation" is associated with allocating tasks to those with appropriate specialization and capabilities. The proposed mechanisms for performing task allocation are selected based on appropriate capability, resources, and other advantages [16]. The process of task allocation can be impacted by both external and internal influences such as competition, environment, and resources [25].

"Information flow" implies the supply of information that a member in the ecosystem may require to perform the operation and development [9]. Furthermore, in the digital startup, the information flow also relates to the protection of sensitive commercial information that directly relates to the intellectual property inside each startup organization [7]. The information flow constructs the connection among parties to integrate efforts that facilitate the collaboration and information exchanges [15]. The technological communities such as the digital startups' ecosystems play a fundamental role as a place for information exchange and collaboration [16, 26, 27].

3 Methodology

A large and growing body of case-based research has investigated the digital entrepreneurship and entrepreneurship ecosystem [15, 16, 26, 27]. This study adopts Flyvbjerg [8]'s critical case study methodology, and aims to highlight the supporting role of QTSC for the digital start-ups in Vietnam. The adoption of critical case research facilitates the investigation of the "how" research question, and is suited for conducting research with the aim of theory contribution and development in a new phenomenon, i.e., the digital entrepreneurship ecosystem in Vietnam. In addition, the case research method is also appropriate for exploring complex phenomena such as how entrepreneurship including start-ups organization and entrepreneurs are intricately embedded into the social context of start-ups ecosystems, in which the comprehensive settings of the background can be illuminated [17, 19].

We choose QTSC as a critical case target as the digital entrepreneurship ccosystem for a number of reasons. First, QTSC is typical of a technological park with given incentives and support from the government in terms of development strategy, infrastructures, human resources, intellectual, and financial capitals. In addition, organization members gathered in QTSC have supported the development of QTSC as well as the entrepreneurship ecosystem in QTSC. Second, most infrastructures, communities, and activities in QTSC are related to the technological development, digital business, and entrepreneurship in the technological area. Besides, QTSC is a successful digital business park in Vietnam and is well-known as a typical example of the digital ecosystem, thereby other areas in Vietnam try to imitate QTSC's development agenda to develop their own entrepreneurship ecosystems.

3.1 Data Collection

While the qualitative critical case study had been adopted as the primary research method, our data collection includes two main stages. In the first stage, which took place from January 2021 to March 2021 we gathered archival documents and published information regarding the development, business operation, and engagement with entrepreneurship and the development of digital start-ups. After collecting and synthesizing the data source of archival records, a holistic picture was created about QTSC's operation in the context of Vietnam's digital transformation and business environment.

In the second phase, informal interviews have been conducted in terms of conversation; informal conversations are conducted without the use of any structured interview guide of any kind. The research team either takes note or tries to remember content in conversations with respondents in the field. According to Cassell et al. [6], informal interviews should be conducted in the early stages of development of a research, where there are a few studies describing the field and the issue of interest. Through informal interviews, the researcher is able to develop the foundation of rapport and build an understanding of the field [17]. A total of 10 informal interviews were conducted with two main groups from March 2021 to May 2021, the first group includes the founders, business managers, and technological experts from digital start-ups at QTSC; and the second group consists of a number of managers and staff members of QTSC. Each conversation lasted between 45 min to an hour and was conducted by at least two researchers. These archival records, published information, and interviews yield 85 pages of documentation and notes.

3.2 Data Analysis

Data analysis began in August 2021, whereby the qualitative data analysis techniques including open coding, axial coding, and selective coding were adopted to systematically analyze all data sources [3]. While the open coding is used to segment data into meaningful expressions and then classified into terms or short sequence, different relationships and connections among all of the categories are developed through axial coding. Finally, selective coding is adopted to select a typical category and link other categories to the typical one in order to construct a consistent storyline of a phenomenon of interest. In detail, open coding is employed to highlight the fundamental themes from all data sources such as "market orientation experienced by startups", "ambiguous prototype design", "lack of involvement of potential customer", and "inconsistent visions". Axial coding and selective coding are conducted together, and this requires the review of previous literature, so that findings are supported by relevant literature. This analysis stage requires the researcher to identify a connection among the themes, for instance, "ambiguous prototype design", "lack of involvement of potential customer", and "inconsistent visions" to reflect the difficulties and challenges that start-ups have faced during the completion of their products and services, thus we linked and organized them as "completion of digital products and services".

To ensure a certain level of reliability, data were triangulated by interviewing and reviewing available literature and archival records. In order to achieve validity, we adopted the Intercoder procedure, whereby two researchers were involved in the data analysis stage and they coded material and data sources independently. Following this, these researchers presented their results to other researchers to get feedback, thus subsequently enhancing the validity of our results.

4 Case Narrative

4.1 Overview

Quang Trung Software City (QTSC) has been established since March 2001, and was intended to operate as a business and technology park covering an area of 43 ha (or

43 ha). In 2017, QTSC was ranked third out of the eight technology parks in Asia in terms of providing preferential policies and incentives for attracting investors, technology firms and also digital enterprises. In 2018, QTSC was the first state-owned enterprise in Ho Chi Minh City to be recognized as the science and technology enterprise. Currently, after nearly 20 years of operation, there are 165 technology companies, including 6 corporations with over 1000 staff members, 52 foreign enterprises, and several technology universities and research centers have operated and been located in this park. These organizations have combined to build and provide more than 250 digital products, services, and solutions for various sectors. The products and solutions have been exported to over 20 foreign countries. Up to now, QTSC is the first, largest, and most successful software park in Vietnam. Besides, QTSC has currently and officially become a "software learning city" serving approximately 22,000 experts, engineers, and students, who are working and studying regularly.

Given a clear intention from the very beginning, QTSC was planned, designed, and built as an urban model of a software city with three main infrastructure foundations, including:

1. Technology infrastructure: this comprises elements related to value creation, value-added for the IT industry as well as other technologies such as the internet infrastructure, data centers, R&D departments, IR applications and experimental areas, software business incubation centers, technology research institutes, and universities and colleges.
2. Urban infrastructure: this is the technical infrastructure foundation designed and constructed to create the environment and basic amenities for production and business activities of enterprises, roads, office buildings, parks, power sources, fiber optic infrastructure, and waste treatment system.
3. Service infrastructure: this is a set of utilities serving the needs of the community which is living, working and studying in the area such as finance and banking services, sports areas, restaurants, cafes, convenience stores, and apartments.

At the preliminary time in 2000, the design of QTSC was an outstanding, boldly designed, and planned model, with a long-term strategic vision. This planning of this model was based on these three foundations and it is the foundation to help QTSC develop, connect and provide support to Vietnam, foreign digital businesses, and start-ups to grow continuously.

Along with the sustainable development of businesses in the community organized by QTSC, the number of technical experts, IT engineers, scientists, and software enterprises has increased continuously over the years, which is the premise and foundation for QTSC to make fundamental changes in alignment with the latest trend in global innovations such as the emergence of the fourth industrial revolution, which introduces a new phase in the design, organization and supervision of the industrial value chain.

Besides the primary roles of performing as a data center and ensuring cybersecurity for the city of Ho Chi Minh's e-government programs, QTSC has participated in the Start-up of Seeding Programs proposed by the Vietnamese government with the overreaching aim to support digital start-ups in Vietnam, due to a number of incomparable advantages: (i) QTSC is among the top technology parks in Asia; (ii) QTSC owns the largest IT business community ecosystem in Vietnam with hundreds of technical products, solutions and services, connecting with partners around the world; (iii) QTSC has a community of highly qualified IT human resources, including experts, IT engineers, and scientists; (iv) QTSC has a modern IT infrastructure, which is synchronized with the internet infrastructure directly connected to many international gateways; the Wi-Fi network system covers the entire buildings and the optical fiber system is underground; (v) QTSC is designed and built with a software city model as a miniature city, providing full technical infrastructure and utility services for the community.

4.2   Start-Ups Development Agenda at QTSC

To support digital start-ups, the management team at QTSC outlines a strategy with several layers with the aim being to support start-ups to complete their digital products or services, as well as supporting them through the market orientation and growing stages. At the core of the operation and development of QTSC are the available infrastructures and technical communities. As a corporation is responsible for ensuring the provision of services related to data center and information security for the e-government and smart city activities of Ho Chi Minh city and some southern provinces, QTSC must fully meet the highest requirements for the technology and business park, meeting the international standards. Besides, the fact that the strong technical community of software engineers and technical experts has been continuously growing over the years, it has become a premise and powerful human resource for QTSC to make a fundamental foundation to support digital businesses.

In order to provide the support for digital start-ups, QTSC develop and implement a fully integrated system including technology development, technology connection, and analysis and sharing of information, which allows both QSTC to support technology completion, and also digital start-ups to connect to partners and segments, as well as analyzing and providing feedback and ideas for digital start-ups for completing products and penetrating markets, toward the three highest goals of the digital start-ups supporting process. These aspects are improving the quality of management and internal operations, increasing customer satisfaction, and developing the brand, which therefore contributes to the success of the Vietnamese digital business sector.

5 Findings

5.1 Challenges Faced by Digital Start-Ups

Completion of digital products and services

Ambiguous prototype design

The first challenges that respondents from start-ups have faced were the ambiguous prototype designs. In the initial stage of digital start-ups, long-term planning for the prototype is usually disregarded, and instead, the designer aims to create prototypes that either attract attention from the users or quickly satisfy market orientation needs. Nonetheless, the main challenge of swift prototyping came from the great efforts needed to spend to advance the prototype conception sufficiently. When each prototype is designed to serve different ad-hoc purposes without considering the number of required prototypes as well as the essential criteria, it may lead to an increase in expenses, risks, and waste of time and effort. The ambiguous prototype design has appeared in several start-ups, in which entrepreneurs and their working teams have worked without pre-determined goals or detailed planning with an optimal product roadmap. As a result, when processing ideas into real products or services, many different prototypes were created. In other words, the roadmap of product/service development has diverged from the original thoughts, where prototypes were developed one after another, which led to a long prototype development process with additional costs, thus wasting effort and time.

Inconsistent visions

The idea of an inconsistent vision between the entrepreneurial team have also been indicated by respondents as a critical challenge for product/service completion. The founder team of start-ups is typically a set of talented members with diverse expertise, perceptions, and experience. Entrepreneurial idea development requires a lot of discussions and conceptualization. A diverse group with different business and technical expertise and experience may lengthen the development of the entrepreneurial idea and prototypes. Similarly, internal communication among people with diverse expertise and experience during development stages is time-consuming and sometimes unsuccessful due to misunderstandings. Furthermore, the diversity in experience and expertise in entrepreneurial groups may lead to diverged ideas and development strategies among the founders. Thus, the completion of digital products, services and prototype development time should also take into account the time taken to pursue, convince, and create harmonization between the start-up team members.

Lack of involvement of potential customers

The final idea related to the completion of digital products and services raised by informants was the lack of understanding of the customer need from start-ups. To understand and identify end users fully, the start-up must be able to solve two problems, first to identify potential lead users, and second, to understand whether there is an actual market for their products or services. This idea came from the fact that not all customers' experiences are valuable input for the prototype development. Findings gathered from typical user groups are vital for developing market-driven digital products or services. Those users are defined as the lead customers, and they can play as a trigger for a new market segment through their experience of new technology at the early development stage. Accessing those potential customers and the market segment is not an easy task for start-ups. Instead, most entrepreneurs believe that this is a bottleneck for their start-ups to identify potential market segments. Challenges from finding the potential market segment may reflect the limitation of the capability in business and communication experience of founders, or it came from the fact that the products and services of start-ups can only satisfy small demands from the user, otherwise it is difficult to find the relevant potential customers.

Market orientation

In addition to the challenges related to digital products and service completion, market orientation was another significant concern highlighted by the respondents. Market orientation is one of the main obsessions relating to customer demands and competitors' strategies and activities. It is an approach for the enterprise to understand and identify the desires and requirements of customers clearly and to create or enhance products/services to satisfy these demands. The founders of start-ups consider the desires of the customer as a significant component of their design, research, and development (R&D) for new products and services. While market orientation is vital for every business, it is even more essential for new enterprises, because regardless of their particular type of business structure, they all need to develop their own market segment and to compete with the existing competitors in the market.

Market orientation is considered as the most conventional and appropriate strategy for start-ups in terms of marketing strategy as well as product development, as the existing enterprises focus on a typical marketing strategy which develops the main selling points to promote existing products and services, rather than creating or enhancing products/services with characteristics that desired by the consumer, thereby maintaining a high level of customer satisfaction and promoting brand loyalty and corporate reputation, leading to a long term competitive advantage. To be successful in market orientation, the entrepreneurial team need to identify the stakeholders' experience and demands, including customer needs, competitors' strategies and activities, employees and corporate performance, so that a future agenda can be developed to address the insights gathered from these assessments. In addition, the management team also need to ensure that all business functions and units can understand and proceed with the market orientation so that market orientation can become a part of corporate culture. These concerns have moved beyond matters of profit and loss, and emphasize that firms need to satisfy stakeholders' needs from where the future benefits will come. In case of digital businesses, this involves a number of technical and managerial aspects which do not currently exist in regular firms such as technical expert communities, digital customer management platforms, and virtual value chain management.

Market orientation in digital start-ups can be distinguished from regular start-ups through a number of aspects. First, digital start-ups require and demand technological skills and competencies. The more that start-ups developed, the more advanced the demand was for the technological features of their products or services. Thus, entrepreneurs and their enterprises can be allured to the improvement of technological advancement, causing them to ignore the fundamental aspect of market orientation. Second, although the advance in some technological applications such as a business intelligence and analytics system can be developed in a few start-ups to report insights of customer needs and forecast customer expectation, the digital area is information-rich and contains far more insights than the regular market. Besides, given the limitation in input data, experience and knowledge of the existing business environment, these applications may not deliver accurate results.

5.2 How QTSC Can Support Digital Start-Ups

Through the corporation and partnership with QTSC, a number of challenges from operations, management and technological capabilities of digital start-ups can be addressed and improved.

Management capabilities

Management capability is one of the significant challenges for start-ups only in the initial stage, although it is also a challenge in managing development in start-ups toward a mature business. In many start-up cases, founders are not equipped with managerial experience to lead their digital enterprises. Although the initial competitive advantage of digital start-ups came from unique technological features, products, and services, when the start-ups began to grow older, their innovative features and business models need to be managed in an appropriate balance. The growing start-ups should have different experts in both technical and management areas which may trigger innovative and entrepreneurial capabilities for a start-up. The lack of experts with the knowledge of an entrepreneurial mindset have been recognized in many digital startups. However, a connection with QTSC can deliver useful management knowledge through interaction and consultancy with a network of founders and experts from other successful digital start-ups and enterprises, as it allows managers from start-ups to learn from each other continuously about succeeding while completing digital products or services as well as penetrating the market.

These results are consistent with those of other studies by Puranam et al. (2014) and Thomas and Autio [23], which suggest that the continuous learning from founders and experts from startups can help to reduce the redundancy among subtasks as well as sustaining the co-specialization and collaboration between new and existing startups in the digital ecosystem.

Intellectual management, exchange, and protection

The management, exchange and protection of intellectual knowledge is critical to maintaining business development and success. New ventures need to develop an organizational learning culture, in which managers and staff members are able to learn from past experiences, gather and utilize information from both internal and external aspects, exploit the intellectual systems developed by their expertise, and join a knowledge exchange network which also protects start-up's sensitive digital knowledge and intellectual property. For start-up businesses, knowledge and intellectual exchange and acquisition are fundamental resources for them to develop into a mature company; knowledge and intellectual ability are unable to transform into technological creations or be competitive themselves (and then take advantage of that competitiveness). They need to integrate with another capability through interaction and collaboration with other partners and experts. These findings match those observed in earlier studies of Baldwin and Clark [2], Thomas and Autio [23] and Li et al. [16], which highlight the collaboration between existing firms with startups as an essential feature for reducing the efforts for entrepreneurs as well as other staff in startups.

Furthermore, intellectual protection is also a critical point for the success of a digital business, because cyber-attacks and other related risks may damage the rest of the company, which create both a threat on the intellectual and also a loss of sensitive knowledge and business know-how. QTSC have supported their start-ups by developing communities of digital mature businesses and start-ups, in which leaders can exchange intellectual knowledge with the aim of building learning organizations and a culture of digital knowledge sharing. The findings observed in this study mirror those of the previous studies which indicated that a digital entrepreneurship ecosystem comprises a technology-enabled infrastructure and available support to facilitate the development of digital startups [7]. Moreover, the cyber security procedures and corresponding applications have also been developed and introduced by experts from QTSC, who are able to help managers from start-ups to build the appropriate cyber security procedures for their start-ups. This support helps to sustain start-ups' capabilities during the completion of digital products and services processes, and it also offers cyber-protection methods for start-ups during their initial development as well as the market orientation stages. These results agree with the findings of previous research which distinguish the digital entrepreneurship ecosystem from other entrepreneurship eco-systems as the digital entrepreneurship ecosystem enables digital enterprise-chasing opportunities based on the advancement of innovative technologies rather than other regular business and institutional aspects, enabled by the regular entrepreneurship ecosystem.

Measurement of performance and KPIs

Another concern from the start-ups' founders was the development of appropriate KPIs and business performance measurements. Unlike regular corporate types, digital start-ups grounded their business on unique and creative technological products and services, thus KPIs and performance may need to be customized to meet specific organizational contexts. In addition, it is vital to measure the influence of corporate performance continuously to understand whether creative products or services are able to deliver valuable outcomes, and also consider the possible actions to be introduced to enhance the business performance. Furthermore, in the growing stage, the other business indicators should be more focused to ensure that the start-ups continue to develop and become mature firms. In these cases, QTSC have helped start-ups to address this concern by introducing the technological application to facilitate the KPIs and business performance measure, thereby allowing the management team to understand their start-up's performance, which means allowing management to take further valuable actions during the market orientation stage. These findings match the "task allocation" aspect, which referred to the allocation of appropriate specialization and capabilities for fulfilling the development of digital startups [16]. The process of task allocation is influenced by the infrastructure and available resources provided by the digital startups ecosystem [25].

Networks development

In the initial establishment stage and the transformation stage toward mature business, the networks of investors, support, and people of know-how have a strong impact for all of the new ventures. From the very beginning, the management team in a start-up needs to develop external connections with potential consumers, investors, business partners, and also with people of know-how in the digital area. Such networks both allow start-ups to create and expand the market segment, and they also allow them to receive support from experts to complete their digital products and services, adding valuable features and possibilities, thereby enhancing the competitiveness advantage for their company. Network development is a critical feature and support that QTSC has delivered for their start-up partners and, in addition to multiple teams of technology experts and information technology engineers, QTSC has developed collaborative programs with several training centers and universities specializing in technologies in QTSC, including FPT University, Hoa Sen University and SaigonTech (University of Houston branch). Given the great human resource and expert support, digital start-ups can receive tremendous chances and opportunities for network development. Thus, support from the network achieved through collaboration with QTSC can help start-ups with technical insights for product or service completion, and also offer opportunities to reach and expand market segments to deal with market orientation concerns. This study produced results which corroborate the findings of a great deal of previous work in this field, such as Li et al. [16] and Zaheer et al. [26, 27], by highlighting the role of QTSC in enhancing the connection among parties to integrate efforts that facilitate the collaboration and information exchanges [15].

6 Conclusion

Our chapter indicates the current challenges faced by digital start-ups and highlights the supporting role of QTSC for the digital start-ups in Vietnam through enhancing management capabilities; intellectual management, exchange, and protection; developing measurement of performance and KPIs; and network development. Our work also documents the start-ups development agenda at QTSC and indicates antecedents for digital start-ups development, including available infrastructure and strong technology communities which can contribute significantly, and makes ground for the development of digital businesses and start-ups at QTSC. While this chapter highlights a detailed investigation of how QTSC is able to support the digital start-ups to overcome these challenges, which therefore facilitates the development of digital start-ups, the results are not directly generalizable. However, as a critical case research, our findings can be transferred to other similar contexts with similar settings in Vietnam.

This chapter makes a number of contributions to research into digital start-ups and the start-ups ecosystem in Vietnam. First, we indicate two main challenges being faced by digital start-ups, including completion of digital products and services and market orientation. Through this, we demonstrate that digital start-ups have faced significant business and management challenges such as inconsistent visions and seeking potential market segment rather than technical difficulties during their initial development stage. In addition, findings from our work suggest that, given the available advantages such as digital infrastructure and a strong community of experts, scientists, and business leaders, QTSC is able to support digital start-ups to deal with both technical competition and development, as well as business issues such as market orientation. Finally, our research also identifies explicit resources and processes inside QTSC, giving great internal resources, a clear development agenda and vision. As well as incentives and support from the government, QTSC has become a place to nurture and support the development of digital business and start-ups in Vietnam.

References

1. Allen, J. P. (2019). *Digital entrepreneurship*. Routledge.
2. Baldwin, C. Y., & Clark, K. B. (2006). The architecture of participation: Does code architecture mitigate free riding in the open source development model? *Management Science, 52*(7), 1116–1127.
3. Belk, R. W. (Ed.). (2007). *Handbook of qualitative research methods in marketing*. Edward Elgar Publishing.
4. Bertola, P., & Teixeira, J. C. (2003). Design as a knowledge agent: How design as a knowledge process is embedded into organizations to foster innovation. *Design Studies, 24*(2), 181–194.
5. Bougrain, F., & Haudeville, B. (2002). Innovation, collaboration and SMEs internal research capacities. *Research Policy, 31*(5), 735–747.
6. Cassell, C., Cunliffe, A. L., & Grandy, G. (Eds.). (2017). *The SAGE handbook of qualitative business and management research methods*. Sage.
7. Elia, G., Margherita, A., & Passiante, G. (2020). Digital entrepreneurship ecosystem: How digital technologies and collective intelligence are reshaping the entrepreneurial process. *Technological Forecasting and Social Change, 150*, 119791.
8. Flyvbjerg, B. (2006). Five misunderstandings about case-study research. *Qualitative Inquiry, 12*(2), 219–245.

9. Gawer, A., & Cusumano, M. A. (2014). Industry platforms and ecosystem innovation. *Journal of Product Innovation Management, 31*(3), 417–433.
10. Hoang C. V., Hoang T. G., Vu N. H., & Le D. A. (2021a) Innovation and sustainability. In D. Crowther & S. Seifi (Eds.), *The Palgrave handbook of corporate social responsibility* (pp. 1245–1267). Palgrave Macmillan. https://doi.org/10.1007/978-3-030-42465-7_42
11. Hoang, C. V., Hoang, T. G., & Kane, V. (2021b). Technological approaches to sustainability. In D. Crowther, & S. Seifi (Eds.), *The palgrave handbook of corporate social responsibility* (pp. 355–380). Palgrave Macmillan. https://doi.org/10.1007/978-3-030-42465-7_37
12. Hoang, T. G., Nguyen, G. N., & Le, D. A. (2022). Developments in financial technologies for achieving the sustainable development goals (SDGs): FinTech and SDGs. In U. Akkucuk (Ed.), *Disruptive technologies and eco-innovation for sustainable development* (pp. 1–19). IGI Global. https://doi.org/10.4018/978-1-7998-8900-7.ch001
13. Hull, C. E. K., Hung, Y. T. C., Hair, N., Perotti, V., & DeMartino, R. (2007). Taking advantage of digital opportunities: A typology of digital entrepreneurship. *International Journal of Networking and Virtual Organisations, 4*(3), 290–303.
14. Joensuu-Salo, S., Sorama, K., Viljamaa, A., & Varamäki, E. (2018). Firm performance among internationalized SMEs: The interplay of market orientation, marketing capability and digitalization. *Administrative Sciences, 8*(3), 31.
15. Kraus, S., Palmer, C., Kailer, N., Kallinger, F. L., & Spitzer, J. (2018). Digital entrepreneurship: A research agenda on new business models for the twenty-first century. *International Journal of Entrepreneurial Behavior & Research, 25*(2), 353–375.
16. Li, W., Du, W., & Yin, J. (2017). Digital entrepreneurship ecosystem as a new form of organizing: The case of Zhongguancun. *Frontiers of Business Research in China, 11*(1), 1–21.
17. Myers, M. D. (2019). *Qualitative research in business and management.* Sage.
18. Nambisan, S. (2017). Digital entrepreneurship: Toward a digital technology perspective of entrepreneurship. *Entrepreneurship Theory and Practice, 41*(6), 1029–1055.
19. Nguyen, H. T., Hoang, T. G., & Luu, H. (2019). Corporate social responsibility in Vietnam: Opportunities and innovation experienced by multinational corporation subsidiaries. *Social Responsibility Journal, 16*(6), 771–792.
20. Nguyen, H. T., Hoang, T. G., Nguyen, L. Q. T., Le, H. P., & Mai, H. X. V. (2021). Green technology transfer in a developing country: Mainstream practitioner views. *International Journal of Organizational Analysis, 65*(4), 11–21.
21. Quinton, S., Canhoto, A., Molinillo, S., Pera, R., & Budhathoki, T. (2018). Conceptualising a digital orientation: Antecedents of supporting SME performance in the digital economy. *Journal of Strategic Marketing, 26*(5), 427–439.
22. Steininger, D. M. (2019). Linking information systems and entrepreneurship: A review and agenda for IT-associated and digital entrepreneurship research. *Information Systems Journal, 29*(2), 363–407.
23. Thomas, L., & Erkko Autio. (2012). Modeling the ecosystem: a meta-synthesis of ecosystem and related literatures. In *DRUID 2012 Conference, Copenhagen (Denmark).*
24. Wang, J. (2014). R&D activities in start-up firms: What can we learn from founding resources? *Technology Analysis & Strategic Management, 26*(5), 517–529.
25. Wijnberg, N. M. (2004). Innovation and organization: Value and competition in selection systems. *Organization Studies, 25*(8), 1413–1433.
26. Zaheer, H., Breyer, Y., & Dumay, J. (2019). Digital entrepreneurship: An interdisciplinary structured literature review and research agenda. *Technological Forecasting and Social Change, 148*, 119735.
27. Zaheer, H., Breyer, Y., Dumay, J., & Enjeti, M. (2019). Straight from the horse's mouth: Founders' perspectives on achieving 'traction' in digital start-ups. *Computers in Human Behavior, 95*, 262–274.
28. Zhang, Y., Khan, U., Lee, S., & Salik, M. (2019). The influence of management innovation and technological innovation on organization performance. A Mediating Role of Sustainability. *Sustainability, 11*(2), 495.

Organizational Change and Enterprise Architecture Adoption: A Case Study in the Public Sector

Duong Dang and Samuli Pekkola

Abstract Enterprise architecture (EA) adoption initiates broad changes in organizations and organizational functions. However, the existing literature on how and what factors influence the changes in EA adoption remains limited. Our study aims to fill in this gap. We study how the EA-initiated changes occur and what are the factors influencing it. Our process-oriented perspective, our data from a qualitative case study, and the lens of organizational change illustrate how the changes occur in organizations, what the factors are, and how especially managers and their activities influence the change. We show that the change is both sociotechnical and punctuated, oscillating between different organizational levels.

Keywords Enterprise architecture · Organizational change · Public sector

1 Introduction

Enterprise architecture (EA) adoption refers to how the organizations get introduced and start to use and use EA [1]. It takes place through EA programs, schemes, or projects that develop and operationalize EA features and functionalities into the organization's real-life practices. Many organizations have adopted EA to improve their operations, such as strategic management, decision making, information technology (IT)–business alignment, and IT consolidation. Also, public sectors in several countries, for example in the United States, Netherlands, and Denmark, have implemented laws or master plans to advance EA adoption [1].

Although EA is said to improve organizational operations, EA initiatives are struggling with several challenges, including slow utilization, ineffective adoption, and even failures [2]. To facilitate EA initiatives, an in-depth understanding about EA

D. Dang (✉)
University of Vaasa, 65200 Vaasa, Finland
e-mail: duong.dang@uwasa.fi

S. Pekkola
Tampere University, 33720 Tampere, Finland
e-mail: samuli.pekkola@tuni.fi

adoption and its practices is needed [3, 4]. Like other large-scale implementations [5, 6], EA adoption initiates changes in organizational functions and forms [7, 8]. However, the relationship between EA adoption and organizational change is unclear because both EA adoption processes and organizational change unfold over years [9].

The EA literature mostly focuses on EA, on EA concepts, or its frameworks and success factors [1, 10]. In addition, EA research often concentrates on a specific phase of adoption, such as the design [11], implementation [12], or post-implementation phase (e.g., EA management [EAM] usage [13]). Little emphasis has been placed on the adoption process or the relationships between EA adoption and the organization. As a result, cross-sectional studies taking, for example, a process-oriented perspective spanning from the EA investment decision to its implementation and full legitimization, are missing. We attempt to fill this gap. We aim at answering the following research question: How does the change unravel in organizations when they adopt EA?

We present a qualitative case study on a large EA project in Vietnam, interviewing the EA project's key personnel. We supplement the interview findings with several documents, informal discussions, and observations to deepen our understanding of the relevant political, social, and contextual issues. Organizational change theory is employed as an analytical lens because it provides an appropriate means of examining exogenous and endogenous factors in the adoption process. We analyze the stakeholder activities and behaviors in relation to the EA project's activities and events throughout the project. Our analysis ranges from the macrolevel (sector level) to the microlevel (e.g., organizational level and even individual level) to provide comprehensive understanding about the relation between EA adoption and organizational change [14].

The paper continues with the literature review and theoretical framework section, followed by the research context and methods section. Then, we present our empirical findings, and the paper continues with the discussion. Finally, the paper ends with a concluding section.

2 Related Research and Theoretical Framework

2.1 Conceptual Basics

EA is "an approach to improve the alignment between the organization's business and their information technologies. It attempts to capture the status of the organizations' business architecture, information resources, information systems, and technologies so that the gaps and weaknesses in their processes and infrastructures can be identified, and development directions planned" [1, p. 130]. The term EAM refers to "management activities conducted in an organization to install, maintain and purposefully develop an organization's EA" [13, p. 412]. In this respect, the EA project and its activities can be understood as being a part of EAM.

EA stakeholders range from users to project members and managers. They produce, use, or facilitate EA artefacts, which include models, principles, strategies, and EA layers (e.g., architectures). EA artefacts can be understood as project products.

2.2 EA Adoption and Organizational Change

EA adoption studies focus on concepts and frameworks, and how EA is used [1, 10]. Some specific phases of EAM are also usually considered [11–13]. They contribute to outcomes [3], benefits, and value [13] in those phases. The literature also takes the IT perspective [12] or the project or organizational level of analysis [13]. We extend this by adopting a process-oriented perspective instead of focusing on some specific phase of EA adoption, and concentrate on macro- (e.g., sector) and microlevels of analysis (e.g., individuals, projects, and the organizational level), from both the business and IT perspectives. Thus, in the spirit of EA, we adopt a holistic view.

EA adoption is argued to help in changing organizations [7, 9]. However, those studies often neglect the issue of how the change actually occurs. One reason for this ignorance is the multidisciplinary characteristics and longitudinal nature of EA adoption [9, 15], which makes the phenomenon difficult to study. The key contributions of EA adoption and organizational change studies are summarized in Table 1.

2.3 Theoretical Lens

There are several factors to be considered when examining change [21]. We adopted [14]'s approach to study change management in public organizations. This approach helps to identify the process, content, leadership, context, and outcomes of change in our context, the public sector. The process of change indicates the interventions and processes that are involved in the change implementation. The content refers to what the change is about, such as the organization's strategies, structures, and systems. The leadership of change explains the leaders' influence on the change. The change context and outcomes describe the settings and results of change.

Table 1 Summary of enterprise architecture (EA) adoption and organizational change literature

Selected reference	Focus; main contributions	Stake-holders	Scope
[16]	Whole EA process; methods for managing EA changes	All stakeholders	Organization, project
[17]	Design of EA; technical framework for analyzed changes in an EA model	EA designers	Project
[18]	Design decision in information systems (IS) change projects; dimensions and characteristics of design decisions in IS change projects	Decision makers	Project
[19]	EA adoption process (preparing for implementation stage); EA success model based on the organizational change framework	Various roles involved in the EA adoption process	National
[20]	EA design (business and information architecture); EA for integration, agility and the ability to change	Various roles involved in EA design	Project

3 Research Context and Methods

3.1 Research Methodology

We conduct a single case study in a province in Vietnam. We call this province *Ceta*. We follow an interpretive research approach, as this will allow us to understand the phenomenon thoroughly in its context [22]. It also allows us to understand internal and external factors, including organizational rules, stakeholders' behavior and activities, and the cultural context. The approach equips us with a comprehensive understanding of the topic in a case organization. Consequently, our focus on the process in EA adoption is studied through an EA project and by considering factors in relation to the organizational change when the organization adopts EA [23].

To support our findings from a single case, we also analyze 16 other provinces in Vietnam with a similar administrative structure as Ceta, those provinces adopted EA only after Ceta's EA project and products were legitimated. This is done by analyzing the provinces' EA project documents and other secondary data sources [23].

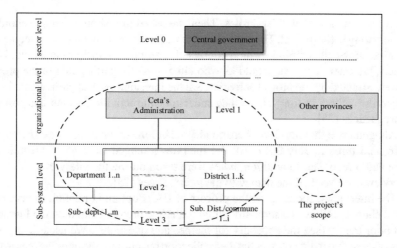

Fig. 1 Administrative structure and scope of Ceta's EA project

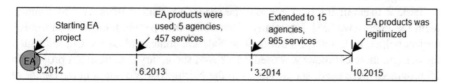

Fig. 2 Timeline of the EA project

3.2 Case Sites and Their Context

Ceta is a Vietnamese province with about 2 million inhabitants. EA was adopted there as one of the first provinces in the country. An EA project was established as a response to the state administration reform, encouraged by a master plan to use information and communication technology (ICT) to promote electronic government (c.f., Decision No. 1605/QD-TTg, 2010). Ceta's EA project covers the whole administrative structure (Fig. 1) [23].

Ceta's EA products include strategy, plans for IT–business alignment, a new model for administrative services (cf., CPS model), and new IT (hardware and software). Figure 2 illustrates the project timeline we followed [23].

3.3 Data Collection and Analysis

We first contacted a senior manager in Ceta to secure top management support and gain access to data collection. We then interviewed the Head of ICT department. He was also the Ceta's chief information officer (CIO) so he understood the project activities and the stakeholders' roles. Then, we asked him about other stakeholders participating in the project. They were interviewed in a similar manner. Consequently, we used snowball sampling, which continued until no new insights emerged. Ultimately, we interviewed stakeholders who either directly participated in the project or were affected by the project activities. All the interviewees had participated in the project throughout its lifecycle, so they understood the activities, events, and possible consequences [23].

Altogether, eight interviews were conducted in June–August 2015, two in August 2016, and three in July 2017. All the interviews ranged from 45 to 60 min and were audio recorded. In addition, notes were taken during the interviews. After the interviews, we verified the data with the interviewees [23].

The interviews, focusing on the process of EA adoption in relation to organizational change, followed a semi-structured interview protocol based on the literature and prior theory (see the appendix for themes and questions). We used theory in a loose way so that it did not steer the data collection but allowed the interviewees to talk freely about the topic and different issues [22]. This approach ensured appropriate knowledge to us.

Table 2 lists our interviewees and the secondary data sources used to complement the interviews [23]. Especially discussions with people familiar with the EA project helped us to interpret political, social, and contextual issues. Consequently, the triangulation technique was used. Moreover, secondary data from EA projects in 16 provinces were used: six provinces in the North, four provinces in the center of the country, and six southern provinces were included.

Data analysis was begun by transcribing the data and uploading it to ATLAS.ti software to help us in analyzing the unstructured data. The first author initially coded the data (open coding technique). The findings were then discussed among the authors to generate insights and interpretations. The coding process was refined when we decided to focus on the change through EA adoption and the factors influencing the change. As a result, the data were coded thematically following the interpretive research approach.

Table 2 Main data source

Interviewees (job role, no. of interviews)	Selected main secondary sources
CIO, 3	Ceta's documents
Project manager, 2	Project plans
Enterprise architect, 1	Project proposals
Enterprise architect, 1	Deliverables reports
IT specialist, 2	Project reports
IT specialist, 2	Project diaries and internal meetings
Civil servant, 1	Regulations and news in official sites
Civil servant/user, 1	Ceta's informal discussion

Table 3 Example of the coding data

Selected quotation	Category	Theoretical concept
"According to the basic ideas [from the Decision No. 1605/QD-TTg, 2010] we [Ceta's information and communication technology (ICT) department] have proposed solutions based on our skills, experiences [and socio-political conditions, financial status, and IT infrastructures]. The proposal then was chosen and approved by the board manager." CIO	Leadership of change	*Explains the leaders' influence on the change* [14]
"The EA project is an unprecedented project as it helped [Ceta] to successfully reform [their administrative] procedures and the way to provide [public] services. The product of the project was approved by the Prime Minister, which rarely happens [in this country]." CIO	Content of change	*Refers to what the change is about, such as the organization's strategies, structures, and systems* [14]

Table 3 illustrates an example of our coding process. During this, we moved between the transcripts, secondary data sources, and theoretical lens to check for inconsistencies between the sources and explanations with the theoretical lens. Finally, we grouped the issues into larger themes (axial coding). Three distinct themes emerged from the case. These were the process, the content of change, and the leadership of change.

4 Findings

To understand the process and content of change in the relation to EA adoption, we analyzed the EA's timeline, especially the process and content of change in EA adoption. We constructed an EA adoption change model as the change was initiated at the organization level (e.g., EA adoption causing changes in Ceta's strategy and planning), which then spread out to subsystem level (e.g., the organizations materialize their strategies to establish projects in subsystems level causing physical changes), and finally expanding the change to the sector level (e.g., other provinces adapt Ceta's model). Each phase of the change has its own content and leaders. For example, at the organizational level, the role of the business department is emphasized while at the subsystem level, the IT department is a key factor when it comes to the leadership of changes.

4.1   Process and Content of Change in EA Adoption

To understand the process and content of change, we examined the EA project timeline. Four main events regarding the organizational change are listed in Table 4.

Change initiated at the organization level. The project was initiated in September 2012. The deputy director of the ICT Department acted as the director of the Project Management Unit. However, project responsibility was quickly transferred to the deputy mayor, making him a project manager that oversees all project activities.

The EA team was granted permission to use all necessary resources in Ceta (e.g., from level 1 to level 3; Fig. 1). For example, the Project Management Unit was allowed to employ people from other state agencies in Ceta and recruit highly skilled people when needed (Decision No. 3152 by Ceta's mayor).

The lack of common standards and practices caused difficulties and challenges when choosing tools, techniques, and approaches. To cope with them, an external consultant was hired to propose new solutions and conduct feasibility studies. In addition, a business trip to other areas where similar projects had been deployed was organized.

This helped Ceta to facilitate their work better because they were expected to deploy the new model (cf. CPS model) for their services as a part of the EA products. This was a result of the agency leaders participating in the project and supporting the project teams in problem solving. They were also allowed to choose appropriate

Table 4 Changing status and main project activities in Ceta

Timeline	Main activities	Change status
2012.9–2013.6	Standardizing procedures and services, proposing centralized model for services	No operational changes but plans and documents how to do them. Change level: 2
2013.6–2014.3	Reforming and standardizing services; one agency in level 1 and five agencies in level 2 successfully used enterprise architecture (EA) products, including CPS model, and went live on 457 services there	Changes in the central administration (level 1) and five agencies (level 2). Change level: 1 and 2
2014.3–2015.10	Reforming, standardizing services; expanding 15 agencies, and going live on 965 services	Changes in 15 agencies. Change level: 1 and 2
2015.10–	The authority approved the EA products, including CPS model and its services and procedures; Ceta's approach now became applicable to all state agencies; Ceta's approach was approved as being effective for services providers, e.g., time to process applications was reduced by 70%	Services model in Ceta have been changed completely; The change was approved by the authority; Other provinces used Ceta as a model for their EA. Change level: 1, 2 and 3

services for experimentation that were standardized later in their agencies. Thus, their work focused on the standardization of services and administrative procedures for internal and external stakeholders. By June 2013, there were no operational changes but only strategies, plans, and documents on how to do them.

The change spread from organizational level to subsystem level. The EA products were then deployed in the agencies by implementing different EA products, including a CPS model. This took place from June 2013 to March 2014. Ceta established four CPS instantiations in four agencies (level 2) and one at the administration center (level 1) and went live on 457 services. This solved many previously faced problems: different services being provided by different agencies, or enforcing the customers to visit numerous agencies several times for accessing the services they wanted. Ceta reformed procedures, aligned business and IT, and established a proxy agency via the CPS model, making single-time visits possible. Austin, a project manager, stated, "This [approach, including the CPS model] not only differs from the old ones, but it also differs from some recent electronic government models [in Vietnam]. For example, in the model of a "one desk government" the customers' applications are received in the administrative section, and then [the employees] transfer them to other agencies. In contrast, [in our model, we] received and processed applications at CPS by instructing, checking, receiving, processing, deciding and returning them. We eliminated "intermediate" steps that just passed the applications from one agency to another".

By implementing EA products, the changes took place at the organizational level (second order) and subsystem level (first order). All services were put online, and senior managers and agency leaders were able to manage every step of each application taken by the civil servants. An enterprise architect articulated, "Our management activities completely changed with the EA products (CPS). First, our new slogan is "services provision with highest citizen satisfaction." This indicates that our staff have to change their attitude, improve their professional skills, and gain training carefully. Second, now citizens can directly assess the person in charge of their applications. Third, top officials are able to know the status of every application at any time. They also know the status of each agency or section so that they can make appropriate decisions or establish solutions".

The management style changed significantly. Although new processes were appreciated by the citizens, sometimes the agency employees disagreed. They feared losing their jobs as the new model required less manpower. This was further emphasized when the activities related to the citizens' applications were recorded, and the managers could monitor and manage the processes and progress. The fear was not groundless—the agency leaders moved employees to other sections or even laid them off if their performance and customer satisfaction did not meet the expectations.

EA products received a positive response from the customers and professional groups, as well as visibility in the press. The number of agencies using EA products in Ceta expanded to 15 and the number of services to 965 in just 20 months. Ceta's EA approach became an example of how to use ICT in state agencies. The project report summarized this as follows, "EA products in central administration [level 1 in Fig. 1] processed 38,890 applications with an on-time-rate being almost 99%. Fourteen agencies [levels 2 and 3 in Fig. 1] processed 110,280 applications and their on-time rate was more than 98% […] the [average] time to process the applications decreased by 70% in comparison with the previous model. For example, the time to handle the investment certification applications was reduced from 25 working days to 7–10 days, and applications in the place of investment decreased from 40 working days to 9 days".

The EA adoption changed how the organization provides services and communicates with customers. It also significantly changed the management style, with a move from a distributed approach to centralized, monitored, and controlled operations.

Change expanding to the sector level. The Ministry of Information and Communications (MIC) considered Ceta's EA practices and products (including the CPS model) as recommendations and suggested them to other provinces in October 2015. This legitimized Ceta's process and the content of change. This affected not only Ceta but also all provinces with similar administrative structures, political systems, and services in Vietnam. The change could now happen in other provinces. In other words, the change has become a sector change, causing a "revolution" for using ICT as a tool for administrative reform. A part of the success can be explained in that the model combines both business and IT perspectives with the organization's management structure. It has changed the administrative procedures and services completely. Ceta's CIO put this, "The EA project is an unprecedented project as it helped [Ceta] to successfully reform [their administrative] procedures and the way to provide [public] services. The product of the project was approved by the prime minister, which rarely happens [in this country]".

4.2 Leadership of Change in EA Adoption

The central government (level 0, Fig. 1) had a master plan on reform administrative procedures and business services. It suggested that using ICT in the state agencies is one of the key priorities for achieving these aims (cf. Decision No. 1605/QD-TTg, 2010). However, the master plan did not include instructions or formal regulations to adopt EA. As there was no law or policies on EA or its implementation, Ceta chose EA as an approach to respond to the master plan independently from their perspective and objectives. This emphasizes the role of senior managers in choosing the approach for how EA is interpreted and implemented. The lack of defined or agreed frameworks, standards or software leaves a lot of room and responsibility for senior managers for choosing suitable EA approaches. This was voiced by the CIO, "According to the basic ideas [from the Decision No. 1605/QD-TTg] … we have proposed solutions based on our skills, experiences [and sociopolitical conditions, financial status, and IT infrastructures]. The proposal was then chosen and approved by the top manager".

Similarly, many local governments (provinces) proposed new IT projects or approaches in response to the master plan. However, they usually mimicked each other and adopted similar approaches for their needs. For example, they purchased single, disconnected software applications for managing electronic documents, upgrading web portals or digitalizing services, as they had done before. In that sense, they took an IT perspective without considering the business perspective.

Like Ceta, some local governments chose EA (16 provinces). They focused on both business and IT issues to reform their services and procedures. These attempts can be seen as responses to the policies from the central governments, as their ultimate aim was to secure resources (e.g., finance, political will). In doing so, they perceived that EA improves citizens' services, increases enterprises' convenience, and makes administrative procedures more effective, efficient and transparent. The CIO stated, "Speeding up the administrative reform and using IT in the agencies through an EA project to transform paper-based services to on-line services reduced the number of times the customers have to visit the agencies for their services". This also emphasizes the role of leadership in adopting EA and deciding its directions and products.

5   Discussion

5.1   Triggers of Change

The change can be initiated and triggered by various factors, such as increasing customer satisfaction, enhancing the organizational core, or responding to external pressures [24]. The change may also start with social upheaval, technological change, market forces, or legislative change [25]. Although these factors were not explicit in Ceta, they appeared in some forms of policies.

First, policies influence the organizations when they choose EA as an approach to reforming administrative procedures and services. This was indeed the case in Ceta, where the project proposal referred to two central government policies, as follows: a master program on administrative reform and the master plan on IT applications. However, these policies did not enforce the organizations' use of EA in general or any specific EA framework or approach.

Second, market force did not seem to be the main source of the change. However, later, when Ceta was regarded as an example of successful EA implementation in the country, it was constantly referred to, "One of the objectives [of the EA project] is that Ceta becomes the leading local government [top 10] in using and developing IT applications in operations". (Ceta's project report). This quotation refers to one of the most prominent indexes in Vietnam, the Vietnam ICT Index. It ranks the state agencies by IT infrastructures, IT applications within the agency, online services, human resources, policies for IT applications, and portals/websites. It also provides a basis for benchmarking. The index is regularly followed and reflected in our interviews.

Senior managers and leaders played important roles as forms of regulative pressure, driving and influencing the change in the early stages of the change process. For example, the senior managers chose EA. Their expectations and assumptions gave directions to the EA projects in terms of frameworks and products, emphasizing leadership in EA adoption.

When looking at the content of change, EA adoption took place first at the organizational level, as Ceta standardized and reformed its business model. Ceta then implemented the model in selected agencies. At the same time, different strategies and IT plans were proposed. This triggered the change in the organizational culture from the "ask-given" approach to the "be ready to serve" approach and started to change the stakeholders' behavior. Civil servants had to be more responsive than before, and their services had to be more professional and transparent. Furthermore, organizational level change, that is, second-order change, triggered the standardization of business services and administrative procedures in the physical system when the agencies deployed the physical model (CPS). In other words, it triggered the first order of changes [24].

5.2   Process of Change

From the viewpoint of the process of change, that is, how the content is implemented in organizations, it seems that EA adoption follows incremental change [14], as it is continuous, incremental, and cumulative [14, 24]. The change began with new procedures, top-down driven services, and bottom-up emerging structures that were later legitimized. For example, the first set of 457 services in five agencies in Ceta were legitimized in June 2013. The number of services was later increased to 965 services in 15 agencies in March 2014. This means that the new approach was first tested out and improved in smaller settings and then expanded to broader audiences. Ultimately, more than 98% of the citizens and enterprises were pleased.

New procedures, services, and structures become norms. For example, when the central government approved CPS, EA practices became legitimized and normative. This was a significant step, as now, all state agencies throughout the country perceived they could use Ceta's approach. As a result, the EA project not only had an impact on a certain organization, but it also influenced the sector in the country. The secondary data from other provinces show that 10 provinces (out of 16) mimicked Ceta's approach. Thus, Ceta's EA adoption influenced other organizations and the public sector throughout the country (third order of change).

We illustrate this development in Fig. 3. We mapped the main events of Ceta's EA adoption with the change process (e.g., time and project phases on the horizontal axis) and the level of change (vertical axis). The change was triggered and started by an organizational level model, where from it got gradually spread out to the subsystem level when the EA initiatives were implemented. This took place in the implementation phase (period 2012–2013), the content of change mainly focusing on strategies and plans. Then, the model was expanded to a broader scope in both organizational

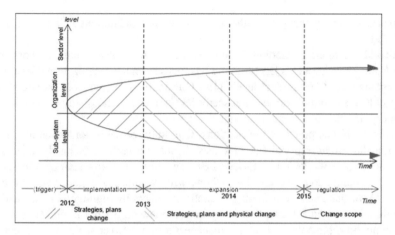

Fig. 3 Changes in EA adoption: process and content of changes

level and subsystem level. In our case, this means that one agency (level 1) and its four agencies (level 2) went live with 457 services, and 15 agencies went live with 965 services. Also, the content of change evolved: now it included strategies, plans, and sets of processes (e.g., CPO model—a new administrative services). Finally, EA expanded to the sector level when the positive signal of EA adoption was approved. In our case, the MIC took Ceta's model to other provinces within the country in October 2015 and those other provinces were started to implement Ceta's model.

6 Conclusions

We study the change in organizations when they adopt an EA approach. We emphasized that the change is triggered by senior managers who act under some form of external forces, which in turn, were caused by the broader policies and plans. As with most large-scale change endeavors, EA change begins at the organizational level. Yet, prior literature has argued that the change starts from social upheaval, technology change, market forces, or legislation change [25]. While these factors have their effects, the importance of senior managers is evident. Their role is emphasized in situations where the change is voluntary to the organization, that is, it is driven by the organization causing negative psychology inertia or socio-cognitive inertia [26], in comparison with situations where EA adoption is compulsory [27].

We illustrated that EA adoption and the changes there are complex phenomena. At the early stages of the EA adoption process, the change takes place from the top down, and later, it occurs from the bottom up when new EA features and functionalities are implemented, expanded, and regulated. This means that the change can be seen as a punctuated change in the subsystem levels of the organizations [24]. However, EA-driven change is also a situated sociotechnical change. This finding can also help understanding changes in other large-scale implementations as in digitalization [28, 29].

In addition to understanding the unravelling of EA enabled change, we contribute to EA literature. Previous EA literature has focused on the organizational level [12], or organizational and project levels [13]. Our analysis ranged from individual and project levels to organizational and sector levels to comprehensively understand EA adoption in relation to organizational change.

This study has practical implications. Our study provides understanding about the real-life organizational EA practices, which are seen as being dominated by normative frameworks (e.g., TOGAF, FEA) describing top-down EA practices, one-way communication, and control of how, why, where, and what should be done [30, 31]. In that sense, our findings benefit managers by highlighting the need for additional views on EA adoption as the current view on EA norms and frameworks might not be applicable. Instead, the managers also need to consider other directions of adoption as shown in Fig. 3, in a flexible way.

A single case study has limitations. This underscores the need for more research in a broader set of cases—in different countries, cultures, and contexts. For example, future research can utilize our findings in analyzing and comparing them to countries where EA is mandatory, such as Finland or the United States. From this perspective, examining and comparing our findings with different models of changes in IS can be a starting point for a broader set of qualitative studies to validate or revise them. Future research can also focus on different angles (e.g., sectional, subsectional changes) or look at stakeholders' roles and behaviors in the EA adoption.

Acknowledgements A previous version of this paper was presented at the 21st Pacific Asia Conference on Information Systems (Langkawi, Malaysia) as completed research paper #71, "Enterprise Architecture and Organizational Reform: A Project Debrief", PACIS 2017 Proceedings, https://aisel.aisnet.org/pacis2017/71. For more information about the conference, please see https://aisnet.org/page/Conferences.

References

1. Dang, D. D., & Pekkola, S. (2017). Systematic literature review on enterprise architecture in the public sector. *Electronic Journal of e-Government, 15*, 130–154.
2. Bloomberg, Jason. 2014. Is Enterprise Architecture Completely Broken? *Forbes.* July.
3. Boh, W. F., & Yellin, D. (2006). Using enterprise architecture standards in managing information technology. *Journal of Management Information Systems, 23*, 163–207. https://doi.org/10.2753/MIS0742-1222230307
4. Foorthuis, R., van Steenbergen, M., Brinkkemper, S., & Bruls, W. A. G. (2016). A theory building study of enterprise architecture practices and benefits. *Information Systems Frontiers, 18*, 541–564. https://doi.org/10.1007/s10796-014-9542-1
5. Thai, D. M., Duong, D., Falch, M., Xuan, C. B., & Thu, T. T. A. (2021). Factors affecting the sustainability of telecentres in developing countries. *Telecommunications Policy*, 102265. https://doi.org/10.1016/j.telpol.2021.102265

6. Dang, D., Pekkola, S., Vartiainen, T., & Pham, S. (2022). Platformization practices of health information systems: A case of National eHealth platforms. In *Proceedings of the 55th Hawaii International Conference on System Sciences*, Hawaii, US.

7. Banaeianjahromi, N., & Smolander, K. (2019). Lack of communication and collaboration in enterprise architecture development. *Information Systems Frontiers, 21*, 877–908. https://doi.org/10.1007/s10796-017-9779-6

8. Dang, D. (2021). Institutional logics and their influence on enterprise architecture adoption. *Journal of Computer Information Systems, 61*, 42–52.

9. Ross, J. W., Weill, P., & Robertson, D. (2006). *Enterprise architecture as strategy: Creating a foundation for business execution.* Harvard Business Press.

10. Simon, D., Fischbach, K., & Schoder, D. (2013). An exploration of enterprise architecture research. *Communications of the Association for Information Systems, 32.*

11. Bruls, W., van Steenbergen, M., Foorthuis, R., Bos, R., & Brinkkemper, S. (2010). Domain architectures as an instrument to refine enterprise architecture. *CAIS, 27.*

12. Schmidt, C., & Buxmann, P. (2011). Outcomes and success factors of enterprise IT architecture management: Empirical insight from the international financial services industry. *European Journal of Information Systems, 20*, 168–185.

13. Lange, M., Mendling, J., & Recker, J. (2016). An empirical analysis of the factors and measures of Enterprise Architecture Management success. *European Journal of Information Systems, 25*, 411–431. https://doi.org/10.1057/ejis.2014.39

14. Kuipers, B. S., Higgs, M., Kickert, W., Tummers, L., Grandia, J., & Van Der Voet, J. (2014). The management of change in public organizations: A literature review. *Public Administration, 92*, 1–20. https://doi.org/10.1111/padm.12040

15. Dang, D., & Pekkola, S. (2020). Institutional perspectives on the process of enterprise architecture adoption. *Information Systems Frontiers, 22*, 1433–1445.

16. Ruta, P., & Grabis, J. (2015). Integrated methodology for information system change control based on enterprise architecture models. *Information Technology and Management Science, 18*, 103–108.

17. Dam, H. K., Lam-Son, L., & Ghose, A. (2016). Managing changes in the enterprise architecture modelling context. *Enterprise Information Systems, 10*, 666–696. https://doi.org/10.1080/17517575.2014.986219.

18. Brosius, M., & Aier, S. (2016). The impact of enterprise architecture management on design decisions in IS change projects. In V. Nissen, D. Stelzer, S. Straßburger, & D. Fischer (Eds.), Bd. (vol. 3, pp. 1405–1416). Ilmenau: Universitätsverlag Ilmenau.

19. Nam, K., Oh, S. W., Kim, S. K., Goo, J., & Sajid Khan, M. (2016). Dynamics of enterprise architecture in the Korean public sector: Transformational change vs. transactional change. *Sustainability, 8*, 1074. Multidisciplinary Digital Publishing Institute. https://doi.org/10.3390/su8111074

20. Hoogervorst, J. (2004). Enterprise architecture: enabling integration, agility and change. *International Journal of Cooperative Information Systems, 13*, 213–233. World Scientific Publishing Co. https://doi.org/10.1142/S021884300400095X

21. Forman, C., King, J. L., & Lyytinen, K. (2014). Special section introduction—Information, technology, and the changing nature of work. *Information Systems Research, 25*, 789–795. INFORMS. https://doi.org/10.1287/isre.2014.0551

22. Walsham, G. (2006). Doing interpretive research. *European Journal of Information Systems, 15*, 320–330. https://doi.org/10.1057/palgrave.ejis.3000589

23. Dang, D., & Pekkola, S. (2017). Enterprise architecture and organizational reform: A project debrief. In *PACIS 2017 Proceedings.*

24. Lyytinen, K., & Newman, M. (2008). Explaining information systems change: a punctuated socio-technical change model. *European Journal of Information Systems, 17*, 589–613. Taylor & Francis. https://doi.org/10.1057/ejis.2008.50

25. Greenwood, R., Suddaby, R., & Hinings, C. R. (2002). Theorizing change: The role of professional associations in the transformation of institutionalized fields. *Academy of Management Journal, 45*, 58–80. Academy of Management. https://doi.org/10.5465/3069285

26. Besson, P., & Rowe, F. (2012). Strategizing information systems-enabled organizational transformation: A transdisciplinary review and new directions. *The Journal of Strategic Information Systems, 21*, 103–124. 20th Anniversary Special Issue. https://doi.org/10.1016/j.jsis.2012.05.001
27. Hjort-Madsen, K. (2007). Institutional patterns of enterprise architecture adoption in government. *Transforming Government: People, Process and Policy, 1*, 333–349.
28. Dang, D., & Vartiainen, T. (2019). Digital strategy patterns in information systems research. In *PACIS 2019 Proceedings*.
29. Dang, D., & Vartiainen, T. (2020). Changing patterns in the process of digital transformation initiative in established firms: The case of an energy sector company. In *PACIS 2020 Proceedings*.
30. Hylving, L., & Bygstad, B. (2019). Nuanced responses to enterprise architecture management: Loyalty, voice, and exit. *Journal of Management Information Systems, 36*, 14–36. Routledge. https://doi.org/10.1080/07421222.2018.1550549
31. Dang, D., Vartiainen, T., & Pekkola, S. (2019). Patterns of enterprise architecture adoption in the public sector: A resource-based perspective. In *Proceedings of the 27th European Conference on Information Systems (ECIS)*, Stockholm & Uppsala, Sweden (17).

Blockchain-Enabled Traceability in Sustainable Food Supply Chains: A Case Study of the Pork Industry in Vietnam

Chi Pham, Thanh-Thuy Nguyen, Arthur Adamopoulos, and Elizabeth Tait

Abstract Blockchain-enabled traceability has been widely touted as having a great potential for improving food supply chains. Proposed benefits include: outbreak tracing, verifying ingredient origins, monitoring environmental compliance and automating payments. Blockchain-enabled food supply chains have not been widely studied in developing countries. Therefore, a comprehensive evaluation of blockchain-enabled traceability in food supply chains was conducted to gain a deeper understanding of the potential impacts on food supply chain sustainability. A case study of a pork supply chain in Vietnam was analysed to understand the context in a developing country. The analysis was conducted through the lens of a triple-bottom-line blockchain framework for supply chains.

Keywords Blockchain traceability · Blockchain technology · Food supply chain · Triple-bottom line

1 Introduction

Blockchain technology (BCT) applications have been implemented in a wide range of industries such as: pharmaceuticals [1], construction [2], reverse logistics [1, 3], manufacturing/distribution [1, 4], food sectors [4, 5], diamonds, art, and valuables [1, 4], energy [4, 6], tourism [4, 7] and financial services [1, 4, 6]. The most important BCT features identified are traceability, provenance, immutability, transparency, disintermediation, and the automation potential through smart contracts [6, 8 and 9].

In supply chains and food supply chains specifically, it is proposed that BCT can significantly contribute to the supply chain by facilitating improvements in accountability, transparency, and traceability [1, 10]. Blockchain-enabled traceability is the main application of blockchain in food sectors, enabling sustainable food supply

C. Pham · T.-T. Nguyen (✉) · A. Adamopoulos
RMIT University, 124 La Trobe, Melbourne, VIC, Australia
e-mail: thuy.nguyen21@rmit.edu.au

E. Tait
Charles Sturt University, Boorooma, North Wagga, New South Wales, Australia

© The Author(s), under exclusive license to Springer Nature Singapore Pte Ltd. 2023   65
N. H. Thuan et al. (eds.), *Information Systems Research in Vietnam*,
https://doi.org/10.1007/978-981-19-3804-7_5

chains [5]. Blockchain traceability not only empowers the control of safe food practices, as distributed blockchains can inform the entire supply chain of any incidents and mitigate potential damages [5, 10], but also enhances trust, monitoring and eases supply chain friction [11].

Blockchain implementations have not been widely studied in developing countries, despite the fact that food supply chains are crucial elements of their economies. Blockchain adoption in developing countries may face more challenges, such as lack of information technology infrastructure, financial and human resources, power distribution between actors and regulatory change of institutions [5, 12].

To provide a deeper understanding of blockchain implementation, this study investigated a case study of blockchain adoption in the pork supply chain in Vietnam. This study reviewed the literature to identify the challenges in implementing blockchain enabled traceability (BET) in food supply chains (FSCs). Then the study determined the key indicators to examine BET adoption in FSCs for sustainability. Finally, the study developed insights of pork industry practices in Vietnam from the case study.

2   Literature Review

To examine the literature, the researchers conducted a review of articles on the Web of Science and Scopus databases to get insights on blockchain adoption or blockchain implementation in FSCs. Papers were grouped into five areas: (1) the overview of BCT, (2) BCT adoption in supply chain management, (3) BET implementation in FSCs, (4) challenges in the adoption of BCT and BET in sustainable FSCs, and (5) Triple bottom line perspective in sustainable FSCs. In total, 35 relevant references were selected and analysed.

2.1   Blockchain Technology

Blockchain technologies are peer-to-peer, decentralised and immutable database networks with smart contracts [1, 8, 9]. According to Wamba et al. there are 13 intrinsic characteristics of BCT, namely "secure, shared, immutable, decentralised, distributed, authenticated, encrypted, open-source, incorruptible, integrated, publicly visible, chronological and permanent" [6]. Among those, 'distributed/decentralised ledger' and 'trust, security and transparency' were the most widely mentioned features in the literature [4, 9, 12]. According to [8, 13], the most important BCT features are immutability, transparency, disintermediation, irreversibility, and the automation potential through smart contracts. In conclusion, blockchain definitions are varied and described by different synonyms [6].

2.2 Blockchain Technology Adoption in Supply Chain Management

BCT adoption in supply chain management shares similar traits to adoptions in other industries, which have been categorised into four domains: Digital registry of assets, Identity, transactions and traceability and data security (see Table 1).

The first domain is blockchain adoption in digital registry of assets, in which blockchain is integrated with Internet of things (IoTs), radio frequency identification data (RFID), and other sensors for the digital registration of ownership (i.e. property, farm animals, certificates, and intellectual properties) [14, 15]. The secure and accurate records of asset information on blockchain enable a clear history of assets [15]. The second domain is the digital identity of people and private records (i.e. IDs, health records, contracts), which also can be securely encoded on blockchain and enables smart contract execution and further functions [1, 4, 6and 14]. The third domain is to register and confirm supply chain-related transactions through blockchain applications, including orders, inventories, products, services and payments [4, 7]. This makes it possible for all relevant stakeholders to trace back all transactions, ensuring transparency for auditing purposes [1, 4and 16]. Contract and payment activities can be more transparent, minimising risks of abuses and fraud [2, 16]. Accepting cryptocurrencies eases cross-border payments for global trading [1, 4and 6], tourism and

Table 1 Applications of blockchain in supply chain management

Blockchain adoptions	Specific adoptions/applications	Publications
Digital registry of asset—machine, animal, intellectual property	Smart product IoT configuration	[14, 15]
	Digital rights management	[14, 15]
Identity—materials, people, machines, distributors	Identity management	[6, 14]
	Dynamic smart contract	[1, 14]
	Letters of credit	[1, 4]
	Part of quality records	[4, 14]
Transaction and traceability	Inventory control transactions	[1, 4, 14, 16]
	Product origin assurance	[14, 16]
	Supply chain traceability	[1, 2, 14, 16]
	Smart grids of solar energy	[4, 9]
	Manage booking and reconciliation	[4, 7]
	Contract management, project funding Crypto payment—cross border	[2, 16] [1, 4, 6]
	Customer loyalty	[4, 7]
Data security	Protection of IoT data/personal information	[1, 4]

Source Literature

loyalty programs [4, 7]. Finally, the fourth domain provides data security solutions for data exchange from internal software and IoTs to external business parties [1, 4].

2.3 Blockchain-Enabled Traceability Applications in Food Supply Chains

Food traceability has been one of the most sought-after applications of blockchain because food contaminations and outbreaks prevail and impact society [5, 17]. There have been various blockchain-enabled applications proposed and developed to address food supply chain traceability problems: QR code traceability, B2B platforms, resource management and automated verification and payment (see Table 2).

The first application is QR code or RFID code-based traceability, which are attached to the food packaging and scanned via a smartphone-based blockchain application. This application helps stakeholders trace back the ingredients, verify food safety certifications and identify sources of contamination quickly [10, 11and 18–21]. Such an application supports FSC operation controls, prevent counterfeits and increases customer confidence in food products [10, 11].

The second application is using a B2B blockchain platform for a consortium of business parties to share data, which enhances trust, monitoring and eases supply chain friction [11]. This includes traceability data and enables parties to track real-time operational data and monitor other stakeholders [4, 10, 11, 18 and 22].

The third application aims to record sustainability-related data [4, 11], in which the sustainable traceability aims to efficiently manage the sustainable resources and monitor environmental issues [4, 5and 11].

Finally, the fourth application is to use smart contracts to quickly verify transactions and process payments. This can ensure faster and fairer payments to support the living of small farmers and fairly distribute value along the FSC [1, 4].

Table 2 Blockchain-enabled traceability applications in FSC

Applications	Publications
QR code traceability: food provenance, ingredients' safety certificates, food recall	[10, 11, 18–21]
B2B platforms: location, temperature tracking, management of scheduling, supply—demand marketplace, logistics and delivery tracking, suppliers' compliance standards	[4, 10, 11, 18, 22]
Resource management: water management, environment standards, animal welfare, recycling	[4, 5, 11]
Automated verification and payment: decentralised crop insurance, fair selling price for small farmers	[1, 4]

Source Literature

2.4 Challenges in the Adoption of Blockchain Technology and Blockchain-Enabled Traceability in Sustainable Food Supply Chains

Challenges in the adoption of blockchains in food supply chain have been categorised into three groups: BCT performance, FSC management, and value (see Table 3).

Blockchain technology performance

Lack of storage and processing capability (scalability limitations). Blockchain platforms can have limitations in recording sensor data and FSC traceability transactions [6]. Such limitations are due to low throughput, low data storage capability and latency in record processing in blockchain environments [4, 6, 13].

Data format inconsistency. A traceability solution integrates data from multiple stakeholders in the FSC, requiring data format compatibility and high data quality [17, 18, 22]. However, when technologies are not equally advanced among stakeholders' firms, ranging from manual records to sensor data, the format of data records can be inconsistent [22]. Also, there are no comprehensive interoperability standards to support blockchain integration [1, 6, 13].

Lack of confidence in data security and privacy. Blockchain technologies are still emerging and immature. Traceability solutions, however, have complex requirements such as sensor data [5, 20]. If a blockchain-enabled traceability solution is not well

Table 3 Challenges of blockchain-enabled traceability in sustainable FSCs

Aspects	Challenges	Publications
Blockchain technology performance	Lack of storage and processing capability (scalability limitations) Data format inconsistency (enterprise systems to blockchain, and between blockchains) Lack of confidence in data security and privacy Energy consumption of blockchain	[4, 6, 13] [1, 6, 17, 18, 22] [4, 5] [1, 6]
Food supply chain management	Lack of expertise and knowledge Conservative mindset Different systems of standards and regulations Lack of trust and collaboration for data sharing	[4, 5, 22] [17, 18, 22] [5, 21] [4, 22]
Value	High costs (IT infrastructure, implementation) Low benefits and returned values (poor productivity, buyers not willing to pay)	[4, 5] [11, 22]

Source Literature

developed, data privacy and security are not ensured both on the blockchain and the application layers, creating cyber attack risks [4, 5].

Energy consumption. Blockchain solutions can potentially make the supply chain more efficient and use less energy [3]. However, the energy consumption of blockchain operations is still a question for blockchain adoption [1, 6].

Food supply chain management

Lack of expertise and knowledge in using blockchain in food supply chain. Stakeholders in FSC—particularly small organisations—need skilled staff and knowledge in blockchain [4, 5, 22]. It is not only essential to employ them to develop the blockchain-enabled solutions, but they must know how to adopt and use blockchain in specific FSC traceability contexts [4, 5, 22].

Conservative mindset. Stakeholders in FSC may be resistant to change or transforming to such a new technology as blockchain [17, 18, 22], due to the pressures from disintermediation, job loss and converting from familiar methods to a digital blockchain application, impacting many stakeholders [4, 5, 17].

Different systems of regulations and standards. When regulations and standards are different among countries, and the data required to be captured can be different for the safety of different food types, a blockchain solution has no guideline from governments and associations to follow [5, 21].

Lack of trust and collaboration for data sharing. The issue of trust among stakeholders is serious in collaboration and data sharing [4, 22]. Stakeholders are only confident to join if the blockchain-enabled FSC consortium is reliable and trustworthy [5]. However, this can be a challenging negotiation among stakeholders to share data, while balancing transparency and privacy [5, 21].

Value

Low benefits and returned value. It can be challenging to tailor BET solution in FSC that can be beneficial and sustainable to all FSC stakeholders [22]. There are also concerns about inefficiency and unproductivity when adding more steps (i.e. scanning, data entry and verification) into the operation process [22]. Traceability for premium products is accepted as customers are willing to pay more to ensure food provenance, but it is questionable whether customers will pay more for common food products [11].

High cost. The cost used to implement blockchain and peripheral technologies (i.e. IoT, sensors) for traceability solutions can be expensive in some FSC contexts and for developing countries [4, 5].

2.5   Theoretical Framework: Traceability in a Triple-Bottom-Line Context

Triple-bottom-line (TBL) has been widely adopted to measure sustainability under three dimensions: economic, social and environmental [23]. Various indicators or

Table 4 Indicators for triple bottom line sustainability

Economic indicators	Social indicators	Environmental indicators
1. Total costs and returned profit 2. Organisational resources 3. Flexibility, responsiveness, on-time delivery 4. Reliability of services, forecast and products 5. Quality of products, service capability 6. Returned goods, customer satisfaction	1. Employment practices 2. Health and safe standards 3. Respect of policy and justice 4. Fair trade, animal welfare, community influence and responsibility 5. Stakeholder engagement and satisfaction	1. Natural environment 2. Green SC management and processing

Source Literature [24–26]

goals to achieve sustainability under the TBL dimensions have been used in various industries, for instance, foods [24], plastic film [25], fuel oil [26], etc. These indicators are presented in Table 4.

There have been relatively few previous studies introducing a specific TBL list of indicators focusing on BET solutions [3, 27]. Therefore, for this study, the researchers developed a theoretical framework by categorising the indicators of blockchain-enabled FSC traceability under the context of the TBL perspective (see Fig. 1). This was done by mapping out and combining the important aspects from BET (Table 2), challenges of BET (Table 3) with the common indicators from previous studies in TBL (Table 4).

Dimensions & Indicators	Publications
Economic dimensions	
Costs of IT infrastructure and transaction	[4], [5]
Cost of stakeholders	[11], [22]
Blockchain technology	[4], [6], [22]
Service productivity and efficiency	[4], [22], [25]
Customer satisfaction	[11], [22], [26]
Social dimensions	
Stakeholder engagement and satisfaction	[4], [5], [25]
Respect of policy and regulation	[5], [21], [26]
Human resource development practices	[4], [5], [26]
Environmental dimensions	
Natural environment management	[4], [5], [7],
Food infected outbreak tracking and tracing	[25], [26]

Fig. 1 Framework and Indicators for blockchain-enabled FSC traceability in TBL context, *Source* Literature

3 Methodology

The TBL model in supply chains is implemented as a literature review-based framework Fig. 1 from a wide range of research disciplines researching blockchain technologies in supply chains. The study uses a qualitative case study approach to explore the gap between the literature and practice in blockchain adoption, focusing on BET in FSCs. Theoretically, a case study explores a phenomenon within a particular context and undertakes the situational evaluation to examine various facets of the phenomenon that can contribute to the topic [28, 29]. Because the purpose of this study was to analyse and understand the under-explored aspects of BET in emerging country FSCs, a case study of the pork industry in Vietnam was chosen. The case study approach was deemed to be suitable for conducting an in-depth investigation on the research phenomenon.

3.1 Case study—The Pork Industry in Vietnam

Vietnam is a developing country, in which the economy consists of three main sectors: services, industry, and agriculture/forestry/fishery. According to official statistics, the agriculture, forestry and fishery industries have steadily grown and account for 23.52% of Vietnamese GDP in 2021 [30], despite the Covid-19 pandemic.

Vietnam is transitioning towards an industrial economy and urban development in Vietnam is burgeoning. Husbandry plays an important role to support consumption and social development [31]. The pork industry has transitioned from collective farming to smallholder farming and more recently to larger-scale industrial farming [31]. However, the pork industry is still a mixture of small-scale and large-scale farms.

Among meat industries in Vietnam, pork production plays a critical role in the food market. For the first 9 months of 2021, pork production was 3,060,000 tonnes, compared to beef production of 332,000 tonnes and poultry production of 1,402,000 tonnes [30]. These increased by 5%, 2.4% and 4.3% respectively compared to the same period in 2020 [30]. Pork is the most consumed meat in Vietnam [31]. Therefore, the pork industry in Vietnam was selected as the case study for this research.

In Vietnam, the pork production process usually contains six key stakeholders: suppliers (farmers), traders (middlemen), producers (slaughterers), wholesalers, retailers, and end-customers. Veterinary control is conducted at critical stages of the supply chain. In the traditional pork supply chain (from farms to wet-markets), farms are mainly small-household farms. Middlemen procure pigs from many households, to send to the slaughterhouse. In contrast, modern farms raise pigs in large numbers and have contracts to supply directly to producers or supermarkets. The modern chain (from modern-farms to producers/supermarkets) is operated as a closed-cycle supply chain (Fig. 2).

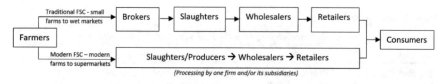

Fig. 2 Diagram of pork supply chain in vietnam, *Source*Literature

The existing loopholes in the pork supply chains in Vietnam contain some serious risks and pork traceability for quality and food safety assurance is still an issue [32]. The fragmented small farm and middlemen supply chain results in poor traceability and transparency [32]. For example, traders can deliver pigs to other provinces for processing, or the intermediaries may mix pork products of unknown origin in with well-regarded sources. At any stage before slaughter, hazardous chemicals for pig fattening can be used [32].

3.2 Data Collection

Due to the limited BET applications in the pork industry in Vietnam, the researchers collected both primary data and secondary data following a specific pork supply chain. This guaranteed that the data was triangulated from different sources and reflects ideas raised from many perspectives, ensuring data accuracy and minimising bias [29].

Data Collected From Interviews
There are three blockchain providers in Vietnam for food traceability. The researchers selected the largest and most well-known blockchain provider associated with pork supply chains to interview for this study. At the same time, to compare the contexts of developed countries with Vietnam as a representative of developing countries, the researchers also conducted individual interviews with international experts working on BET in FSCs. In total, 12 interviews were conducted. Each interview was from 45 min to an hour. The backgrounds of the interviewees are provided in Table 5.

Data collected from secondary sources of interview
The secondary data collection was conducted by sourcing interviews done by journalists relating to a selected blockchain provider and its' pork supply chain, published in Vietnamese newspapers. The stakeholders in the articles included three farmers, two traders, two processing firms, two slaughterhouses, two end consumers and eight government officials (animal health, food safety and local government).

Table 5 Background of interviewees

Interviews with stakeholders associating with the BET in a pork SC in Vietnam

Stakeholders in SC	Position	Type of company
Supplier (farmer)	Project executive (I1)	Feeding, manufacturing
Blockchain provider	Chairman (I2)	Blockchain developer
Retailer	Director (I3)	Supermarket
Government Agency	Innovative manager (I4)	Feeding, manufacturing, retailing
	Project executive (I5)	Province department
	Deputy Director (I6)	

Interviews with international experts in BET in food supply chains

Stakeholders in SCs	Position	Type of company
Supplier	Innovation manager (I7)	Agriculture association
Blockchain providers	Chairman (I8)	Blockchain solution (BS)-beef traceability
Retailer	Founder (I9)	BS—agriculture traceability
	CEO (I10)	Traceability solution—agriculture
	CEO (I11)	BS–seafood traceability
	COO (I12)	E-commerce platform—chicken traceability

CEO: Chief executive officer, COO: Chief operating officer.

3.3   Data Analysis

The researchers split the data into three groups: primary data of Vietnamese interviews, primary data of international experts' interviews and secondary data of journalist interviews and articles. Each group was coded independently, which enabled later triangulation and comparison. The indicators proposed in the theoretical framework in Fig. 1 were used as the initial coding scheme [33]. To analyse the data, the researchers firstly read and analysed line by line to identify relevant concepts of the research interest. At this stage, the researchers employed the NVivo 12 software tool to assist with the analysis. Searches were performed for word cluster and word frequency, which provided further codes at the beginning of the coding process. This phase, known as open coding, aimed to identify, name and describe events, keywords, phrases, or sentences where appropriate, to reflect the in-depth meaning of concepts within each interview [34]. In the axial coding phase, the fractured data from the open coding phase was constantly compared and contrasted to identify relationships between concepts and to re-assemble these concepts into themes [34]. The selective coding phase was replaced by the analysis of the arising themes following the TBL context in Fig. 1. This process enabled the researchers to close the analysis cycle by comparing the meaning of the findings with the theoretical lens [33, 35]. The themes and categories that arose from the analysis are presented in the next section, along with a comparison with the literature and appropriate discussion of implications.

4 Findings and Implications

The study's findings are discussed following the BET framework in the TBL context, associating the literature outcomes, interviews of international experts, and Vietnamese experts for implications.

4.1 Economic Dimension

Cost of Blockchain Infrastructure and Transaction

The literature illustrates that BCT implementation can be extremely costly for a traceability solution in FSCs when the FSCs have many transactions [4, 5, 12, 13].

In practice, all the experts from developed countries confirmed the high cost of blockchain transactions regarding a specific blockchain network. While three of them recommended using a private blockchain as a lower cost solution, the other experts advised to minimise the cost by using cloud-based environments, using on-chain/off-chain mechanism and posting only essential data on the blockchain (I7–12). In Vietnam, the interviews with the Vietnamese blockchain developer confirmed that if the blockchain solution in the FSC is costly there would be no clients willing to pay to use it, due to the developing country context. Nevertheless, the cost for IoT devices and AI for animal face recognition as an identification method could be high at the beginning. The suggested solution is to "*build a separate and private system—a trust chain to lower the solution cost, not a pure blockchain*" (I2) while the secondary data mentioned the on-chain/off-chain mechanisms.

Therefore, both groups of interviewees were concerned with ensuring the cost of the blockchain solutions was minimised.

Cost for Stakeholders in FSCs

When implementing BCT, each stakeholder in SC requires modifications of IT infrastructure, changes in organisational processes, use of IoT devices, maintaining and training employees, which adds cost to all stakeholders in the FSC [4, 22]. In addition, remote smallholder farmers may have to tolerate extra costs [12].

In developed countries, almost all experts (I7–11) believe that IoT can be a solution for premium food provenance, which is costly but can provide a much higher return value to stakeholders if adopted. The cost of IoT, however, is expected to be lower in the future. The majority agreed that the government, association or the host of the solution should sponsor the traceability solution to alleviate cost impacts on farmers.

In Vietnam, according to the blockchain provider, pork products using traceability solutions are more expensive than the traditional methods, requiring additional devices such as tracing bracelets. Such costs are shared among farmers, processors and other middlemen, so that the cost for farmers is reasonable and much lower than that of the processors and other beneficiaries (I2, 3). However, the secondary data reveals that the investment for each IoT device of BET can be a challenge for small and medium enterprises. Even if the government supports fully or partly the cost for the farmers, the traders and wholesalers must bear the cost themselves.

> Our priority is not to make money on farmers, but I will allocate them the cheapest cost and I will share that cost with richer stakeholders…to reduce costs for all (*I*2).

Blockchain Technology

As mentioned in the literature, there are number of major challenges in BCT adoption. The first challenge is the lack of storage and processing capability, which means the limitation of data storage on blockchain may restrict the speed of processing high numbers of transactions in FSC [4, 6]. In developed countries, this issue still exists. The solution is to split data into on-chain and off-chain layers or using big data and AI to filter data and solve the bottleneck issue (*I*9–11). In Vietnam this problem was bypassed by relying on the traceability solution that already existed (QR code, DNA test kits, near field communication (NFC), big data and cloud computing) and integrating it with a blockchain layer to only record critical events.

> Without blockchain, a traceability solution still works fine. In 2016, we did not have blockchain, until 2018 we developed blockchain (*I*2).

The second challenge named in the literature is that blockchain immaturity results in risks to security and data privacy [4, 5]. Most blockchain vendors in the developed countries are confident with their security solution, even though there are still concerns about the quality of the data posted on the blockchain by stakeholders (*I*9–11). Unexpectedly, the Vietnamese blockchain provider indicates that the blockchain is the most secured part of their technology now. The traceability data of FSC have quite low value making them not worth the hacking effort.

> No one would be crazy enough to change the information that a food product wasn't from a specific farm on the blockchain (*I*3).

The third challenge relates to the data format inconsistency due to the wide range of data formats derived from enterprise systems [17, 18, 22], and data manipulation [12]. The solution of the developed countries is to integrate the enterprise systems with blockchain via a global standard language such as Global System of Supply chain standards (GS1) (*I*7, 9–11). However, the blockchain experts indicate the need to direct IoT data into the blockchain network to mitigate the risk of fraud when integrating enterprise systems to blockchain (*I*9–11). In Vietnam, this challenge exists specifically when stakeholders do not have equally advanced systems. The solution is to prescribe GS1 as an international product language to collect and standardise products' information. It also solves the problem of data exchange between blockchains, particularly when blockchain interoperability is not possible or desired (*I*1, 3).

> We're working with a firm that exports to China. China doesn't want to use our traceability system… They just want the data from us to be compatible with their system. It also happens within Vietnam… supermarkets have their own system (*I*2).

Service Productivity and Efficiency
By its' nature, BET adds more steps in operational processes (i.e. scanning, data entry and verification), which constrains the productivity of FSC [4, 22]. The interviews with both Vietnamese and international experts agree with the literature relating to the reduction of productivity. There is also the problem of data entry errors that can happen at any stage, even when using IoT devices (*I*1–5, *I*7–12). For instance, in Vietnam the farmers must make records at each step, which can consume a lot of time. They may use tracing devices for pigs (bracelets) but if they do not enter data using the mobile app, the traceability solution is useless. In the case of data entry errors, they must be reported to the blockchain provider to fix (*I*1–5).

> Now the farmers have to do one more stage…take a phone to record the process! It is time-costly for them… they are not used to it and a lot of people do it wrong (*I*3).

Customer Satisfaction with Blockchain Solutions
In the literature, it is commonly reported that customers are willing to pay for premium products and food safety, thanks to the use of blockchain [11, 32]. The reason being that BET products ensure customer trust, which increases the revenue and reputation of the brand [5, 19]. The international interviews agreed with the literature in relation to premium products, that customers demanding transparency and provenance monitoring and are willing to pay more (*I*6–12). However, the Vietnamese context provides a different conclusion in that end-consumers do not pay much attention to traceability solutions. Pork prices at supermarkets are fixed, and therefore manufacturers and suppliers absorb the blockchain cost. Even though QR codes are imposed under regulations for food safety, consumers do not pay much attention (*I*1–5).

> Vietnamese consumers have little understanding of blockchain traceability. They buy goods mainly based on emotions… from a store that is up-market, the price is a bit higher, the packaging is a bit nicer, they automatically believe it is good (*I*3).

4.2 Social Aspects

Stakeholder Engagement and Satisfaction
In the literature, trust is an important factor for stakeholders collaborating and sharing data on a blockchain, and lack of trust is a serious issue in collaboration and data sharing [4, 22]. The international expert interviewees had differing opinions on this. Some thought that only FSC consortiums with a high level of trust can implement blockchain solutions, while others believe that the blockchain solutions themselves create trust by providing more transparency among stakeholders. In Vietnam, stakeholders and government officers believe that collaborative standards should be established among all SC members, and it is the responsibility of the Animal Husbandry Association and provincial veterinary offices to encourage engagement. The case study also confirms that traceability activities are more successful in a high trust environment.

The government participates to build trust, but they must create the consensus among the society and the supply chain (*I*2).

One of the biggest challenges for the stakeholder engagement is the conservative mindset of stakeholders in transforming towards a blockchain solution [17, 18, 22]. Even in the context of developed countries, there is challenge in changing existing practices and business processes to using BET in their FSCs. If the stakeholders do not see real benefits, they will not accept such a transformation. In the Vietnamese context, changing the mindset of the farmers is the most critical task. This task is more easily achieved in large farms, when the values brought to the farmers are visible (e.g. greater opportunity to export aligned with the stringent export standards).

General managers see blockchain as a way to compete with other companies... so the adoption of blockchain is a long-term investment (I5).

However, small household farmers, traders and slaughterhouses may not accept this transformation due to the higher cost and more working time (*I*1).

Respect of Policy and Regulation

When implementing BET, it could be problematic in proposing policies and regulations because blockchain adds more dimensions to control [5, 21]. Both international experts and Vietnamese interviewees agree with the literature. Each country has its own food standards and food safety programs, and the digital transformation in which converting paper to digital documents experiences challenges as *"meat supply chains are still heavily reliant on paperwork"* (*I*7, 8). In Vietnam, the regulation on traceability is not detailed and each organisation has its own interpretation. Both paper forms and BET are used, which causes duplication. Regulation of traceability for pigs is not mandatory, so farmers still do not fully comply. Data entry into the traceability mobile app is not always complete, which brings less traceability values (*I*1, 2, 3, 4 and 5).

The bureaucratic system is arranged in written documents, which must be stamped and signed, which takes time. The regulations are only for prior technologies of the last century— but this century the technologies are different (*I*2).

Human Resource Development Practices

Because blockchain is an emerging technology which is not well understood by many stakeholders, training is a must [4, 5, 22]. The interviews with experts in the developed countries confirm that many development staff must find documents online, attend webinars and self-learn from peers (*I*7, 8 and 10). There is also considerable collaboration between academia and blockchain practitioners (*I*9, 10 and 12).

In Vietnam, it is the blockchain provider who established the training programs to support other stakeholders including B2B users, farm managers and veterinarians. These trainees can then train their workers. *"The veterinarians can understand the solution data entry and circulate it to the farmers"* (*I*5). In the manufacturing organisation, *"IT department employs new staff yearly to develop the capacity and knowledge"* (*I*5) to gradually improve their staff competency.

4.3　Environmental Aspects

While most of the literature widely discusses a dilemma between the energy consumption of blockchain and potential benefits for the environment [1, 3, 6], the interviewees reported that other environmental solutions are considered when implementing BET in FSCs. For instance, a common discussion of the international experts was the potential to measure environmental issues by using BCT to track sustainability data. However, these are not prioritised in their current projects (I7–12).

In Vietnam, beside pork traceability for food safety the blockchain provider states that "*tracking and tracing an animal disease outbreak was a proud experience and an important lesson for the husbandry industry*" (I3). According to the journalists' interviews, in 2019 the blockchain solution was used to prevent the "African swine cholera outbreak" in pigs in Vietnam. Farmers used the mobile app to report their infected pigs and this allowed authorities to track, control and prevent the disease. This new technique is extremely useful for developing countries where infectious diseases can spread quickly due to traditional husbandry methods (I2, 3, 5 and 6).

Also, the blockchain solution supports verifying that environmental standards have been followed, which is essential for certified organic and export products, "*we know the coordinate-latitude of that farm, the climate, soil, whether the area is near a garbage factory, as well as information about fertilisers and seeds*" (I4,6).

5　Conclusions

BET has been widely considered as having a great potential for improving FSCs. The most well-known potential benefits are the visibility for efficient operation, checking ingredient origin, monitoring environmental compliance, and automated payments. This study examined and qualitatively evaluated BET adoption in FSCs generally, and in the pork industry in Vietnam specifically, to gain a deeper understanding of the impacts on FSC sustainability in a developing country. Theoretically, the study provides a comprehensive literature review and literature-based framework with key indicators regarding BET adoption in FSCs under the TBL context. While blockchain is still a new concept, this analysis can be used to overcome the lack of expertise and experience of relevant staff. The proposed indicators in the framework can be used to diagnose problems in practice and develop suitable measures.

Practically, the case study shines more light on the adoption of BET in pork supply chains in the developing country context, which has not been thoroughly discussed in current academic and practical literature. Through the challenges and innovations introduced in the case study, other organisations could gain insights for their future practices. While the wet market (or traditional supply chain) is a part of Vietnamese culture, the case study shows that the adoption of blockchain and the returned values of traceability are more significant in the modern supply chain (supermarkets) than those of the traditional supply chain. In conclusion, BET is a tool to facilitate food safety control, to enhance the SC management capability, and promote the collaboration amongst all the stakeholders of the SC and the government. The FSCs generally and the pork SC specifically will be more sustainable when there is higher demand for food safety in communities.

Acknowledgements We would like to express our special thanks to TE-FOOD, Vietnamese and international participants for supporting this project.

References

1. Wang, Y., Han, J. H., & Beynon-Davies, P. (2018). Understanding blockchain technology for future supply chains: A systematic literature review and research agenda. *Supply Chain Management: An International Journal, 24*(1), 62–84.
2. Kiu, M. S., Chia, F. C., & Wong, P. F. (2020). Exploring the potentials of blockchain application in construction industry: A systematic review. *International Journal of Construction Management*, 1–10
3. Zhang, A., Zhong, R. Y., Farooque, M., Kang, K., & Venkatesh, V. G. (2020). Blockchain-based life cycle assessment: An implementation framework and system architecture. *Resources, Conservation and Recycling, 152*, 104512.
4. Dutta, P., Choi, T.-M., Somani, S., & Butala, R. (2020). Blockchain technology in supply chain operations: Applications, challenges and research opportunities. *Transportation Research. Part E, Logistics and Transportation Review , 142*, 102067
5. Kamilaris, A., Fonts, A., & Prenafeta-Boldú, F. (2019). The rise of blockchain technology in agriculture and food supply chains. *Trends in Food Science Technology, 91*, 640–652.
6. Wamba, S. F., Kala Kamdjoug, J. R., Bawack, R. E., & Keogh, J. G. (2019). Bitcoin, blockchain and fintech: A systematic review and case studies in the supply chain. *Production Planning & Control, 31*(2–3), 115–142.
7. Vinod, B. (2020). Blockchain in travel. *Journal of Revenue and Pricing Management, 19*(1), 2–6.
8. Pournader, M., Shi, Y., Seuring, S., & Koh, S. C. L. (2020). Blockchain applications in supply chains, transport and logistics: A systematic review of the literature. *International Journal of Production Research, 58*(7), 2063–2081.
9. Queiroz, M. M., Telles, R., & Bonilla, S. H. (2020). Blockchain and supply chain management integration: A systematic review of the literature. *Supply Chain Management: An International Journal, 25*(2), 241–254.
10. Kshetri, N. (2018). Blockchain's roles in meeting key supply chain management objectives. *International Journal of Information Management, 39*, 80–89.
11. Rogerson, M., & Parry, G. C. (2020). Blockchain: Case studies in food supply chain visibility. *Supply Chain Management, 25*(5), 601–614.
12. Kshetri, N. (2021). Blockchain and sustainable supply chain management in developing countries. *International Journal of Information Management, 60*, 102376.
13. Babich, V., & Hilary, G. (2020). OM forum—Distributed ledgers and operations: What operations management researchers should know about blockchain technology. *Manufacturing & Service Operations Management, 22*(2), 223–240.
14. Helo, P., & Hao, Y. (2019). Blockchains in operations and supply chains: A model and reference implementation. *Computers & Industrial Engineering, 136*, 242–251.
15. Sun, H., Wang, X., & Wang, X. (2018). Application of blockchain technology in online education. *International Journal of Emerging Technologies in Learning, 13*(10), 252–259.

16. Perera, S., Nanayakkara, S., Rodrigo, M. N. N., Senaratne, S., & Weinand, R. (2020). Blockchain technology: Is it hype or real in the construction industry? *Journal of Industrial Information Integration, 17*, 100125.
17. Kamble, S., Gunasekaran, A., & Sharma, R. (2020). Modeling the blockchain enabled traceability in agriculture supply chain. *International Journal of Information Management, 52*, 101967.
18. Bumblauskas, D., Mann, A., Dugan, B., & Rittmer, J. (2020). A blockchain use case in food distribution: Do you know where your food has been? *International Journal of Information Management, 52*, 102008.
19. Köhler, S., & Pizzol, M. (2020). Technology assessment of blockchain-based technologies in the food supply chain. *Journal of Cleaner Production, 269*, 122193.
20. Feng, H., Wang, X., Duan, Y., Zhang, J., & Zhang, X. (2020). Applying blockchain technology to improve agri-food traceability: A review of development methods, benefits and challenges. *Journal of Cleaner Production, 260*, 121031.
21. Behnke, K. & Janssen, M. F. W. H. A. (2019). Boundary conditions for traceability in food supply chains using blockchain technology. *International Journal of Information Management, 52*, 101969
22. Sternberg, H. S., Hofmann, E., & Roeck, D. (2020). The Struggle is real: Insights from a supply chain blockchain case: The struggle is real. *Journal of Business Logistics, 42*(1), 71–87.
23. Elkington, J. (1999). *Cannibals with forks: The triple bottom line of 21st century business* (1st ed.). Capstone.
24. Yakovleva, N., Sarkis, J., & Sloan, T. (2012). Sustainable benchmarking of supply chains: The case of the food industry. *International Journal of Production Research, 50*(5), 1297–1317.
25. Xu, J., Jiang, X., & Wu, Z. (2016). A sustainable performance assessment framework for plastic film supply chain management from a Chinese perspective. *Sustainability, 8*(10), 1042.
26. Narimissa, O., Kangarani-Farahani, A., & Molla-Alizadeh-Zavardehi, S. (2020). Evaluation of sustainable supply chain management performance: Indicators. *Sustainable Development, 28*(1), 118–131.
27. Venkatesh, V. G., Kang, K., Wang, B., Zhong, R. Y., & Zhang, A. (2020). System architecture for blockchain based transparency of supply chain social sustainability. *Robotics and Computer-Integrated Manufacturing, 63*, 101896.
28. Kaarbo, J., & Beasley, R. K. (1999). A practical guide to the comparative case study method in political psychology. *Political Psychology, 20*(2), 369–391.
29. Yin, R. K., & Campbell, D. T. (2018). *Case study research and applications: Design and methods* (6th ed.). SAGE Publications.
30. General Statistics Office of Vietnam. https://www.gso.gov.vn/en/data-and-statistics/2021/10/socio-economic-situation-in-the-third-quarter-and-nine-months-of-2021/, Last Accessed 2021/10/31.
31. Hansen, A. (2018). Meat consumption and capitalist development: The meatification of food provision and practice in Vietnam. *Geoforum, 93*, 57–68.
32. Khuu, T. P. D., Saito, Y., Tojo, N., Nguyen, P. D., Nguyen, T. N. H., & Matsuishi, T. F. (2019). Are consumers willing to pay more for traceability? Evidence from an auction experiment of vietnamese pork. *International Journal of Food Agricultural Economics, 7*(2), 127–140.
33. Klein, H. K., & Myers, M. D. (1999). A set of principles for conducting and evaluating interpretive field studies in information systems. *MIS Quarterly, 23*(1), 67–93.
34. Strauss, A. L., & Corbin, J. M. (1998). *Basics of qualitative research: Techniques and procedures for developing grounded theory* (2nd ed.). Sage Publications.
35. Silva, L., Goel, L., & Mousavidin, E. (2009). Exploring the dynamics of blog communities: The case of Meta Filter. *Information Systems Journal, 19*(1), 55–81.

Protecting Organizational Information Security at Home During the COVID-19 Pandemic in Vietnam: Exploratory Findings from Technology-Organization-Environment Framework

Duy Dang-Pham, Hiep Pham, Ai-Phuong Hoang, Diem-Trang Vo, and Long T. V. Nguyen

Abstract While prior research has examined the cognitive factors that influenced the information security behaviors of remote workers, little was known about the impact of the different work environments on these behaviors. Moreover, organizations and employees were abruptly forced to embrace working from home due to the ongoing COVID-19 pandemic, which created unprecedented problems and inconvenience in how employees perform daily work at home that could jeopardize organizational information security. This study adapts the technology-organization-environment (TOE) framework to investigate the factors that influence how employees in Vietnam protect organizational information security while working from home during the COVID-19 pandemic. Our qualitative findings drawn from in-depth interviews with 20 respondents reveal several factors that influence the employee protection of organizational InfoSec at home, such as the use of secure software for remote work, the flexible yet distracting work environment at home, and the lack of social interactions with colleagues that could demotivate personal information security efforts. We offer practical recommendations for organizations to prepare for flexible and secure workplaces in the future, especially to meet the continuing demand for working from home after the COVID-19 pandemic. In terms of theoretical implications, future studies are encouraged to focus on exploring the contextual and situational factors that influence employee information security behaviors.

Keywords Information security behavior · Behavioral information security · Work from home · WFH · COVID-19 · Technology-organization-environment framework

D. Dang-Pham (✉)
School of Business and Management, RMIT Vietnam, Ho Chi Minh City, Vietnam
e-mail: duy.dangphamthien@rmit.edu.vn

H. Pham · A.-P. Hoang · D.-T. Vo · L. T. V. Nguyen
RMIT University Vietnam, 702 Nguyen Van Linh Street, Ho Chi Minh City, Vietnam

N. H. Thuan et al. (eds.), *Information Systems Research in Vietnam*,
https://doi.org/10.1007/978-981-19-3804-7_6

1 Introduction

The COVID-19 pandemic has changed every single aspect of our lives. In Vietnam, the first case of COVID-19 was reported on January 23, 2020. The country is experiencing the fourth wave of infection, in which Ho Chi Minh City is the epicenter [37]. Many organizations were abruptly forced to work-from-home (WFH) since April 2021. While organizations are struggling to sustain operation with this working mode, the employees face many challenges in both work and life. In the new work environment at their own home, employees may not be well protected by adequate information security (InfoSec) measures, and thus exposed to various InfoSec risks.

Prior to the pandemic, there were mixed opinions regarding the future of remote working. On one side, there is ample evidence to support this work mode at the individual and organizational levels. Working remotely can increase productivity, job satisfaction, and performance [2, 16]. Remote workers are also reported to be more committed, though the level of commitment depends on the telecommuting arrangement [26]. It is worth noting that telecommuting is associated with reduced turnover rates and reduced absenteeism across firms with different characteristics [27]. The non-work environments, however, pose many challenges for workers. Burnout, defined as "a prolonged response to chronic emotional and interpersonal stressors on the job" is common during the WFH period [25]. The lack of a professional working environment and the distractions from family make it difficult for workers to stay focused [21]. In addition, many of them experience social isolation which hinders collaboration and teamwork [7].

An increasing number of sophisticated cybersecurity threats, aiming at at-home workers during the pandemic have been reported [17, 23]. Prior studies have focused on exploring employees' information security practices in the professional workplace, such practices in non-work environments are not thoroughly examined [24, 29]. Non-work environments can influence InfoSec behaviors of remote workers in more nuanced ways. Our research complements the scarce literature on InfoSec behavior across different working environments. In particular, we examine the factors that influence how Vietnamese remote workers protect organizational InfoSec while working from home. Understanding how InfoSec behaviors differ across contexts provides practical implications for organizational leaders to adjust their work policies and offer suitable support for remote workers.

2 Literature Review

2.1 Information Security Challenges of Working from Home

Recent advances in technology have made telecommuting a viable option for employees around the world. In the broad term, telecommuting refers to the use of telecommunication technology to partially or completely replace the need to commute to and from work [3]. Numerous studies also have shown the positive impacts of telecommuting on job satisfaction, organizational commitment, and identification with the organization [25]. Working remotely can reduce work-role stress and work exhaustion [16, 34]. However, this work mode requires individuals to have self-discipline, self-motivation, and adaptability [19].

Scholars have examined different cyber security challenges of working from home and highlighted the need for training and interventions [5, 15]. While virtual programs have been shown to increase productivity and decrease cost, virtual employees often experience social isolation as they are separated temporally and spatially from their colleagues [30]. As they feel excluded and isolated from other organizational members, they are more likely to perceive themselves as immune to any deterrence program, thus lowering perceived sanction costs of violating InfoSec policies [11]. Similarly, compliance intentions are influenced by the external cues of situational support, verbal persuasion, and vicarious experience, which makes the discrepancies between remote and in-house employees towards policy compliance exist [38]. For example, although virtual employees indicate that they feel some pressure, but overall are fairly neutral on pressure from co-workers to adhere to InfoSec policies and practices [18].

When employees work virtually, they rely on digital technology for work and communication [11]. Digital technology makes it easier for managers and subordinates to contact each other at all times, thus increases productivity [2]. However, this leads employees to the situation of constant workplace monitoring due to being on the job continuously [14]. Employees may feel technostress as they have to learn to use new technologies, be available on mobile device for work at almost all times, and cope with multi-tasking [14]. These demands create time pressure, task overload, and stress to their primary tasks, which are the root causes of InfoSec violation [6, 10]. As employees may share the living space with their families, the risk of a cyberattack is also shared among the family members [28]. When organizations change work practices to enable employees to work from home, there is a risk that children may click on malicious links on their parents' computers [28].

The lack of WFH experience and pandemic pressure are other challenges for InfoSec compliance. Studies have discussed the necessities of organizations' awareness and support sessions to avoid attacks from cyber criminals [1]. This is because not all employees have the skills and experience with working remotely, which create opportunities for attackers [1]. In fact, 44.44% of the employees have no virtual working experience before the crisis, and they receive no InfoSec advice on their new working reality [17]. In addition, COVID-19 has brought personal stress and anxiety to workers, which can increase the chance of them being a victim of cyberattacks [23] For example, cyber criminals may claim to have a cure for COVID-19, or offering financial support to attract people and ask them to click on malicious links or attachments [1]. Victims are more likely to share unverified information due to information overload and online information trust [22], in which such an attack may result in data loss on a big scale [1].

Although the pandemic brings numerous challenges that may impede InfoSec compliance, not all organizations have paid sufficient attention to this change [25].

While companies have to improvise new working structures, some leave corporate assets less protected than before for the sake of inter-operability [23]. About 53% of the participants report not having received any InfoSec guidelines from their employers regarding working from home. More than 50% of hardware assets with no strict InfoSec rules and apparent surveillance are used for remote working gaining access to corporate networks [17]. The inadequate uses of InfoSec tools have limited their effectiveness [32]. Recent studies have also discussed the importance of organizations applying InfoSec updates to protect their networks [1, 32]. This is because network gateway devices and virtual private networks (VPN) are vulnerable targets to ransomware campaigns, which allow attackers to steal credentials and access to compromised networks [1]. When organizations had to obtain new technological solutions to facilitate their operations in the new working reality, employees were requested to use applications or services that they were unfamiliar with while working remotely [17].

2.2 Technology-Organization-Environment (TOE) Framework

Technical and administrative measures are two key components of organizational InfoSec management. The former refers to the enforcement of InfoSec practice on users of IT systems through implementing authentication, authorization, data encryption and antivirus software. The second component, administrative measures, refers to encouraging safe InfoSec practice while deterring malicious computer abuses, through InfoSec policies and procedures, awareness training, and supervision [9]. Employee self-efficacy in performing InfoSec behaviors is required to achieve InfoSec compliance [36]. InfoSec awareness and skills are generally referred to as self-efficacy, which encompasses one's belief in their capability to protect information systems from InfoSec threats [36]. Employees who have a high level of self-efficacy can effectively and frequently carry out InfoSec tasks. On the other hand, those who report to lack self-efficacy were found to disengage from compliance with InfoSec policies [29]. The awareness about InfoSec of the employees and their compliance with InfoSec policies are commonly regarded as key determinants of administrative measure effectiveness. To improve InfoSec awareness and compliance with InfoSec policies, it is necessary for companies to nurture an organizational culture that encourages knowledge sharing among employees [12, 33]. Given the increasing number of InfoSec risks, effective knowledge sharing can help employees to stay vigilant against those risks [33].

Despite the relevance of these theories in exploring employees' compliance behavior, general deterrence theory, protection motivation theory, and theory planned behavior focus on the cognitive processes and attributes, rather than other important factors of organizational InfoSec protection by individuals such as the work environment and technology. The surging COVID-19 pandemic has brought significant influences at macro and micro levels which impact both businesses and employees. This justifies the need to investigate further the protection of organizational InfoSec by employees, not only by examining their cognitive processes and attributes but also the larger picture including the different contexts and environmental factors. To this end, our study uses the Technology-Organization-Environment (TOE) framework to analyze how employees protect organizational InfoSec while being forced to work from home during the COVID-19 pandemic.

Originally, the TOE framework is used to explain how organizations make the decision to adopt information systems [13]. The framework suggests that existing technology (e.g. IT resources and technology dissemination), organizational charac-teristics (e.g. organizational structure and culture, governance, size, and geographic location, IT leader behaviors), and environmental factors (e.g. industry charac-teristics, government regulations, organization's relationships with its partners, customers, and competitors) could affect an organization's decision to adopt IS [13]. These three categories of factors not only affect the adoption decision but also interact with and influence one another [13]. By drawing on the TOE framework, this research aims to explore the factors that influence the employee protection of organizational InfoSec from technology, organization, and environment aspects, which then provide managerial implications to improve InfoSec during the COVID-19 period.

3 Research Method

We follow the qualitative research approach to obtain rich insights into the phenomenon under investigation [8]. Purposive sampling was used to recruit these employees from our professional networks, who were forced to work from home by their company during the pandemic. We conducted online interviews with open-ended questions with a total of 20 employees in various industries until theoret-ical saturation was reached i.e. the respondents stopped providing significantly new insights. The online interviews lasted 1.5 h on average.

The demographics of the respondents are summarized as follows. The gender ratio, comprising male and female respondents, is balanced. The average age of the sample is 30 years old. On average, each respondent lives with three other family members and has no children. Half of the respondents reported to share a large amount of daily chores with their family members during the WFH period. We asked the respondents to rate their WFH environment suitability and IT skill on a scale ranging from 0 (most inadequate) to 10 (most adequate). The average scores for both these questions are 7.25 out of 10. Most of the respondents work in either education (6 respondents), banking and finance (4), advertising and marketing (3), or IT (3).

Interview transcripts were reviewed by the research team and consolidated into a single spreadsheet, where each column stored the respondent answers provided for a specific interview question. Thematic analysis was performed to detect prevalent concepts and themes that naturally emerged from the data. We followed the five-phase process of thematic analysis proposed by [4]. This inductive analysis approach allowed the key concepts and themes to naturally emerge from the data.

We used the qualitative data analysis software NVivo 12 Pro for our analysis. Two researchers in our team conducted the thematic coding process independently from each but followed a similar process: they both began with open and inductive coding to generate an initial set of key concepts. This initial set contained generic concepts related to respondents, such as the difficulties they encountered in regard to technology, work environment, and organizational procedures. Then, the researchers carefully reviewed each coded concept to identify more specific and prevalent themes that repeatedly appeared across the respondents. This review process was performed iteratively to refine the themes, by merging similar concepts and removing those with a low number of occurrences in the cases. Finally, the whole team met to discuss and consolidate the themes.

4   Findings

We first explored the differences in terms of the work arrangement at home as compared to at work. Almost all respondents, except respondent #3, reported to have sufficient technologies to work from home. The mentioned WFH technologies include laptops (either personal or provided by their company), smart device (smartphones and tablets), home Internet, VPN software, communication software (e.g. Microsoft Teams, Telegram, Google Meet, Zoom, Webex). Two respondents (#7 and #14) said that their companies did not provide any specific requirements regarding WFH equipment. Respondent #8 shared that her company encouraged employees to use work-issued equipment, but employees may also use their own device if it satisfies the company's requirements.

Fourteen out of 20 respondents reported to feel confident about protecting organizational InfoSec while working from home. Respondents #12 and #14, whose company enforced InfoSec policies and daily tasks involved handling strictly confidential information, believed that they are well-equipped to perform work securely at home. Respondents #9 and #15 felt unsure about ensuring InfoSec at home, since their companies did not provide any formal guidelines and protecting organizational InfoSec had so far relied on individuals' own awareness.

In general, most—except four—respondents believed that there was no major difference in protecting organizational InfoSec in office (before the lockdown took place) and at home during the forced WFH period. Some reasons for this indifference include the fact that several work routines had been carried out both in office and at home before the lockdown (respondent #1), and the WFH equipment is secured by the company's InfoSec software (respondent #4). Respondent #6 explained that the protection of organizational InfoSec relies on personal InfoSec awareness rather than the work environment. Moreover, respondent #5 explained that she lives by herself, and thus the cyber risks associated with sharing work device are minimized.

Four respondents mentioned some differences between protecting organizational InfoSec at work and at home. For instance, respondents #9 and #10 experienced a more complicated work process with extra steps to ensure InfoSec when trying to access work data remotely. In contrast, respondents #14 and #15 found accessing work data to be easier, and they warned about the risk of leaking confidential information to people outside of work e.g. family members and friends. Despite their self-reported responses to not find any difference in protecting organizational InfoSec across the two contexts i.e. at work and at home during the pandemic, the respondents identified several factors that could affect the protection of organizational InfoSec when working from home.

4.1 Technological Factors

The availability of the technologies that enable communication and sharing of data in a secure manner was highlighted by most of our respondents as one of the most significant factors for protecting organizational InfoSec at home. Specifically, respondents #7 and #8 suggested that companies need to provide technological solutions to classify information and establish different layers of security for each type of information, so that unintended exposure of critical information can be avoided. Respondent #2 further concurred that the information needs to be filtered and only shared with relevant employees. To respondent #2, the uncontrolled distribution of information not only creates InfoSec risks but also information overload, which may lead to employees ignoring important communication such as announcements of InfoSec risks that are directly related to their work.

Respondents #3, #4, #9, and #14 agreed that companies must provide appropriate support for working remotely, including InfoSec software on personal computers and management systems for remote work. They believed that these solutions would block InfoSec threats and warn employees about risky actions, as well as enable them to work from home comfortably while maintaining productivity. Several respondents also mentioned the lack of effective communication methods when working from home besides using email. To overcome this limitation, they used social media platforms such as Facebook and Zalo for communicating and sending files, which would create more InfoSec risks of leaking important information.

4.2 Organizational Factors

Organizational culture was mentioned by the respondents as an important factor for InfoSec compliance when working from home. According to respondent #2, an oppressive organizational culture would make employees disclose confidential information of the business. Moreover, respondents #3, #5, and #7 shared that a well-developed InfoSec policy, including strict sanctions for violations, is critical for ensuring compliance with InfoSec requirements at home. Instructions and supervision from managers, who can provide timely advice and explanations for unclear policies, are also vital for InfoSec compliance (respondents #3 and #13). InfoSec training programs are recommended, especially those that focus on identifying confidential information and devices that are allowed to connect to the company networks while working from home (respondent #8). Respondents #2, #4, and #10 highlighted the importance of taking into consideration the impact of workload on InfoSec compliance at home. Managers should be mindful about the disadvantages and disruptions that employees may encounter while working from home, and thus offer the flexibility in workload and work deadlines to maintain employee motivation and work efficiency (respondents #2, #4, and #10).

4.3   Environmental Factors

The respondents identified several factors of the work environment at home that are advantageous for ensuring the protection of organizational InfoSec while working from home. According to respondent #9, working from home provides a safe working environment which minimizes InfoSec issues such as eavesdropping and the accidental reveal of confidential information. Respondents #5 and #8 also enjoy their working environment at home, where they can focus on work and are not distracted by unscheduled meetings or occasional requests from colleagues. This focused environment allows these respondents to complete the work faster while paying attention to avoid InfoSec threats. Moreover, the respondents can flexibly adjust their work pace without the pressure of being under constant supervision, which reduces their cognitive load and helps them to focus more on meeting InfoSec requirements (respondents #1, #4, and #7). Other benefits, such as the freedom to wear flexible clothes and not being required to physically meet other people, thus reduces the risk of COVID-19 infection, all contribute to the pleasant WFH experiences, according to the respondents.

Nonetheless, not all respondents could receive the advantages offered by working from home. For instance, respondents #1 and #8 experienced difficulties when trying to seek IT support, while others reported to have low bandwidth and unstable Internet connection at home (respondents #3, #7, and #8). For inexperienced IT users, inappropriate and careless troubleshooting may expose themselves to more InfoSec risks. Although some respondents mentioned the benefit of not being under close supervision all the time, respondents #3, #7, #8, and #12 found themselves to be more easily distracted and less productive without the supervision pressure when working from home. Since accessing business information from home is restricted, some employees may try to find workarounds that allow them to access the necessary information, which can expose organizational InfoSec to more risks (respondents #4 and #5).

The flexibility of working from home also works against some respondents, as they reported to feel more stress from working overtime. One respondent complained that "there is almost no 'stop' on a working day; there is only the end of the day but never the end of work" (respondent #12). Other respondents also shared that they often received business calls and additional tasks outside of business hours. Respondents #3, #9, and #10 found it difficult to keep the mood for work outside of the office atmosphere, while respondents #12 and #13 were distracted by the noises at home and having to share daily chores. All these negative experiences discourage the respondents to pay attention to meeting InfoSec requirements when working from home.

4.4   Individual Factors

Ten out of 20 respondents mentioned that individual factors contribute to the protection of organizational InfoSec while working from home. Most of these mentions highlight the importance of having a strong sense of responsibility over organizational InfoSec and the employees' personalities. Respondent #14 explained that people may feel more relaxed when working at home, and depending on their personality, they may access any websites without considering the risks of that. InfoSec skills were mentioned by respondents #4, #5, #13, and #20, such as knowing how to make file backups in secure places, check for security indicators of networks and websites when making important communication and transactions.

5   Discussion

As shown in Fig. 1, the issues mentioned in one category were identified to relate to one another. For instance, respondents highlighted the importance of being well-equipped with secure technologies such as VPN and online systems for classifying information, which was related to the organization category since there was also need for management to provide clear guidelines about acceptable use of technologies as well. Likewise, low bandwidth and poor Internet connection, or restricted access to work resources, are technology-related issues, but they only take place in the home context i.e. belonging to the work environment category. Therefore, there is a dependency between the technology and work environment categories. According to the respondents, although the work environment at home provides flexibility, it also results in the feelings of being disconnected from the work atmosphere and interactions with colleagues and supervisors, leading to poor attention to work and InfoSec tasks. The individuals play the central role in making use of the tools, InfoSec knowledge and skills, and their work environment at home to determine the effective protection of organizational InfoSec while working from home.

Before the COVID-19 pandemic, research has examined how remote employees perceive organizational InfoSec requirements and perform InfoSec behaviors outside of the office. Our findings about the feeling of social isolation, which affects the employees' perceptions of organizational InfoSec, mirror those of prior studies such

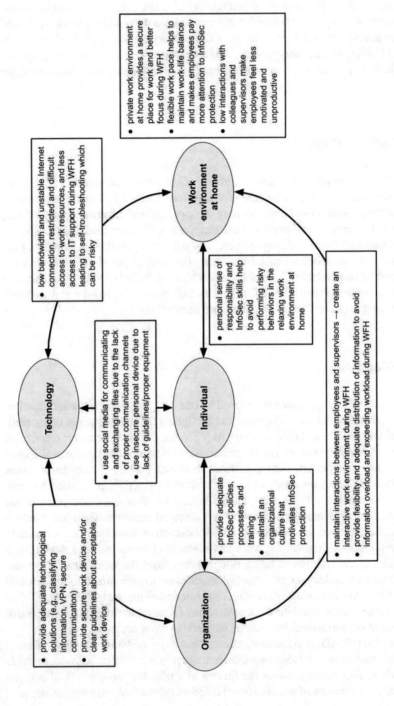

Fig. 1 Summary of research findings

that employees feel under less supervision while working from home [11, 18, 30]. The abrupt demand for WFH caused by the pandemic left organizations with little time to equip employees with adequate resources to ensure their protection of organizational InfoSec at home [17]. The stress associated with working from home, which is caused by the distractions and reduced work-life balance, adds to the technostress that further distract employees from performing secure behaviors [14]. Our findings reveal that in such situation, the protection of organizational InfoSec relies much on the employees' personal sense of InfoSec duty and work ethic to ensure that their performance of daily work at home is safe and secure.

Many companies have announced their permanent post-COVID remote work or hybrid home/office policies, and adoption of WFH practice is expected to be 75% higher than the current situation [20, 35]. As such, our findings about the impact of WFH on InfoSec compliance at home would remain relevant even when the pandemic fades and people adapt to the new normalcy. Organizations should focus on preparing for flexible and adequate arrangements for remote work that allow employees to work either at home or in the office. Organizations also need to review their business processes to determine the operations and activities that would be significantly impacted or altered by the continuing demand for WFH. These operations and tasks may need to be re-designed to fit the employees' capabilities and work contexts outside of the regular office environment, so that work-life balance and effective InfoSec can be achieved.

Our study calls for more managerial attention to maintain an adequate level of social interactions for remote workers e.g. through providing leadership, frequent communication, or leveraging technologies for managing virtual workplaces. Our analysis shows that there is little variation in the impact of WFH on the employee InfoSec compliance, despite their different demographics such as age, gender, the number of children they have, and the self-rated quality of their work environment at home. Such indifference might have been due to the limited sample size of our qualitative study, which does not reveal the variations that would take place if a larger sample is surveyed quantitatively. Moreover, we anticipate that the different impacts of WFH on InfoSec compliance at home would be more profound across job roles whose access to confidential data and InfoSec responsibilities are varied. Future studies are thus invited to continue identifying the contextual determinants of InfoSec compliance at home, which can inform management practices to maintain organizational InfoSec while working from home.

In terms of theoretical implications, we believe that it is timely and practical for behavioral InfoSec research to adopt theoretical frameworks that explain the impacts of task design and the work environment on employees' InfoSec behaviors. Employee compliance with InfoSec policies has been one of the most widely studied factor in the behavioral InfoSec literature. In the post-COVID period, where employees can be expected to work remotely and away from the formal office setting, novel and situational InfoSec behaviors that do not necessarily follow the prescribed actions may emerge and impact organizational InfoSec differently. As evident in our findings, the respondents exchanged work files and communicated with each other via social media platforms while considering these channels as secure and more convenient than the remote working solutions recommended by their companies. Future behavioral InfoSec research should investigate the situational InfoSec behaviors performed by the employees while working remotely, including their antecedents and consequences. Another research direction that may be worth pursuing is examining management models that can maintain the synergy between remote and onsite employees in protecting organizational InfoSec, especially by helping them to achieve work-life balance and reducing the stress associated with the increasing demand for InfoSec in any work context.

6 Limitations and Conclusion

By following the qualitative research approach, our study inevitably has some limitations. First, our qualitative findings, which are drawn from a small sample size, would not be generalizable to a larger population. By doing so, we focus on extracting in-depth and rich understanding about the examined phenomena from the small sample rather than aiming for statistical generalization. This limitation subsequently leads to an opportunity to conduct quantitative research to further validate these findings. For instance, future research may employ statistical analysis techniques to determine the antecedents of employee InfoSec compliance and misuse while working from home. Second, the sample of our study comprises young professionals (with an average age of 30 years old) who work in Vietnam, and therefore, our findings would reflect most accurately the unique characteristics of this sample. Future studies are thus invited to examine the InfoSec behaviors of employees having different demographics and cultural traits while working from home.

From the respondents' perspectives, the majority of them did not see any major difference in performing secure behaviors while working from home, as compared to working in the office. Nevertheless, they identified several factors in four areas, technology, organization, work environment, and individual, that influenced their InfoSec behaviors at home (see Fig. 1). Based on these findings, we offer practical recommendations to organizations, which aim to provide flexible and secure work arrangements in different contexts to meet the continuing demand for WFH after the pandemic. Future research is also encouraged to explore further the contextual and situational factors that influence employee InfoSec behaviors beyond the formal work context.

References

1. Alzahrani, A. (2020). Coronavirus social engineering attacks: Issues and recommendations. *International Journal of Advanced Computer Science and Applications, 11*(5), 154–161.
2. Ayyagari, R., Grover, V., & Purvis, R. (2011). Technostress: Technological Antecedents and Implications. *MIS Quarterly: Management Information Systems, 35*(4), 831–858.

3. Bélanger, F., Watson-Manheim, M. B., & Swan, B. R. (2013). A multi-level socio-technical systems telecommuting framework. *Behaviour and Information Technology, 32*(12), 1257–1279.
4. Braun, V., & Clarke, V. (2006). Using thematic analysis in psychology. *Qualitative Research in Psychology, 3*(2), 77–101.
5. Chigada, J., & Madzinga, R. (2021). Cyberattacks and threats during COVID-19: A systematic literature review. *SA Journal of Information Management, 23*(1), 1–11.
6. Chowdhury, N. H., Adam, M. T. P., & Skinner, G. (2019). The impact of time pressure on cybersecurity behaviour: A systematic literature review. *Behaviour and Information Technology, 38*(12), 1290–1308.
7. Cooper, C. D., & Kurland, N. B. (2002). Telecommuting, professional isolation, and employee development in public and private organizations. *Journal of Organizational Behavior, 23*, 511–532.
8. Creswell, J.W. a., & Creswell, J.D. (2018). In *Research Design: Qualitative, Quantitative, and Mixed Methods Approaches*. 5th ed. SAGE Publications, Inc.,.
9. Crossler, R. E., Johnston, A. C., Lowry, P. B., Hu, Q., Warkentin, M., & Baskerville, R. L. (2013). Future directions for behavioral information security research. *Computers & Security* (32), Elsevier Ltd, 90–101.
10. D'Arcy, J., Herath, T., & Shoss, M. K. (2014). Understanding employee responses to stressful information security requirements: A coping perspective. *Journal of Management Information Systems, 31*(2), 285–318.
11. D'Arcy, J., & Hovav, A. (2008). Does one size fit all? Examining the differential effects of is security counter measures. *Journal of Business Ethics, 89*(S1), 59–71.
12. Dang-Pham, D., Pittayachawan, S., & Bruno, V. (2017). Why employees share information security advice? Exploring the contributing factors and structural patterns of security advice sharing in the workplace. *Computers in Human Behavior, 67*, 196–206.
13. Depietro, R., Wiarda, E., & Fleischer, M. (1990). The context for change: Organization, technology and environment. *The Processes of Technological Innovation, 199*, 151–175.
14. De', R., Pandey, N., & Pal, A. (2020). Impact of digital surge during Covid-19 pandemic: A viewpoint on research and practice. *International Journal of Information Management, 55*(June).
15. Furnell, S., & Shah, J. N. (2020). Home working and cyber security—an outbreak of unpreparedness? *Computer Fraud and Security, 2020*(8), 6–12.
16. Gajendran, R. S., & Harrison, D. A. (2007). The good, the bad, and the unknown about telecommuting: Meta-analysis of psychological mediators and individual consequences. *Journal of Applied Psychology, 92*, 1524–1541.
17. Georgiadou, A., Mouzakitis, S., & Askounis, D. (2021). Working from home during COVID-19 Crisis: A cyber security culture assessment survey. *Security Journal* (2021).
18. Godlove, T. (2012). Examination of the factors that influence teleworkers' willingness to comply with information security guidelines. *Information Security Journal, 21*(4), 216–229.
19. Hobbs, D., & Armstrong, J. (1998). An experimental study of social and psychological aspects of teleworking. *Facilities, 16*(12–13), 366–371.
20. Jain, T., Currie, G., and Aston, L. (2021). COVID and working from home: Long-term impacts and psycho-social determinants. *Transportation Research Part A: Policy and Practice, 156*, 52–68.
21. Kazekami, S. (2020). Mechanisms to improve labor productivity by performing telework. *Telecommunications Policy, 44*(2), 101868.
22. Laato, S., Islam, A. K. M. N., Islam, M. N., & Whelan, E. (2020). What drives unverified information sharing and cyberchondria during the COVID-19 pandemic? *European Journal of Information Systems 29*(3), 288–305.
23. Lallie, H. S., Shepherd, L. A., Nurse, J. R. C., Erola, A., Epiphaniou, G., Maple, C., & Bellekens, X. (2021). Cyber security in the age of COVID-19: A timeline and analysis of cyber-crime and cyber-attacks during the pandemic. *Computers and Security, 105*.

24. Li, Y., & Siponen, M. (2011). *A call for research on home users' information security behaviour*. In: 15th Pacific Asia Conference on Information Systems (PACIS).
25. Martin, B. H., & MacDonnell, R. (2012). Is telework effective for organizations? A meta-analysis of empirical research on perceptions of telework and organizational outcomes. *Management Research Review, 35*(7), 602–616.
26. Maslach, C., Schaufeli, W. B., & Leiter, M. P. (2001). Job burnout. *Annual Review of Psychology, 52*, 397–422.
27. Moen, P., Kelly, E. L., & Hill, R. (2011). Does enhancing work-time control and flexibility reduce turnover? A naturally occurring experiment. *Social Problems, 58*, 69–98.
28. Mwagwabi, F., & Jiow, J. H. (2021). Compliance with security guidelines in teenagers: The conflicting role of peer influence and personal norms. *Australasian Journal of Information Systems, 25*, 1–25.
29. Palanisamy, R., Norman, A. A., & Kiah, M. L. M. (2020). Compliance with bring your own device security policies in organizations: A systematic literature review. *Computers and Security 98*.
30. Pearlson, K. E., & Saunders, C. S. (2001). There's no place like home: Managing telecommuting paradoxes. *Academy of Management Executive, 15*(2), 117–128.
31. Pham, H. C. (2019). Information security burnout: Identification of sources and mitigating factors from security demands and resources. *Journal of Information Security and Applications, 46*, Elsevier Ltd, 96–107.
32. Pollini, A., Callari, T. C., Tedeschi, A., Ruscio, D., Save, L., Chiarugi, F., & Guerri, D. (2021). Leveraging human factors in cybersecurity: An integrated methodological approach. *Cognition, Technology and Work*.
33. Rhee, H.-S. S., Kim, C., & Ryu, Y. U. (2009). Self-Efficacy in information security: Its influence on end users' information security practice behavior. *Computers & Security, 28* (8), 816– 826.
34. Safa, N. S., & Von Solms, R. (2016). An information security knowledge sharing model in organizations. *Computers in Human Behavior, 57*, 442–451.
35. Sardeshmukh, S. R., Sharma, D., & Golden, T. D. (2012). Impact of telework on exhaustion and job engagement. *New Technology, Work and Employment, 27*(3), 193–207.
36. Smite, D., Tkalich, A., Moe, N. B., Papatheocharous, E., Klotins, E., & Buvik, M. P. (2022). Changes in perceived productivity of software engineers during covid-19 pandemic: The voice of evidence. *Journal of Systems and Software, 186*, 1–14.
37. *Viet Nam COVID-19 Situation Report #65*, WHO. 30 October 2021. Retrieved 30 October 2021.
38. Warkentin, M., Johnston, A. C., & Shropshire, J. (2011). The influence of the informal social learning environment on information privacy policy compliance efficacy and intention. *European Journal of Information Systems, 20*(3), 267–284.

Technology Readiness and Digital Transformation: A Case Study of Telework During COVID-19 Pandemic and Future Work in Vietnam

Quan Vu Le⭕, Jason Nguyen⭕, and Jasmine Ha⭕

Abstract The COVID-19 pandemic has highlighted how the adaptability to telework has become the key to resilience for businesses and workers. In this chapter, we study how organizations can implement telework effectively to both enhance organizational resilience and improve workers' productivity and welfare. To that end, we conducted a self-administered survey in Vietnam with five-hundred and fifty-four employees across 52 companies based in Ho Chi Minh City and Ha Noi. The quantitative analysis is further supported by informal interviews with by mid-level managers and senior executives in the University of Hawaii—Shidler Vietnam EMBA program. We identify workers' technology readiness as an important driver for the productivity telework in that technology readiness has a positive and statistically significant impact on working from home productivity. Furthermore, adequate equipment and training positively and significantly influenced working from home productivity. This increase in productivity leads to higher individual performance expectations and company performance. Given strong evidence presented in this study supporting telework, senior management and executives participated in the survey recommend digital transformation strategy to cope with the new normal must consider the following tasks: (1) Technical capacity enhancement; (2) Categorize employees into different groups; (3) Change the management mindset; (4) Build a corporate culture for telework; and (5) Organize periodic virtual events such as team building, and open forum.

Q. V. Le (✉)
University of Hong Kong, HKU-Vietnam, Floor 19, Bitexco Financial Tower 2 Hai Trieu, Ben Nghe, D1, Ho Chi Minh City 700000, Vietnam
e-mail: quan.le@hku-vn.org

Shidler College of Business, University of Hawaii, Mānoa, Vietnam EMBA Program, 234 Pasteur St., District 3, Ho Chi Minh City 700000, Vietnam

J. Nguyen
Ivey Business School, Western University, 1151 Richmond St, London, ON N6G 0N1, Canada

J. Ha
Department of Sociology, Western University, 1151 Richmond St, London, ON N6G 0N1, Canada

Keywords Technology readiness · Digital transformation · Telework · Future work · COVID-19 pandemic · Vietnam

1 Introduction

The COVID-19 pandemic has highlighted how the adaptability to telework has become the key to resilience for businesses and workers. Disruptions caused by the pandemic has pushed companies to enable and scale up remote work, as well as to accelerate digitalization [29]. Global business leaders have quickly come to acknowledge the importance of flexible workplaces as a significant factor to maintain productivity and performance to cope with the "new normal" [21]. Anecdotal evidence during the COVID-19 pandemic has shown that telework is a tenable solution for businesses to survive and thrive under the "new normal" of limited travel and restricted face-to-face interactions. Beyond the pandemic, it is expected that telework designs will allow businesses to recruit from a wider pool of talents beyond their corporate bases as traditional physical barriers become less relevant. It can also help organizations develop nimble structures where problems could be addressed in a timely manner through the partnerships of human, virtually instantaneous information communication technology (ICT) and mobile tools. On the flip side, the general challenges of transitioning from the physical space to telework must be adequately addressed to keep remote employees engaged, productive, and connected [25].

The unprecedented availability of large scale remote and flexible works forced by the pandemic presents a unique natural experimental for companies to examine their telework settings and to further reimagine how work could and should be done. This also opens new opportunities for research to systematically examine the complexity of emerging practices and advance fundamental understandings of how teleworks can enhance the resilience of future work and workers. It is, however, noteworthy that not all types and classes of workers may benefit from telework. As Saltiel [23] demonstrates, demographic factors such as educational attainment, employment status in the formal sector and household wealth are positively associated with the possibility of working from home. This creates a concern of employability of various groups of workers during the pandemic. Dingel and Neiman [10] also report that based on occupational classifications in 85 countries, lower-income economies have a lower share of jobs that can be done at home. As such, it is important to understand not only how telework can be implemented effectively across organizations, but also when and how it can benefit a wider set of workers. In this chapter, we look to further that understanding by answering the following research questions.

1. *How can organizations create the most positive telework outcomes for workers?*
2. *How can the concept of telework be expanded to support a wider set of workers and businesses to enhance organizational resilience?*
3. *How to prepare future workers for telework?*

Answering these questions is particularly important for developing countries, where the economy is mostly dominated by lower-skilled jobs within small-and-medium enterprises (SMEs). Before the pandemic, telework arrangement has been a low strategic priority for both the Vietnamese businesses and its workers, given the country's idiosyncratic limited digital infrastructure and a dominating workforce of lower-skilled workers in SMEs. A recent estimate by the market research firm Deloitte indicates that only about 13% of the Vietnamese workforce may switch to remote work, the lowest in the South-East Asian region, trailing behind Thailand (15%), Indonesia (16%), and the Philippines (22%). Singapore leads the region with a potential remote workforce of up to 45% [9]. Cultural preference is an additional barrier for telework adoption in Vietnam, as research has found that workplace culture in East Asia prioritizes managerial control, as well as in-person training and supervision [1].

However, anecdotal evidence shows that Vietnamese businesses have adopted a wide range of telework practices during the on-going pandemic. This started in 2020 when the country experienced the first nation-wide government-mandated lockdown in March, followed by a few additional localized social distancing orders due to case spikes in July and November 2020. Overall, the spread of telework practices in Vietnam in 2020 was unexpected because the country did very well in maintaining a low records of COVID cases as well as COVID-related deaths. During the 2020 lockdowns, the government left it open for the businesses to decide whether they would have their workers work remotely. Those requiring workers to work in person must provide a letter specifying that the worker must travel to the office. Only high-risk settings (such as daycare centers and schools) were required to operate remotely, so all children must stay home.

In Vietnam, the most common form of telework, which is working from home, is adopted by businesses whose work nature lends itself well to home-based offices and virtual meetings. This practice has greatly benefited workers in the big cities, namely Ha Noi and Ho Chi Minh City. The two cities also withstand the hardest pandemic hit in the early waves, as they are major hubs for international arrivals to Vietnam. Beyond the immediate function to support public health social distancing measures, the impacts of the sudden transition to telework in Vietnam on both the workers and the businesses remain unknown. The answers to these questions are key for envisioning how telework can become a strategic priority for businesses in Vietnam to develop in the face of uncertainty, such as in the on-going pandemic.

To address these questions, we conducted a self-administered survey in Ho Chi Minh City and in Ha Noi, in December 2020 and in January 2021, respectively. The questionnaires were circulated to 52 mid-level and senior executives of leading MNCs and local companies, who distributed to 554 co-workers in their organizations. With this diversity in the sample, the survey extracted a wide-range of information from the workers, including productivity, technology readiness, work-life integration, business profitability and individual performance expectations. This dataset helps to shed light on the impact of telework on workers, and ultimately to identify key technology readiness and management practices that can lead to more favorable performance and productivity outcomes. For example, the survey revealed that over

70% of the respondents preferred remote work, and 30% reported that their performance has improved due to working from home. However, indirect estimates suggest that only about 30% of all jobs in Vietnam can feasibly be adapted into telework as the work is done through a computer and does not require face-to-face interactions.

2 Brief Literature Review

The full or partial lockdown measures in 2020 to contain the spread of the coronavirus have impacted 2.7 billion workers, representing around 81% of the workforce worldwide [15]. Before the pandemic, telework has long remained a low-order strategic priority for many organizations for two reasons. First, telework is typically equated to its most common form, which is remote work from home, by definition, the workers live within commuting distance from the office [3]. Within this narrow conception, few jobs can feasibly be reconfigured into remote work, and they typically confer higher pay, allow more schedule flexibility, as well as more work autonomy. Such job characteristics have been shown to correlate strongly with social privileges in terms of social class, gender, race, and ethnicity. The narrow conception of telework thus limits its application and potential contribution to future work. Second, organizations hesitate to adopt telework designs because there are few insights on how telework may interact with organization structure and existing business management practices.

Telecommuting has clear beneficial effects on the workers, including perceived autonomy, lower work-family conflict, stress, and turnover intent; and higher job satisfaction and performance [13]. From a management perspective, productivity is a key concern when considering a more flexible work arrangement for the workers. There is growing evidence during the pandemic that provides positive reassurances on productivity. According to recent research by McKinsey, 80% of the participants in the survey reported that they enjoy working from home, 41% asserted that they are more productive than they had been before, and 28% claimed that they are as productive [4]. Furthermore, Harvard Business Review reports that knowledge workers are more productive working from home [2]. Given a wide-spread adoption of telework, emergent practices have resulted in diverse changes in business management practices. Some management practices are shown to enhance worker's productivity, promote worker's well-being, increase work-life integration, and boost workplace cohesion.

As companies around the world are preparing to bring their workers back to the offices in a new normal conditions, McKinsey has recommended organizations to reclassify the worker segments into four categories based on 'people to work' or 'work to people' ([4], p. 4): (1) fully remote (net positive value-creating outcome); (2) hybrid remote (net neutral outcome); (3) hybrid remote by exception (net negative outcome but can be done remotely if needed); (4) on site (not eligible for remote work). Brynjolfsson et al. [5], and Fadinger and Schymik [11] find that during the pandemic, younger workers in management, professional and related occupations were more likely to switch to telework. These young professionals will continue to have a strong preference for working remotely in the post-pandemic environment. To achieve the highest productivity, integration between these four groups must be achieved. Insights from both individual workers and collective work teams thus are crucial to fully understand the human-technology partnership in telework.

Technology readiness is fundamentally important in a remote working environment. The pool of available information communication technology (ICT) and mobile tools that enable telework has been very well developed, with many user-friendly and easy-to-implement options readily available. This technology readiness has allowed organizations to develop multiple telework designs within a short timeframe to cope with disruptions during the pandemic. Less affected businesses are the ones that have invested on digital transformation, even before the outbreak. The effective use of existing ICT to accomplish needed tasks and maintain productivity is the key determinant of individual performance and company's profitability. However, the abrupt yet wide-spread adoption of telework technology has also exposed several gaps in business management practices, organizational structures, and business models. Existing evidence indicates that the transition to remote work has only been applied narrowly—in relatively more privileged occupations and in developed countries with mature digital infrastructures and high-skilled workforce. According to the World Bank [28], in response to the COVID-19 pandemic, 34% of firms increased their use of digital platforms and only 17% of firms invested in digital solutions. Despite the well-developed pool of user-friendly ICT and mobile tools readily available to support telework, inadequate knowledge on how to successfully integrate technology and telework to optimize work design and organization structure has limited the potential of telework.

3 Survey Methodology and Data

The data collection efforts integrate both quantitative and qualitative data on emergent telework practices and outcomes in Vietnam during the two waves of lockdown in 2020. The first national lockdown was between March and April, and the second partial lockdown was between July and August. Primary quantitative and qualitative data were collected to facilitate conceptual development and rigorous analyses, incorporating well developed measures such as worker's productivity, technology readiness, as well as potential new measures uncovered through in-depth conversations with senior management and executives.

The online survey was conducted between December 2020 in Ho Chi Minh City and January 2021 and Ha Noi. Twenty-eight mid-level and senior executives in the University of Hawaii—Shidler College of Business Vietnam EMBA cohort in Ho Chi Minh City, and twenty-four students from the cohort in Ha Noi supported in designing the questionnaires and distributing the survey to their co-workers. The Shidler Vietnam EMBA has 20 plus years of presence in Vietnam with a large alumni network of more than 1000 leaders across industries. Many of them are currently held

Table 1 Demographic profile of participants—personal

Indicator	Frequency (%)
Age	
20–29	28.2
30–39	43.9
40–49	23.6
50–59	3.8
60 or above	0.5
Gender	
Male	51.0
Female	47.7
Prefer not to say	1.3
Education level	
Post-graduate	13.4
College	72.2
Other education	14.4
Children	
No	37.5
Yes, youngest child under 11	46.4
Yes, youngest child 11 +	16.1
Access to childcare (among those with children)	
No	31.8
Yes	68.2
Commute time from home to office	
Less than 30 min	51.3
More than 30 min	48.7

Note N = 554

senior management positions in leading MNCs, local public and private companies in Vietnam, including IBM, HP, Intel, Cargill, Abbott, HSBC, Vinamilk, FPT, The PAN Group, VNPT, PVN, etc.

Fifty-two students from both cohorts in Ho Chi Minh City and Ha Noi represented a wide range of companies from different industries. In addition to the survey, we asked the students how their companies were responding and adapting to the lockdowns in 2020. The qualitative data is used to support the quantitative results. In total, 554 employees across 52 organizations participated in the survey, of which 277 employees were from Ho Chi Minh City, and another 277 employees were from Ha Noi. Tables 1, 2, 3 and 4 present the demographics of the respondents.

Table 1 reveals that many of the respondents are in the middle-aged group. Fifty-one percent of the respondents are male, 48% are female, and 1% unspecified. Many of them have their youngest child under 11 years old and 68% of them have access

Table 2 Demographic profile of participants—work-related

Indicator	Frequency (%)
Position	
Executive	12.0
Manager	30.0
Supervisor	19.0
Staff	39.0
Time with the company	
Less than 1 year	11.6
1–3 years	28.2
>3–5 years	19.0
>5–10 years	21.0
>10 years	20.2
Work arrangement	
Mostly office-based	69.9
Flexible	22.7
Mostly factory/site-based	7.4
Work outside of the office	
Not at all	27.6
10–30% of work hours	48.6
31–50% of work hours	14.7
51–70% of work hours	5.1
Over 70% of work hours	4.0
Work overtime	
No	9.7
Sometimes	59.3
Frequently	31.0

Note N = 554

to childcare. Fifty-one percent of the respondents spend less than 30 min commuting between home and office. In Table 2, 30% of the respondents reported they are in a management position, only 12% reported they are in executive position. The remaining 58% are in supervisors and staff positions. About 40% of the respondents have 5–10 plus years with the company, while 60% have between 1 to less than 5 years. Seventy percent of the respondents have an office-based work schedule, while 23% have a flexible work schedule. About half of the respondents spend 10–30% of work hours outside of the office for work-related activities, while 28% spend all their time in the office. Less than 10% of the respondents spend between 50% to more than 70% outside of the office. Many of the workers reported that they sometimes or frequently work overtime. In terms of education level, over 70% of the

Table 3 Company profile

Indicator	Frequency (%)
Sector	
Private	51.1
Public	30.7
FDI	18.2
Industry	
Finance/accounting/insurance	15.3
IT	23.8
Healthcare	5.2
Real estate/construction	9.4
Marketing/management/consulting	8.3
Manufacturing	10.6
Education	9.4
Others	18.01
Number of employees	
Less than 50 employees	21.0
51–100 employees	15.3
101–200 employees	11.0
200+ employees	11.7
500+ employees	13.2
1000+ employees	27.8

Note N = 554

Table 4 Work arrangement during and after COVID-19 social isolation

Indicator	Frequency (%)
A. *Work arrangement during COVID-19 social isolation*	
Was given the choice to work from home	38.4
Was required to work from home	40.3
No change	18.8
Other arrangement	2.5
B. *Work arrangement after COVID-19 social isolation*	
The company went back to pre-pandemic arrangement	49.5
The company kept the during-pandemic arrangement	24.4
The company created a new work arrangement	26.1

Note N = 554

respondents are college-educated, 13% have post-graduate education, and 14% has other education (such as high school and vocational certificates).

Table 3 reports approximately 51% of the respondents work in the private sector, 31% work in the public sector, and the remaining 18% work in the FDI sector. A quarter of the respondents work in the IT-related industry, 15% work in finance, accounting, and insurance industry. Other industries represented less than 10% of the respondents. About 28% of the respondents work in companies with more than 1000 employees, and 21% work in companies with less than 50 employees. Other respondents work in companies with 51 to 500+ employees.

In Table 4, we provide the responses on the work arrangement during and after COVID-19 social isolation period. Forty percent of the respondents reported that they were required to work from home during social isolation, 38% were given the choice to work from home, while 19% reported no change in the work arrangement. After the social isolation period, about half of the respondents reported that their companies returned to the pre-pandemic arrangement, 24% kept the during-pandemic arrangement, and 26% created a new work arrangement for the employees.

Having physical infrastructure at home to create an effective working environment is important to productivity. In Table 5 Part A, using Likert type five-point scales with 5 indicating "strongly agree" and 1 indicating "strongly disagree", the respondents reported a mean score 3.77 on the question "I have adequate equipment and training to effectively perform my work at home". This implies that the respondents are not behind on technology and training when working from home during the lockdown.

Utilizing a set of indicators based on Bloom et al. [3], the survey asked the respondents on the perceptions of working from home productivity. The respondents answered the questionnaires on Likert type five-point scales with 5 indicating "strongly agree" and 1 indicating "strongly disagree". Accordingly, at the aggregate level, a mean score higher than 3 indicates more likely towards agreeing with the question. Table 5 Part B reports the results with the mean scores ranging between 3.10 and 3.63 on the perceptions of working from home productivity. The respondents reported the highest mean score on happiness, while reporting the lowest mean score on productivity. They are more likely to agree that working from home leads to lower stress, and less likely to take time off from work.

In terms of technology readiness, selected indicators based on Parasuraman and Colby [19]; and Parasuraman [20] were employed to ask the respondents using similar Likert type five-point scales defined in Part B. The authors define technology readiness as the tendency to embrace and use new technologies as an important factor affecting adoption and usage of technology in various contexts. The mean scores for technology readiness ranging between 3.28 and 4.17 are reported in Part B of Table 5. The respondents reported the highest score on the importance of technology and efficient in their work. They also reported high score on technology gives them more control over their daily lives. In general, the respondents are comfortable with using new technology and they receive benefits from it.

Regarding the perceptions of returning to work in the office or continuing working from home under the new normal conditions, the respondents reported a higher mean score for the status quo, being 3.60 versus 3.24. However, they reported a highest

Table 5 Descriptive statistics of indicators

Indicator	Mean	Std. deviation
A. *Infrastructure*		
I have adequate equipment and training to effectively perform my work from home	3.77	1.06
B. *Working from home productivity*		
Working from home leads to an increase in performance	3.17	1.05
People who work from home report higher productivity	3.10	1.02
People who work from home are more likely to report lower stress	3.57	1.05
People who work from home are less likely to take time off from work	3.48	1.06
People who work from home periodically are happier	3.63	0.96
C. *Technology readiness*		
I can usually figure out new hi-tech products and services without help from others	3.64	1.03
I like the idea of working via computers because I am not limited to regular business hours and location	3.81	0.96
Technology gives people more control over their daily lives	4.03	0.86
Technology makes me more efficient in my occupation	4.17	0.78
In general, I am among the first in my circle of friends to acquire new technology when it appears	3.28	0.99
D. *Perceptions of status quo or the "new normal"*		
I prefer to return back to work in the office under the status quo conditions prior to the pandemic	3.60	1.02
I prefer the working from home conditions under the new normal, using technology to connect with colleagues, instead of being in the office 8 h a day	3.24	1.08
I prefer a balance and flexible option between working from home and in the office	4.13	0.93

Note N = 554
Likert scale: 5 = Strongly agree; 4 = Agree; 3 = Neutral; 2 = Disagree; 1 = Strongly disagree

mean score for the preference of a balance and flexible option between working from home and in the office as revealed in Table 5 Part D.

To measure company performance, indicators based on Wiklund and Shepherd [27] were utilized to compare the current business performance to the condition prior to the pandemic: net profits, value, cash flows, and sales. These indicators are generally considered to have validity and have been successfully used in other studies in the Vietnamese context [16, 17, 22]. Not all participants have access to

Table 6 Performance and outlook

Indicator	N	Mean	Std. deviation
A. *Company performance*[1]			
Your company's net profits	506	3.11	0.97
Growth of the company's value	505	3.28	0.92
Your company's cash flow	503	3.08	0.96
Your company's sales	506	3.04	0.96
B. *Company outlook*[2]			
What is your outlook on the prospect for growth of your company in the post-pandemic period? Would you say you are ...	554	3.76	0.80
C. *Individual performance expectation*[3]			
In general, in terms of productivity during COVID-19 pandemic and now compared to the pre-pandemic period, my performance:	554	2.26	0.75

Notes (1) 5 = Much better; 1 = Much worse; (2) 5 = Optimistic; 1 = Pessimistic; (3) 4 = Significantly exceeds the expectations; 3 = Exceeds the expectations; 2 = Meets the expectations; 1 = Does not meet the expectations

the company's financial information, thus N is around 500. The Likert type 5-point scales were used, where 5 implies "much better" and 1 implies "much worse". In general, the mean score is slightly above 3 on business performance as reported in Table 6 Part A, despite low economic activities during the lockdowns, indicating that the respondents have a relatively positive view of the company performance at the aggregate level.

Surprisingly, in terms of company outlook reported in Part B, the respondents are relatively optimistic (mean score = 3.76) about the prospect for growth of the company in the post-pandemic period. However, the respondents reported a mean score slightly above 2 in Part C, suggesting that they only meet expectations in terms of individual performance during the pandemic and at the time of the survey compared to the pre-pandemic period.

Principal components analysis (PCA) described in Nardo et al. [18] is employed to construct three indices, depicting: (1) working from home productivity index, (2) technology readiness index; and (3) company performance index. Varimax rotation with Kaiser normalization is utilized to uncover the latent dimension of a set of indicators. All items loaded over 0.70 using Cronbach's alpha reliability test.

The working from home productivity index is constructed from a set of five indicators presented in Table 5 Part B. PCA indicated the computed measure is unidimensional. Cronbach's alpha indicated this measure had a satisfactory reliability of 0.80. The technology readiness index is constructed using PCA on a set of five indicators presented in Table 5 Part C. Cronbach's alpha indicated technology readiness index had a satisfactory reliability of 0.73 and the measure is unidimensional.

Company performance index is measured by four indicators presented in Table 6 Part A. PCA indicated the computed measure is also unidimensional. Missing values were replaced with the mean score. Cronbach's alpha indicated this measure had a satisfactory reliability of 0.92.

4 Analysis and Results

This section analyzes how technology readiness and management practices create positive work from home outcomes for the workers and companies, and how the concept of telework be expanded to enhance organizational resilience in the post-COVID-19 pandemic. In addition, we discuss how to prepare future workers for telework. The results for the multivariable regressions are reported in Tables 7 and 8.

Technology readiness index has a positive and statistically significant impact on working from home productivity as revealed in Table 7. Thus, accelerating digitalization and supporting the workforce are important success factors of working from home during and post-COVID-19 pandemic. Having adequate equipment and training to work effectively from home positively and significantly influenced the productivity of the workers. It is important to provide workers with adequate equipment and offer continuous training to increase productivity as part of the companies' digital transformation strategy. Anecdotal evidence from the mid-level managers and senior executives in the Vietnam EMBA program strongly support the empirical results. One executive of a manufacturer noted, *"In the early stage of COVID-19 productivity was relatively low. However, after investment in technology, productivity and overall company performance soared."*

In addition to technology readiness, cybersecurity readiness is another concern in remote work [14]. The respondents raised pressing issues of data privacy and cybersecurity, particularly individuals who work in the IT and financial industry. Information privacy and security of both individuals and organizations need further investigation in the post-pandemic working environment. A manager who works in the consulting industry expressed this concern as follows, *"Company needs to ensure the availability of equipment and the quality of the internet access as well as necessary applications to ensure security, data privacy, and fraud protection."* This is also recommended by another executive in a payment processing center, *"The company purchased the best cybersecurity solutions globally to access internal systems without losing information."*

Other statistically significant indicators in the model that have a positive impact on working from home productivity are respondents who reported having a college education, working outside of the office 31–50% of work hours, having a youngest child 11+ years old, and spending more than 30 min commuting to work. These statistically significant results are confirmed by the executives as one commented, *"Technology has made it possible for people to work from home, thus increases productivity by reducing the amount of time wasted on the road, mostly for business*

Table 7 Multivariable regression model of technology readiness and working from home productivity

Indicator	Model 1
Constant	−1.295***
	(−4.151)
Technology readiness index (TRI)	0.354***
	(8.456)
I have adequate equipment and training to effectively perform my work from home	0.179***
	(4.617)
In general, people prefer to work alone	0.206***
	(5.957)
Gender (Ref = Male)	
Female	0.070
	(0.913)
Prefer not to say	−0.121
	(−0.381)
Age (Ref = 20–29)	
30–39	0.063
	(0.570)
40–49	0.152
	(−1.071)
50–59	0.098
	(0.415)
Above 60	0.805
	(1.596)
Education (Ref = Postgraduate)	
College	0.145*
	(1.729)
Other education levels	−0.074
	(−0.266)
Work position (Ref = Executive)	
Manager	0.063
	(0.497)
Supervisor	0.078
	(0.560)
Staff	0.181
	(1.322)
Work Nature (Ref = Other arrangements)	
Mostly office-based	−0.151
	(−1.34)
Flexible	−0.058
	(−0.347)

(continued)

Table 7 (continued)

Indicator	Model 1
Work Outside of Office (Ref = Not at all)	
10–30% of my work hours	−0.009 (−0.106)
31–50% of my work hours	0.249** (1.967)
51–70% of my work hours	0.013 (0.068)
Over 70% of my work hours	0.028 (0.135)
Overtime (Ref = No overtime)	
Sometimes	−0.309*** (−2.486)
Frequently	−0.321** (−2.334)
Children (Ref = No children)	
Yes, youngest child under 11	−0.071 (−0.629)
Yes, youngest child 11 +	0.256* (1.670)
Childcare (Ref = No childcare)	
Yes childcare	0.101 (1.172)
Commute Time (Ref = Less than 30 min)	
More than 30 min	0.164** (2.237)
Observations	554
Adjusted R-squared	0.340

Notes Dependent variable: Working from home productivity; t-stats in parentheses; * significant at 10%; ** significant at 5%; *** significant at 1%

meetings." Working overtime negatively influenced working from home productivity and the result is statistically significant. Thus, a senior manager of a securities brokerage recommended, "*Continue focusing on employee assessment based on performance, allowing flexible working schedule instead of rigid work hours.*"

Finally, it is important to recognize that telework is not applicable to everyone. People who prefer to work alone and capable of completing the tasks independently can significantly increase productivity when working remotely. The statistical evidence in the model supports this assessment. Managers tend to agree with the statistical result as noted by an IT manager "*Most of the managers prefer employees to work in office so they can easily supervise. [However], a new managing system must be developed. Training should be carried out periodically to help managers*

Table 8 Multivariable regression model of working from home productivity, company performance, and individual performance expectations

Indicator	Model 2[a]	Model 3[b]
Constant	−1.775*** (−5.689)	0.981*** (3.594)
Working from home productivity index	0.253*** (7.149)	0.157*** (5.063)
Outlook on the prospect for growth of your company in the post-pandemic period	0.391*** (8.902)	0.188*** (4.877)
Sector (Ref = Public)		
Private	−0.310*** (−3.832)	0.071 (0.994)
FDI	−0.035 (−0.325)	0.216** (2.296)
Industry (Ref = Others)		
IT	0.300*** (2.725)	0.233** (2.424)
Real estate/construction	−0.125 (−0.887)	0.088 (0.713)
Marketing/management/consulting	−0.005 (−0.037)	0.345*** (2.729)
Manufacturing	0.182 (1.324)	0.320*** (2.668)
Finance/accounting/insurance	0.414*** (3.437)	0.233** (2.207)
Healthcare	0.033 (0.188)	−2.027 (−0.176)
Education	0.219 (1.567)	0.464*** (3.794)
Number of Employees (Ref = Less than 50 employees)		
51–100 employees	−0.179 (−1.540)	−0.129 (−1.270)
101–200 employees	0.141 (1.080)	−0.177 (−1.550)
200+ employees	0.382*** (3.013)	0.038 (0.343)
500+ employees	−0.013 (−0.101)	0.026 (0.238)
1000+ employees	0.108 (1.034)	0.133 (1.464)
Work Arrangement During Social Isolation (Ref = Other arrangement)		
I was given the choice to work from home	0.257 (1.140)	0.323* (1.634)

(continued)

Table 8 (continued)

Indicator	Model 2[a]	Model 3[b]
I was required to work from home	0.255 (1.124)	0.369* (1.860)
No change	0.555** (2.388)	0.433** (2.128)
Work Arrangement After Social Isolation (Ref = The company created a new work arrangement)		
The company went back to pre-pandemic arrangement	−0.080 (−0.927)	−0.064 (−0.841)
The company kept the during-pandemic arrangement	−0.093 (−0.925)	−0.157* (−1.175)
Observations	554	554
Adjusted R-squared	0.315	0.143

Notes [a] Dependent variable: Company performance index; b Dependent variable: Individual Performance Expectations; t-stats in parentheses; * significant at 10%; ** significant at 5%; *** significant at 1%

be able to supervise employees remotely." Furthermore, "*Under the new normal, company leaders must change their mindset to create a working trend with flexibility, combining work from home and in the office to achieve both goals of productivity and create comfort for employees,*" commented by a senior executive of a manufacturing company.

Table 8 reports the impacts of working from home productivity on company performance, and on individual performance expectations. The results indicate that the coefficient of working from home productivity has a positive and statistically significant impact on company performance, and on individual performance expectations. Anecdotal evidence by a senior manager of a bank seems to support the empirical evidence, "*Allowing employees to work from home means giving them greater autonomy in their job and protect them from the pandemic; therefore, employees feel trusted and cared for by the management. This would motivate them to be more productive.*" The statistical results and supporting evidence from the senior management are consistent with the McKinsey Report by Boland et al. [4].

The coefficient of private sector negatively and significantly affected the performance of the company, indicating that privately-owned businesses were facing difficulties during the pandemic. Respondents in the FDI sector reported a negative and statistically significant impact on individual performance expectations. The coefficients of the industries, including IT, and finance, accounting, insurance industry have a positive and statistically significant impact on company performance. With respect to individual performance expectations, respondents in the industries such as IT; marketing, management, consulting; and finance, accounting, insurance reported to have a positive and statistically significant sign. The results are supported by senior executives in the related industries, "*The impact of a flexible work arrangement was very positive, and the productivity of individuals and organization were higher than prior to the pandemic.*" This is because, "*Employees were willing to handle more workload and maintained a higher quality of work since they had more control over the schedule and the environment,"* noted by an IT executive. Consistent with the findings reported in Harvard Business Review by Birkinshaw et al. [2], which indicate that knowledge workers are more productive working from home.

Other statistically significant indicators are: Mid-size companies with 200+ employees reported to have a positive and statistically significant impact on company performance. Work arrangements during the social isolation period whether by choice, required to work from home, or no change in work arrangement are positively affected individual performance expectations, but only the coefficient of no change in work arrangement has a positive and statistically significant impact on company performance. Interestingly, respondents who reported that the company kept the during-pandemic arrangement after the social isolation period revealed negative and statistically significant impact on individual performance expectations. Further investigation must be done to confirm these findings.

Finally, the positive and significant sign on the coefficient of company outlook in the post-pandemic period suggests that the respondents are optimistic about the recovery of the economy. Vietnam gained international accolades for its successful campaign against COVID-19 in 2020. The country's remarkable success in controlling the first two waves of the pandemic accounted for the government's fast learning and a decisive lockdown in March and April during the first wave of the pandemic, and the partial lockdown during the second wave in July and August. As a result, the Vietnam's economy achieved the second highest economic growth in the region at 3% only after China in 2020.

Within a resilience framework described in Coutu [8], the capacity of organizations and individuals to embrace new technology, innovations, and resourceful practices is the key for future businesses and workers to take an active role, in contrast to a reactive role, when faced with challenges in the fast-changing social and environmental context. The COVID-19 pandemic has redefined the concept of remote work, transitioning from a work-from-home model surveyed in this chapter to a work-from-anywhere model, which provides the workers the opportunity to have more flexibility to choose where to live [7]. Their study reveals that workers experienced higher productivity after shifting from work-from-home to work-from-anywhere mode, with no significant increase in rework. This increase in productivity is a result of geographic flexibility, which allows the workers to relocate to lower cost-of-living locations, thus a higher increase in real wages.

In this context, workers in certain professions in Vietnam are recommended to have the flexibility of working from everywhere. This is well noted by an HR manager of a foreign-owned manufacturer, *"Flexibility in working arrangement is gaining more weight on working professionals, and it is gradually becoming an appreciated benefit that organizations should consider offering in order to attract and retain their talents."* However, adoption of the new working arrangement must also consider, *"Different employees with different nature of work will adopt telework at different level to be most productive,"* noted by a senior analyst at an investment firm. This is further support by another senior manager, *"For those whose job nature is more independent such as data analyst, designers, and those who prefer to work alone, the flexible work arrangement really creates a significant impact on the individual perfor-mance, and thus impact positively on the overall business performance."* Regardless of the workplace model, telework is the future work in the new normal. In a recent study, 38% of companies stated that they will adopt a hybrid model with both remote and office-based work; 27% will reduce staff density in the workplace; only 8% will not change their workplace environment [21].

5 Conclusions

In this chapter, we study how organizations can implement telework effectively to both enhance organizational resilience and improve workers' productivity and welfare. To that end, we conducted a self-administered survey in Vietnam with five-hundred and fifty-four employees across 52 companies based in Ho Chi Minh City and Ha Noi. The quantitative analysis is further supported by informal interviews with by mid-level managers and senior executives in the University of Hawaii—Shidler Vietnam EMBA program. We identify workers' technology readiness as an important driver for the productivity telework in that technology readiness has a posi-tive and statistically significant impact on working from home productivity. Further-more, workers with adequate equipment and training are positively and significantly influenced working from home productivity. This increase in productivity leads to higher individual performance expectations and company performance. These find-ings contribute crucial insights on the worker's perspectives, filling an important gap in the literature on telework which has typically focused more on organizational strategies [24].

The mid-level managers and senior executives surveyed in this study have shared a consensus that businesses will face numerous unpredictable situations caused by the pandemic in the future, thus work-from-home, as one type of agile model, will provide companies with more flexible work arrangements to better prepare for such challenges in the new normal. By allowing periodical work-from- home also helps employees well prepared for future potential catastrophe events similar to the COVID-19 pandemic. The executives also emphasized that the pandemic has proved some weaknesses in the current model of telework and thus, it is also very important not to overlook the significance of this opportunity for developing and implementing new models. In addition, it is important to empower the leadership for managing teams in remote collaboration, and to facilitate the working environment in both virtual and reality.

Given strong evidence presented in the statistical analysis supporting telework, senior management and executives participated in the survey recommend digital transformation strategy to cope with the new normal must consider the following tasks: (1) Technical capacity enhancement for remote workers to improve efficiency; (2) Categorize employees into different groups to prioritize telework arrangement; (3) Change the management mindset to lead in the new work environment; (4) Build a corporate culture for telework to enhance diversity, equity, and inclusion; and (5)

Organize periodic virtual events such as team building, and open forum to support employees' mental health and wellness.

There are some limitations in this study. First, the survey was conducted in only two major cities, Ho Chi Minh City and Hanoi. Future study should also examine other big cities across Vietnam, including Hai Phong, Da Nang, and Can Tho. Second, only technology readiness was addressed in the study. Cybersecurity readiness should also be examined in future study. Third, the current fourth wave of the pandemic started in April 2021 with no sign of ending as the time of writing this chapter in September has posted many challenges to the economy and the workforce. The current nationwide lockdown is imposed with more severe restrictions and limited mobility. It would be interesting to draw a comparison between the Vietnam EMBA cohorts in Fall 2020 with the new cohorts in Fall 2021 on the perceptions of working from home, productivity, and performance.

References

1. Annel, K., Hartmann, D., & Harrington, B. (2007). *Flexible work arrangements in Asia: What companies are doing, why they are doing it and what lies ahead.* A Report Prepared for the Members of the Global Workforce Roundtable, Boston College. https://www.bc.edu/content/dam/files/centers/cwf/research/publications3/res earchreports/Flexible%20Work%20Arrangements%20in%20Asia. Last accessed 05 Feb 2022
2. Birkinshaw, J., Cohen, J., & Stach, P. (2020, August). Research: Knowledge workers are more productive from home. *Harvard Business Review.*
3. Bloom, N., Liang, J., Roberts, J., & Ying, Z. J. (2015). Does working from home work? Evidence from a Chinese experiment. *Quarterly Journal of Economics, 130*(1), 165–218.
4. Boland, B., De Smet, A., Palter, R., & Sanghvi, A. (2020). *Reimagining the office and work life after COVID-19.* McKinsey & Company. https://www.mckinsey.com/business-functions/ organization/our-insights/reimagining-the-office-and-work-life-after-covid-19. Last accessed 10 Sept 2021.
5. Brynjolfsson, E., Horton, J. J., Ozimek, A., Rock, D., Sharma, G., & TuYe, H.-Y. (2020). *COVID-19 and remote work: An early look at US data.* NBER Working Paper 27344.
6. CBRE. (2020). The real estate reset. APAC leadership attitudes towards working location. CBRE APAC, Q4.
7. Choudhury, P., Foroughi, C., & Larson, B. (2021). Work-from-anywhere: The productivity effects of geographic flexibility. *Strategic Management Journal, 42*(4), 655–683.
8. Coutu, D. L. (2002). How resilience works. *Harvard Business Review, 80*(5), 46–55.
9. Deloitte. (2020). *Remote work: A temporary 'bug' becomes a permanent 'feature'.* https:// www2.deloitte.com/content/dam/Deloitte/sg/Documents/human-capital/sg-hc-remote-work. pdf. Last accessed 05 Feb 2022.
10. Dingel, J. I., & Neiman, B. (2020). How many jobs can be done at home? *Journal of Public Economics, 189*, 104235.
11. Fadinger, H., & Schymik, J. (2021). The costs and benefits of home office during the COVID-19 pandemic: Evidence from infections and an input-output model for Germany. Center for Economic Policy Research (CEPR), *COVID economics: Vetted and real-time papers.* CEPR Press 9(24.4), 107–134. https://cepr.org/sites/default/files/news/CovidEconomics9.pdf. Last accessed 10 Sept 2021.
12. Fairchild, C. (2020, August). *WHF is a problem for parents. Returning to the office won't solve it.* LinkedIn News Weekly Series. https://www.linkedin.com/pulse/wfh-problem-parents-ret urning-office-wont-solve-caroline-fairchild. Last accessed 10 Sept 2021.

13. Gajendran, R. S., & Harrison, D. A. (2007). The good, the bad, and the unknown about telecommuting: Meta-analysis of psychological mediators and individual consequences. *Journal of Applied Psychology, 92*(6), 1524–1541.
14. Georgiadou, A., Mouzakitis, S., & Askounis, D. (2021). Working from home during COVID-19 crisis: A cyber security culture assessment survey. *Security Journal* (Open Access).
15. International Labour Organization (ILO). (2020). *ILO monitor: COVID-19 and the world of work* (2nd ed.). https://www.ilo.org/wcmsp5/groups/public/@dgreports/@dcomm/documents/briefingnote/wcms_740877.pdf. Last accessed 10 Sept 2021.
16. Le, Q. V., & Raven, P. V. (2015). Women entrepreneurship in rural Vietnam: Success and motivational factors. *Journal of Developing Areas, 49*(2), 57–76.
17. Le, Q. V., Nguyen-Lisovich, M., & Raven, P. V. (2016). Regional differences in behaviors, attitudes, and motivations related to performance among women-owned microenterprises in Vietnam. *World Development Perspectives, 2*, 17–24.
18. Nardo, M., Saltelli, A., Tarantola, S., Hoffmann, A., & Giovannini, E. (2005). *Handbook on constructing composite indicators: Methodology and user guide*. OCED Statistics Working Papers.
19. Parasuraman, A., & Colby, C.L. (2015). An updated and streamlined technology readiness index: TRI 2.0. *Journal of Service Research, 18*(1), 59–74.
20. Parasuraman, A. (2000). Technology readiness index (TRI) a multiple – Item scale to measure readiness to embrace new technologies. *Journal of Service Research, 2*(4), 307–320.
21. PwC and the Urban Land Institute. Emerging Trends in Real Estate Asia Pacific 2021. https://www.pwccn.com/en/real-estate/emerging-trends-in-real-estate-asia-pacific-2021.pdf. Last accessed 10 Sept 2021.
22. Raven, P. V., & Le, Q. V. (2015). Teaching business skills to women: Impact of business training on women's microenterprise owners in Vietnam. *International Journal of Entrepreneurial Behavior & Research, 21*(4), 622–641.
23. Saltiel, F. (2020). Who can work from home in developing countries? *COVID Economics, 7*, 104–118.
24. Shin, B., Sheng, O. R. L., & Higa, K. (2000). Telework: Existing research and future directions. *Journal of Organizational Computing and Electronic Commerce, 10*(2), 85–101.
25. Sull, D., Sull, C., & Bersin, J. (2020). Five ways leaders can support remote work. *MIT Sloan Management Review*.
26. Vietnam Market Research. (2020, April). *Remote work satisfaction by social distancing*. Q&Me Asia Plus Inc. https://qandme.net/en/report/remote-work-satisfaction-by-social-distancing.html. Last accessed 10 Sept 2021.
27. Wiklund, J., & Shepherd, D. (2003). Knowledge-based resources, entrepreneurial orientation, and the performance of small and medium-sized businesses. *Strategic Management Journal, 24*(3), 1307–1314.
28. World Bank. (2020, October). *Unmasking the impact of COVID-19 on businesses: Firm level evidence from across the world*. Policy Research Working Paper 9434. World Bank Group, Finance, Competitiveness, and Innovation Global Practice. https://openknowledge.worldbank.org/bitstream/handle/10986/34626/Unmasking-the-Impact-of-COVID-19-on-Businesses-Firm-Level-Evidence-from-Across-the-World.pdf?sequence=5&isAllowed=y. Last accessed 10 Sept 2021.
29. World Economic Forum. (2020, October). *The future of jobs report*. http://www3.weforum.org/docs/WEF_Future_of_Jobs_2020.pdf. Last accessed 10 Sept 2021.

Generation X's Shopping Behavior in the Electronic Marketplace Through Mobile Applications During the COVID-19 Pandemic

Bui Thanh Khoa ⓘ

Abstract Thanks to the prevalence of mobile applications (mobile apps), consumer behavior is shifting from conventional to online. Globally, mobile commerce has taken precedence over other forms of transaction due to the impact of the COVID-19 pandemic except for Generation X (Gen X) customers. They have restricted access to modern technologies and are critically impacted by the COVID-19 pandemic. Hence, this chapter applied the Theory of Acceptance and Use of Technology model (UTAUT), and Task-technology fit models (TTF) to determine how the pandemic and Gen X characteristics affect buying behaviors in the electronic marketplace. The primary research method was the quantitative approach, in which data was collected from 467 respondents through a structured questionnaire. The findings indicate that Gen X consumers' mobile commerce buying intentions are influenced favorably by mobile shopping (m-shopping) efficiency, effort expectancy, and the perceived severity of COVID-19. Generation X's shopping behavior in the e-marketplace through mobile apps was also affected by the usability of mobile applications and their desire to purchase online. Additionally, the Gen X consumers' expectation of effort was negatively impacted by the usability of mobile apps.

1 Introduction

Technology changes consumer behavior from traditional to online through mobile applications (apps). Mobile commerce (m-commerce) has become a prior transaction form worldwide. Also, various elements may influence how people use and interact with technology, especially their ages, classifying customers into generational cohorts. Cohorts of people born simultaneously have similar views, goals, values, and behaviors. These differences create a generational identity that can influence how people use technology, interact with it, and behave [1]. There are significant differences in how different generations utilize technology; as a result, the generational cohort may influence how individuals use and interact with technology. In

B. T. Khoa (✉)
Industrial University of Ho Chi Minh City, Ho Chi Minh City, Vietnam
e-mail: buithanhkhoa@iuh.edu.vn

© The Author(s), under exclusive license to Springer Nature Singapore Pte Ltd. 2023   117
N. H. Thuan et al. (eds.), *Information Systems Research in Vietnam*,
https://doi.org/10.1007/978-981-19-3804-7_8

cohort-based categorization, people are often divided into younger members like the millennials (Gen Y) or who?—Generation Z (Gen Z) and older members like those in Baby Boomer and Generation X (Gen X) [2]. As "digital natives" and technologically aware, Gen Y and Gen Z have been proven to be different from previous generations; hence, the bulk of study has focused on perceptions of technology of Gen Y and Gen Z. Research on the motives of previous cohorts, such as Gen X and Baby Boomer, to use and interact with technology is lacking. Gen X is the group of people born between 1965 and 1980 known for their scepticism, pragmatism, and a desire to avoid taking risks [3]. This generation was not exposed to the internet or digital technology from an early age and has recently become proficient users. As personal computers became more common in schools and the internet expanded, Gen X had little trouble integrating new technology into their everyday routines. Gen X, as opposed to Millennials or Gen Z, was not born into the digital age but has embraced many, if not all, of its new features of it as they have progressed through life; as a result, Gen X might be referred to as "digital immigrants," because they were not born into a technologically advanced society but have instead learned to live with it [4].

As the primary method of preventing the pandemic, people have been advised to stay at home while social distance is applied across the globe. The elderly is unquestionably one of the most vulnerable populations throughout this unprecedented pandemic, putting them in danger of bodily and mental harm. Along with the chronic illnesses group, they are dealing with the most significant risk of mortality because of the most severe symptoms, with a mortality rate of 3.6% among those 60–69 years old, rising to 18.6% for those over 80 [5].

In light of the continuing COVID-19 pandemic, mobile apps solutions are now more critical than ever to minimize the danger of cross-contamination from close contact. COVID-19's proliferation has been slowed by various strategies using mobile technologies. Mobile devices, which may help with social isolation, are widely available, accepted, and easy to use. Due to the COVID-19 pandemic, additional evidence suggested the risk and perceived difficulty of utilizing Gen X apps on m-commerce [6]. Hence, Gen X customers have reexamined their purchasing patterns or have developed new ones entirely. As a result of stringent containment procedures and safeguards, customers have been forced to explore alternatives such as internet shopping, home delivery, and cashless payments. In the wake of the COVID-19 issue, Gen X customers have become more reliant on apps in m-commerce to communicate, get information, and cope with the COVID-19 pandemic. The perceived severity of COVID-19 is developing not only in health [7] but also in education [8], and economics [9]. Most Chinese individuals engage in health-protective behaviors such as remaining at home, severely limiting their social life due to the perceived severity of COVID-19 [10]. While individual health-protective activities have effectively prevented the spread of Coronavirus, they have also resulted in a major increase in psychological strain, resulting in varying degrees of mental stress [11]. If COVID-19 spreads extensively across the population, nobody knows what will happen, especially among those who feel they are susceptible or believe the risks are substantial [12]. Evidence supports the hypothesis that social norms contradicting behavior might prevent the implementation of preventive measures. As a result, there are strong arguments for merging the Unified Theory of Acceptance and Use of Technology model (UTAUT) and the Task-technology fit model (TTF) and adding m-commerce characteristics, mobile app characteristics, and COVID-19's perceived severity to study Gen X's buying behavior in the e-marketplace through applications in COVID-19.

Based on UTAUT and TTF, this chapter explored the impact of COVID-19 and the Gen X characteristics on consumers' shopping behavior in the electronic marketplace (e-marketplace) through mobile apps. The research results have theoretical and practical contributions as combining UTAUT and TTF to assess Gen X consumers' shopping behavior. In addition, the study also pointed out the influence of the perceived severity of COVID-19 on shopping intention in m-commerce. Finally, some managerial implications were proposed for businesses in the e-marketplaces to enhance Gen X consumers' shopping behavior.

2   Literature Review

2.1   Theoretical Background

Venkatesh et al. [13] developed the UTAUT model to test technology acceptance and use a more unified approach. UTAUT asserts that behavioral intention is determined by effort expectancy, performance expectancy, and social influence and that these factors, together with facilitating conditions, impact how to utilize technology. It was discovered that UTAUT was the second most common theoretical lens for analyzing consumer acceptance of mobile payment, online shopping, and online education. TTF was first introduced in the mid-1990s by Goodhue and Thompson [14]. Individuals may accomplish specific activities or groups of tasks with the help of technology if task needs and technology features are aligned or fit, according to the model's presumption that technology's value/performance is generated by the alignment or fit. TTF has been extensively utilized to better understand how information systems are used and the outcomes of their usage in a variety of scenarios, including mobile browsers [15], online shopping [16], and social media use [17]. Although UTAUT is considered more efficient than previous models such as the Theory of Planned Behavior, Technology Acceptance Model, And Innovation Diffusion Theory, it still has limitations in explaining technology adoption behavior. For example, even if consumers find technology useful and simple to use, they will not utilize it in the present environment if it does not meet their wants or gadgets. As a result, the combination of TTF and UTAUT will well describe the technological adoption behavior. This combination has been emphasized through the studies related to the banking industry [18, 19], online learning [20], and health care [21].

Task specifies what must be done in response to stimuli, described as a stimulus complex. The instructions specify what subjects should do in response to stimuli and the overall objective. It is following Hackman's "task as behavior description" that information system researchers have usually relied on the viewpoint of "task as behavior requirement" that sees a task in terms of which response should be emitted by the subject [22]. In commerce activities, shopping is the main task of the buyer. The customer always wants to purchase the best product and get a fair price in transactions. In m-commerce activities, shopping in apps is expected to benefit customers who decided to use apps during the COVID-19 pandemic.

Furthermore, e-commerce has come a long way in the past decade and is sure to do so for the foreseeable future. Mobile devices have become the primary purchasing instruments as a result of the unique benefits offered by mobile internet technology, including ubiquity, convenience, localization, and customization; therefore, mobile devices have become the main facility to connect the buyer and seller in m-commerce. The perceived severity of COVID-19 is growing not just in the health business but also in the general public [7] but also in education [8] and economics [9]. Because of the perceived severity of COVID-19, most Chinese individuals engage in health-protective behaviors such as remaining at home, severely limiting their social life, i.e., Chinese citizens' social participation levels have decreased to less than 2 out of 5 [10]. While health-protective practices of individuals have successfully halted the spread of Coronavirus, they have also generated a dramatic surge in psychological strain, leading to various degrees of mental stress [11]. Anyone's guess is what happens when COVID-19 spreads widely across the community, particularly among people who believe they are vulnerable or see the hazards as serious [12]. Evidence supports the theory that social norms that conflict with the behaviour can prevent the implementation of preventative measures. As a result, there are strong arguments for merging TTF and UTAUT and adding m-commerce characteristics, mobile app characteristics, and COVID-19's perceived severity to study Gen X's buying behavior in the e-marketplace through applications in COVID-19. Figure 1 depicts the theoretical model used in this study.

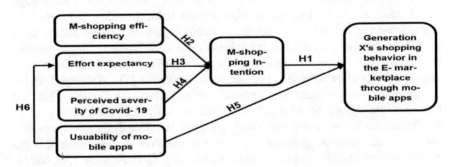

Fig. 1 Theoretical model

2.2　Hypotheses Development

According to previous research, attitudes regarding shopping malls may directly impact purchasing behavior at shopping malls; however, the link between these two constructs is weak. It is conceivable that an intention omits to blame. Several theorists believe that purpose, rather than attitude, is the most closely related cognitive precursor to actual behavioral execution [23, 24]. "The degree to which a person has created conscious intentions to conduct or not execute some specified future activity" is defined as "intention" [25]. A few meta-analyses of empirical research have shown that behavior may accurately predict intentions [25, 26]. Many different forms of behavior have provided evidence for a link between intentions and subsequent behaviors/actions [27]. Their buy intention for online shopping measures the willingness of a customer to purchase in apps. As indicated by theories like the Theory of Planned Behavior, this research aims to learn how Gen X customers use mobile apps to buy products from the e-marketplace. In numerous m-commerce research, intention, first introduced by Ajzen and Fishbein [23], has been employed to predict online purchase behavior or an outcome variable in place of actual buy behavior [28]. According to Taylor and Todd [29], for persons with prior experience and familiarity with technology, User behavior is well predicted by behavioral intention. Hence, this study proposed the H1:

H1: Shopping Intention has a positive impact on Generation X's shopping behavior in the E-marketplace through mobile apps

Shoppers may use their mobile devices to access the wireless internet through mobile shopping (m-shopping), a new sales channel that makes responsive websites available on mobile devices (e.g., location-based technology). M-shopping refers to customers making purchases while connected to the wireless internet on their mobile devices [30]. With their unique characteristics in shopping environments, mobile devices give customers more convenience than conventional online shopping done with desktop or laptop computers, despite privacy and security concerns. Modern customers are increasingly using their mobile devices to pay for things, according to recent research on the topic of "m-shopping" [31]. M-shopping has distinct benefits over traditional e-commerce, such as better convenience, localization, and immediacy, only possible with mobile internet technology [32]. In m-shopping, customers must choose, order, and pay for things on their mobile devices; these activities can be challenging for Generation X; however, Gen X customers ought to use apps to make transactions in COVID-19. M-shopping activities are expected to finish the shopping in the COVID-19 pandemic. Hypothesis H2 was proposed:

H2: M-shopping efficiency has a positive impact on Generation X's shopping intention in the E-marketplace through mobile apps

A user's desire to do a task on a portable device is strongly influenced by perceptions of utility, security, and fun. The perceived ease of use for information system adoption in a workplace and an e-commerce setting has been studied before [33, 34]. The user design in mobile apps is improved day by day, especially for the elders

[35]; consequently, it is easy for Gen X customers to interact with shopping activities. UTAUT pointed out that effort expectancy and performance expectancy will positively impact user intention [13]. Hence, hypothesis H3 was formed as:

H3: Effort expectancy has a positive impact on Generation X's shopping intention in the E-marketplace through mobile apps

Customers' attitudes, interests, and opinions are shaped by their perceptions of things, behaviors, and events. Decisions are influenced by how people perceive risk and safety [36]. The desire to direct activities as travel decreases as the severity of a disease or the associated health risks become more apparent [37]. The COVID-19 pandemic is dangerous to older customers; hence, Gen Z customers intend to shop through mobile apps to ensure their safety. The apparent severity of the COVID-19 epidemic predates internet purchase through an electronic marketplace or mobile applications [9]; hence, the hypothesis H4 was proposed:

H4: Perceived severity of the COVID-19 pandemic has a positive impact on Generation X's shopping intention in the E-marketplace through mobile apps

Mobile apps are often the mobile counterparts of internet sites. Businesses often create and launch applications closely related to their online sites when they extend their operations to the mobile platform [38]. Despite this, cellphones and personal computers continue to have significant disparities. Information search habits on mobile phones vary from desktop computers [39] because mobile material is shown on smaller displays; people only read it when they have time. Ghose et al. [40] came to a similar conclusion because the lower display size of mobile devices raises search costs, making the first search result more attractive than the second on mobile devices than on desktops in the long term. Mobile phone users who value ubiquitous availability choose their phones over desktops [41]. These results highlight the differences between internet and mobile platforms. Inferring mobile behavior from online behavior research, on the other hand, may provide erroneous findings. Consequently, mobile apps characteristics were predicted to decrease Gen X's shopping behaviour and effort expectancy in m-commerce as they purchase from e-marketplace apps. So, the hypotheses H5 and H6 were proposed:

H5: Usability of mobile apps has a negative impact on Generation X's shopping behavior in the E-marketplace through mobile apps

H6: Usability of mobile apps has a negative impact on Generation X's effort expectancy as shopping in the E-marketplace through mobile apps

3 Research Method

The speculative model was examined using a cross-sectional design in this research. To build our sample, we used a non-probabilistic sampling strategy (purposive sampling). The data was acquired in Vietnam for five months, from February to June 2021, for a mobile shopping app of Tiki, Lazada, Sendo, and Shopee, the four leading e-marketplaces in Vietnam. From a total of 500 replies, 467 legitimate and full consumer responses were obtained, and each one was given instructions on how

Table 1 The respondent information

Characteristics		n	%
Gender	Male	258	55.2
	Female	209	44.8
Age group	41–50	201	43.0
	51–56	266	57.0
Times of using m-shopping apps (in months)	1–2	114	24.4
	3–6	111	23.8
	6–12	134	28.7
	>12	108	23.1
Screen size of the mobile device (inches)	≤5	248	53.1
	>5	219	46.9
Occupation	Lecturer	146	31.3
	Office worker	163	34.9
	Housewife	158	33.8

to use the equipment before being asked to complete a brief questionnaire. Table 1 summarizes the participants' sociodemographic characteristics. Participants were asked to complete a questionnaire that contained assessments of the variables under research after being instructed on the goal of the study.

This research used a survey questionnaire that examined 20 different items for six research constructs. The research carefully selected and verified all metrics using data from previous studies to meet the study's objectives. All questions were scored from 1 ("strongly disagree") to 5 ("strongly agree") on a five-pointed Likert scale. Some of the items were slightly reworded to better meet our research's objectives. In addition, the survey asked respondents a series of demographic and app use questions. The detailed scale items and their corresponding sources include m-shopping efficiency (3 items, ME, [32]), Effort expectancy (4 items, EE, [13]), perceived severity of COVID-19 (3 items, PS, [42]), the usability of mobile apps (3 items, US, [43]), shopping intention (4 items, SI, [42]), Generation X's shopping behavior (3 items, SB, [13]).

The results were investigated using Anderson and Gerbing's two-step structural equation modeling technique [44]. At first, the validity and reliability criteria were verified, and then the structural model was evaluated. The data in the study was analyzed using SPSS 21.0 and SmartPLS. The data was processed in two phases. In the first stage, the measurement model's validity and reliability were evaluated. Second, the weight and size of the connections between variables were assessed by evaluating the structural model.

4 Data Analysis

4.1 Measurement Scale Assessment

To begin, this research evaluates construct reliability using Cronbach's Alpha (CA) and the composite reliability measure (CR), both of which had values more than 0.7. The average variance collected was used to test for convergent validity (AVE). According to the findings, all of these components' loads were significant and larger than 0.7, with an average extracted variance (AVE) value greater than 0.5. Furthermore, the outer loading (OL) of all products was greater than 0.708. In view of this conclusion, Fornell and Larcker [45] measurement models show adequate convergent validity. The results in Table 2 allow us to establish the convergent validity and reliability of the scales used to measure the different components in the research model.

The discriminant validity has to be checked using the Fornell and Larcker criteria, which stipulates that the square root of the AVE of each variable must be greater than the correlations between that variable and the other variables in the model. As shown in Table 3, the square root AVE of each construct is greater than its correlation with any other construct; hence, there is discriminant validity between all constructs in the study model.

Table 2 Convergent validity and reliability

	CA	CR	AVE	OL
EE	0.877	0.915	0.73	[0.850–0.862]
ME	0.883	0.928	0.811	[0.863–0.937]
PS	0.917	0.948	0.858	[0.918–0.939]
SB	0.81	0.888	0.727	[0.746–0.925]
SI	0.912	0.938	0.791	[0.868–0.931]
US	0.808	0.887	0.724	[0.805–0.885]

Table 3 Fornell and Larcker criterion

	EE	ME	PS	SB	SI	US
EE	0.855					
ME	0.368	0.901				
PS	0.486	0.419	0.926			
SB	0.607	0.529	0.575	0.852		
SI	0.423	0.404	0.439	0.736	0.889	
US	−0.452	−0.54	−0.556	−0.672	−0.544	0.851

4.2 Structural Model Assessment

The structural model evaluation procedure was followed in this work, which included collinearity assessment, structural model path coefficients, coefficient of determination (R^2 value), effect size (f^2 value), blindfolding, and predictive relevance (Q^2 value) [46].

A standard tool for assessing the degree of collinearity among formative indicators is the variance inflation factor (VIF). If the VIF score is more than 5, there are severe difficulties with indicator collinearity among the assessed components. Even with VIF levels as low as 3, collinearity problems might emerge. The VIF values should ideally be less than or equal to 3. In Table 3, all maximum VIF is 1.434, which is less than 3; hence, there is no collinearity issue in this research.

Next, this study assesses the endogenous construct's R^2 value if collinearity is not a concern. A model's explanatory power may be measured by looking at the R^2, which calculates the variance explained by each endogenous component. Acceptable R^2 levels depend on context, and an R^2 value of 0.20 is regarded as satisfactory in certain areas as a stock return or behavior [47]. Usability of mobile apps explained 20.4% of the change of effort expectancy ($R^2_{EE} = 0.204$); m-shopping efficiency, effort expectancy, and perceived severity of COVID-19 impact 28.9% of the change of m-shopping intention ($R^2_{SI} = 0.289$); finally, the usability of mobile apps and m-shopping intention create 64.6% change in Generation X's shopping behavior in the E-marketplace through mobile apps ($R^2_{SB} = 0.646$).

The Q^2 value may be used to evaluate the predicting accuracy of the partial least squares path model. The Q^2 score for an endogenous construct is more significant than zero; it indicates that the structural model for that construct is accurate ($Q^2_{EE} = 0.144$; $Q^2_{SB} = 0.46$; $Q^2_{SI} = 0.222$).

When a predictive construct is removed, researchers may see how the R^2 value of the endogenous construct changes. This measure is redundant with the f^2 effect size in route coefficients. The relevance of the predictor construct in explaining the dependent construct in a structural model is often equivalent in rank order to comparing path coefficients and effect sizes in f^2 models, which are more precise measurements of effect size. Values larger than 0.02, 0.15, and 0.35, respectively, imply minor, medium, and large f^2 effect sizes. Based on Table 4, m-shopping efficiency, effort expectancy, and perceived severity of COVID-19 pandemic has a negligible effect on m-shopping intention ($f^2_{EE \rightarrow SI} = 0.053$; $f^2_{ME \rightarrow SI} = f^2_{EE \rightarrow SI} = 0.054$); usability of mobile apps has a medium effect on the effort expectancy and shopping behavior ($f^2_{US \rightarrow EE} = 0.256$; $f^2_{US \rightarrow SB} = 0.296$); m-shopping intention has a significant effect size on Generation X's shopping behavior in the E-marketplace ($f^2_{SI \rightarrow SB} = 0.551$).

The Smart PLS 3.2.7 software was used with 5000 subsamples of the original sample size for a Bootstrapping study using partial least squares structural equation modeling to verify the assumptions (PLS-SEM). Table 5 showed that all hypotheses had a 99% confidence level (t-value >2.58).

Table 4 VIF, R^2, f^2, Q^2

	VIF			R^2	f^2			Q^2
	EE	SB	SI		EE	SB	SI	
EE			1.368	0.204			0.053	0.144
ME			1.268				0.054	
PS			1.434				0.054	
SB				0.646				0.46
SI		1.42		0.289		0.551		0.222
US	1.000	1.42			0.256	0.296		

Table 5 PLS-SEM result

Relationship	Beta	Standard deviation	t-value	Hypothesis	Result
SI → SB	0.526	0.046	11.367	H1	Supported
ME → SI	0.222	0.053	4.203	H2	Supported
EE → SI	0.227	0.062	3.642	H3	Supported
PS → SI	0.236	0.059	4.015	H4	Supported
US → SB	−0.386	0.053	7.282	H5	Supported
US → EE	−0.452	0.069	6.533	H6	Supported

5 Discussion

Based on the UTAUT, this research result reaffirmed the relationship between effort expectancy, m-shopping intention, and shopping behavior [13]. To begin, effort anticipation has a favorable influence on Gen X consumers' m-shopping intention (Beta = 0.227, t-value = 3.642, p-value = 0.000); hence, hypothesis H3 was accepted with 99% confidence. Furthermore, m-shopping intention influenced Generation X's purchasing behavior in the E-marketplace through mobile applications (Beta = 0.526, t-value = 11.367, p-value = 0.000); as a result, hypothesis H1 was validated in 99% of cases. In the COVID-19 pandemic, Gen X consumers' choices for using a portable device are inextricably tied to their perceptions of its utility, security, and even entertainment aspects; hence, perceived ease of use for the office and online shopping is critical [33, 34]. The less they effort to learn or use the shopping apps, the more customers want to use them for their shopping activities on mobile. Mobile app user interfaces and functions are becoming better, particularly for the elderly in Gen X, who has a simple time interacting with the online retail environment [35]. A relationship between intentions and subsequent behaviors has been found in a wide range of behaviour [25, 48]. Gen X customers' desire to make purchases via mobile applications is gauged by their buy intention when shopping online, particularly in the COVID-19 pandemic. Gen X shoppers are using mobile applications to acquire things from the e-marketplace, as well as intention was used as a predictor of online purchase behavior or as an outcome variable instead of actual purchase behavior in various m-commerce studies [28, 49].

The result pointed out similarities and differences under the integration of TTF in UTAUT. Firstly, M-shopping efficiency influences m-shopping intention positively (Beta = 0.222, t-value = 4.203, p-value = 0.000); therefore, hypothesis H2 was supported with the 99% of confidence level. M-shopping efficiency can be the performance expectancy in UTAUT [13], which positively impacts the technology adoption intention. In the COVID-19 pandemic, m-shopping helps Gen X customers shop easily and make them safer at home. These benefits have a large impact on the shopping intention of Gen X [50]. For Gen X customers, the mobile apps bring difficulties in usability, which are mentioned as four aspects: navigation, communication, visual recognition, or screen reading. The mobile apps screen is small for Gen X customers to read the product information or touch to shop the product; furthermore, some Gen X users are not familiar with the navigation in the smartphone. Hence, the mobile apps in the e-marketplace do not receive high agreement about usability, which negatively impacts Generation X's shopping behavior in the E-marketplace through mobile apps (Beta = −0.386, t-value = 7.282, p-value = 0.000). Moreover, the negative usability can create many disadvantages for Gen X customers, so the customers in this generation must invest more effort to learn or use the apps. The empirical result in this study supported the H6 as the usability of mobile apps negatively impacts Generation X's effort expectancy as shopping in the E-marketplace through mobile apps (Beta = −0.452, t-value = 6.533, p-value = 0.000).

Lastly, the perceived severity of COVID-19 has a positive factor in improving the m-commerce intention (Beta = 0.236, t-value = 4.015, p-value = 0.000); hence hypothesis H4 was supported by the empirical result. The perceived severity of COVID-19 is the part of threat appraisal, which is popular with Gen X customers. Consumers were more likely to take the copying activity to escape the dangerous scenario when it was severe. Therefore, the perceived severity of COVID-19 strengthened the capacity to regulate one's actions [9]. Consumers' conviction in their ability to manage their conduct grew due to the threat motive to avoid COVID-19 [51]. Because of this, Gen X customers would believe they have more influence over their buying behavior if they experience high risks from COVID-19, such as shopping in the e-marketplace the mobile apps [10].

6 Conclusion

Smartphones, which are becoming more common, provide a third option for shopping and the traditional offline and internet options. A conceptual model was established that considers both the advantages and disadvantages of mobile shopping [52]. Mobile shopping's perceived value rises due to their model's time-related advantages in efficiency, leading to increased buy intent. Gen X's behavioral intention to utilize mobile applications was influenced by the four indicators studied in this research. Research results pointed out that the shopping intention of Gen X customers in mobile commerce is positively affected by shopping efficiency, effort expectancy, and perceived severity of COVID-19.

Moreover, the customer's m-shopping behavior on e-marketplace through m-apps was influenced by the usability of mobile apps and the intention to shop online. In addition, the usability of mobile apps was negative antecedence of the Gen X consumers' effort expectancy. The study's results have theoretical and practical implications for the acceptability and development of mobile applications for individuals with vision impairments.

In theoretical contribution, this study combined the UTAUT and TTF model in generation X's shopping behavior in the E-marketplace through mobile apps. The root of the theoretical model is UTAUT; however, some constructs related to mobile apps, m-shopping, and the COVID-19 pandemic were added to achieve the research objective. M-shopping efficiency and usability of mobile apps as task characteristics and technical characteristics in TTF; and as performance expectancy and facilitating conditions in UTAUT. Moreover, this result discovered the negative relationship between the usability of mobile apps and (1) effort expectancy and (2) shopping behavior in the E-marketplace through mobile apps.

Some managerial implications were proposed for managers who manage the e-marketplace. Regarding effort expectancy and usability of mobile apps, businesses might enhance mobile technology's usability and, in particular, its learnability. Animated training is helpful for Gen X customers who are unfamiliar with touchscreens—because of this, completing the recommended activities will take longer if users are not provided with training sessions on how to utilize the apps. The apps should provide less information on a screen and be easier for new users. Simplified apps do not rely on scrolling or swiping for navigational purposes. Many publications advocate improving usability by making texts more intelligible and increasing font sizes for Gen X customers. In both cases, the text of the apps is a common thread. Applications should utilize terminology that matches that of intended Gen X consumers. E-marketplace businesses should update the information on news, benefits of m-shopping, or coordinate with other businesses to generate promotion campaigns, emphasizing the role and benefit of m-shopping.

Our interpretation was hampered by the study's limitations, which sparked new ideas for future research. Firstly, the findings may not be generalizable to other situations where the circumstances of mobile app users are different because of the online survey and non-probability sample. To find out whether the links between the UTAUT model's variables are constant across various user groups with diverse cultural traits, it would be beneficial to compare them in the same context. Another area that requires investigation is why mobile app performance expectancy is essential. The other three predictors (m-shopping efficiency, effort expectancy, perceived severity of COVID-19) are not as effective at predicting behavioral intention to adopt and use mobile apps in Gen X customers. Further study is needed to determine why some modifiers (such as gender or years of experience) do not affect the link between predictors and behavioral intention.

References

1. Gursoy, D., Maier, T. A., & Chi, C. G. (2008). Generational differences: An examination of work values and generational gaps in the hospitality workforce. *International Journal of Hospitality Management, 27*, 448–458.
2. Kotler, P., Armstrong, G., & Opresnik, M. O. (2021). *Principles of marketing.* Pearson.
3. Khoa, B. T., Ha, N. M., & Ngoc, B. H. (2022). The accommodation services booking intention through the mobile applications of generation Y: An empirical evidence based on TAM2 model. In N. Ngoc Thach, D.T. Ha, N.D. Trung, V. Kreinovich (Eds.), *Prediction and causality in econometrics and related topics* (pp. 559–574). Springer International Publishing. https://doi.org/10.1007/978-3-030-77094-5_43
4. Knezevic, B., Falat, M., & Mestrovic, I. S. (2020). Differences between X and Y generation in attitudes towards online book purchasing. *Journal of Logistics, Informatics and Service Science, 7*, 1–16. https://doi.org/10.33168/liss.2020.0101
5. García-Fernández, L., Romero-Ferreiro, V., López-Roldán, P. D., Padilla, S., & Rodriguez-Jimenez, R. (2020). Mental health in elderly Spanish people in times of COVID-19 outbreak. *The American Journal of Geriatric Psychiatry, 28*, 1040–1045.
6. Dorie, A., & Loranger, D. (2020). The multi-generation: Generational differences in channel activity. *International Journal of Retail & Distribution Management, 48*, 395–416. https://doi.org/10.1108/ijrdm-06-2019-0196
7. Li, J.-B., Yang, A., Dou, K., & Cheung, R. Y. (2020). Self-control moderates the association between perceived severity of coronavirus disease 2019 (COVID-19) and mental health problems among the Chinese public. *International Journal of Environmental Research and Public Health, 17*, 4820.
8. Hai, P. H., & Khoa, B. T. (2021). Lecturers' intention to use online video conferencing tools: The role of perceived severity. In *2021 1st conference on online teaching for mobile education (OT4ME)* (pp. 1–7). https://doi.org/10.1109/OT4ME53559.2021.9638787
9. Deng, S., Wang, W., Xie, P., Chao, Y., & Zhu, J. (2020). Perceived severity of COVID-19 and post-pandemic consumption willingness: The roles of boredom and sensation-seeking. *Frontiers in Psychology, 11*, 567784. https://doi.org/10.3389/fpsyg.2020.567784
10. Li, J.-B., Yang, A., Dou, K., Wang, L.-X., Zhang, M.-C., & Lin, X.-Q. (2020). Chinese public's knowledge, perceived severity, and perceived controllability of COVID-19 and their associations with emotional and behavioural reactions, social participation, and precautionary behaviour: A national survey. *BMC Public Health, 20*, 1–14.
11. Xiang, Y.-T., Yang, Y., Li, W., Zhang, L., Zhang, Q., Cheung, T., & Ng, C. H. (2020). Timely mental health care for the 2019 novel coronavirus outbreak is urgently needed. *The Lancet Psychiatry, 7*, 228–229.
12. Jiang, X., Hwang, J., Shah, D. V., Ghosh, S., & Brauer, M. (2021). News attention and social-distancing behavior amid COVID-19: How media trust and social norms moderate a mediated relationship. *Health Communication*, 1–10. https://doi.org/10.1080/10410236.2020.1868064
13. Venkatesh, V., Morris, M. G., Davis, G. B., & Davis, F. D. (2003). User acceptance of information technology: Toward a unified view. *MIS Quarterly, 27*, 425–478.
14. Goodhue, D. L., & Thompson, R. L. (1995). Task-technology fit and individual performance. *MIS Quarterly, 19*, 213–236. https://doi.org/10.2307/249689
15. Saputra, M. C., Wardani, N. H., Trialih, R., & Hijriyati, A. L. (2018). Analysis of user acceptance factors for mobile apps browser using unified theory of acceptance and use of technology (UTAUT) and task technology fit (TTF) on Generation Y. In *2018 international seminar on intelligent technology and its applications (ISITIA)* (pp. 263–268). IEEE.
16. Valaei, N., Nikhashemi, S., Jin, H. H., & Dent, M. M. (2018). Task technology fit in online transaction through apps. In *Optimizing E-participation initiatives through social media* (pp. 236–251). IGI Global.
17. Li, Y., Yang, S., Zhang, S., & Zhang, W. (2019). Mobile social media use intention in emergencies among Gen Y in China: An integrative framework of gratifications, task-technology fit, and media dependency. *Telematics and Informatics, 42*, 101244.

18. Oliveira, T., Faria, M., Thomas, M. A., & Popovič, A. (2014). Extending the understanding of mobile banking adoption: When UTAUT meets TTF and ITM. *International Journal of Information Management, 34*, 689–703.

19. Zhou, T., Lu, Y., & Wang, B. (2010). Integrating TTF and UTAUT to explain mobile banking user adoption. *Computers in Human Behavior, 26*, 760–767.

20. Wan, L., Xie, S., & Shu, A. (2020). Toward an understanding of university students' continued intention to use MOOCs: When UTAUT model meets TTF model. *SAGE Open, 10*, 1–15. https://doi.org/10.1177/2158244020941858

21. Wang, H., Tao, D., Yu, N., & Qu, X. (2020). Understanding consumer acceptance of healthcare wearable devices: An integrated model of UTAUT and TTF. *International Journal of Medical Informatics, 139*, 104156. https://doi.org/10.1016/j.ijmedinf.2020.104156

22. Hackman, J. R. (1969). Toward understanding the role of tasks in behavioral research. *Acta Psychologica, 31*, 97–128.

23. Ajzen, I., & Fishbein, M. (1975). *Belief, attitude, intention and behavior: An introduction to theory and research.* Addison-Wesley.

24. Khoa, B. T., & Nguyen, M. H. (2022). The moderating role of anxiety in the relationship between the perceived benefits, online trust and personal information disclosure in online shopping. *International Journal of Business and Society, 23*, 444–460. https://doi.org/10.33736/ijbs.4624.2022

25. Ajzen, I. (1991). The theory of planned behavior. *Organizational Behavior and Human Decision Processes, 50*, 179–211.

26. Zhang, Y.-B., Zhang, L.-L., & Kim, H.-K. (2021). The effect of UTAUT2 on use intention and use behavior in online learning platform. *Journal of Logistics, Informatics and Service Science, 8*, 67–81. https://doi.org/10.33168/LISS.2021.0105

27. Chao, C.-M. (2019). Factors determining the behavioral intention to use mobile learning: An application and extension of the UTAUT model. *Frontiers in psychology, 10*, 1652.

28. Dash, S., & Saji, K. (2008). The role of consumer self-efficacy and website social-presence in customers' adoption of B2C online shopping: An empirical study in the Indian context. *Journal of International Consumer Marketing, 20*, 33–48.

29. Taylor, S., & Todd, P. A. (1995). Understanding information technology usage: A test of competing models. *Information Systems Research, 6*, 144–176.

30. Ko, E., Kim, E. Y., & Lee, E. K. (2009). Modeling consumer adoption of mobile shopping for fashion products in Korea. *Psychology & Marketing, 26*, 669–687.

31. Hung, M.-C., Yang, S.-T., & Hsieh, T.-C. (2012). An examination of the determinants of mobile shopping continuance. *International Journal of Electronic Business Management, 10*, 29.

32. Lissitsa, S., & Kol, O. (2019). Four generational cohorts and hedonic m-shopping: Association between personality traits and purchase intention. *Electronic Commerce Research, 21*, 545–570. https://doi.org/10.1007/s10660-019-09381-4

33. Koufaris, M. (2002). Applying the technology acceptance model and flow theory to online consumer behavior. *Information Systems Research, 13*, 205–223.

34. Legris, P., Ingham, J., & Collerette, P. (2003). Why do people use information technology? A critical review of the technology acceptance model. *Information & Management, 40*, 191–204.

35. De Barros, A. C., Leitão, R., & Ribeiro, J. (2014). Design and evaluation of a mobile user interface for older adults: Navigation, interaction and visual design recommendations. *Procedia Computer Science, 27*, 369–378.

36. Rittichainuwat, B. N., & Chakraborty, G. (2009). Perceived travel risks regarding terrorism and disease: The case of Thailand. *Tourism Management, 30*, 410–418.

37. Yang, Y., Zhang, H., & Chen, X. (2020). Coronavirus pandemic and tourism: Dynamic stochastic general equilibrium modeling of infectious disease outbreak. *Annals of Tourism Research, 83*, 102913.

38. Bang, Y., Han, K., Animesh, A., & Hwang, M. (2013). From online to mobile: Linking consumers' online purchase behaviors with mobile commerce adoption. In *17th Pacific Asia conference on information systems, PACIS 2013.*

39. Goh, K.-Y., Chu, J., & Wu, J. (2015). Mobile advertising: An empirical study of temporal and spatial differences in search behavior and advertising response. *Journal of Interactive Marketing, 30*, 34–45.
40. Ghose, A., Goldfarb, A., & Han, S. P. (2013). How is the mobile internet different? Search costs and local activities. *Information Systems Research, 24*, 613–631.
41. Chong, A.Y.-L. (2013). Mobile commerce usage activities: The roles of demographic and motivation variables. *Technological Forecasting and Social Change, 80*, 1350–1359.
42. Baber, H. (2021). Modelling the acceptance of e-learning during the pandemic of COVID-19—A study of South Korea. *The International Journal of Management Education, 19*, 100503. https://doi.org/10.1016/j.ijme.2021.100503
43. Isakovic, M., Sedlar, U., Volk, M., & Bester, J. (2016). Usability pitfalls of diabetes mhealth apps for the elderly. *Journal of Diabetes Research, 2016*, 1604609. https://doi.org/10.1155/2016/1604609
44. Anderson, J. C., & Gerbing, D. W. (1988). Structural equation modeling in practice: A review and recommended two-step approach. *Psychological Bulletin, 103*, 411–423. https://doi.org/10.1037//0033-2909.103.3.411
45. Fornell, C., & Larcker, D. F. (2018). Evaluating structural equation models with unobservable variables and measurement error. *Journal of Marketing Research, 18*, 39–50. https://doi.org/10.1177/002224378101800104
46. Hair, J. F., Jr., Hult, G. T. M., Ringle, C., & Sarstedt, M. (2016). *A primer on partial least squares structural equation modeling (PLS-SEM).* Sage publications.
47. Hair, J. F., Risher, J. J., Sarstedt, M., & Ringle, C. M. (2019). When to use and how to report the results of PLS-SEM. *European Business Review, 31*, 2–24. https://doi.org/10.1108/ebr-11-2018-0203
48. Nguyen, M. H., & Khoa, B. T. (2021). The Google advertising service adoption behavior of enterprise in the digital transformation age. *Webology, 18*, 153–170. https://doi.org/10.14704/web/v18si02/web18064
49. Kalinic, Z., & Marinkovic, V. (2016). Determinants of users' intention to adopt m-commerce: An empirical analysis. *Information Systems and e-Business Management, 14*, 367–387.
50. Kalgotra, P., Gupta, A., & Sharda, R. (2021). Pandemic information support lifecycle: Evidence from the evolution of mobile apps during COVID-19. *Journal of Business Research, 134*, 540–559. https://doi.org/10.1016/j.jbusres.2021.06.002
51. Chan, D. K. C., Zhang, C. Q., & Weman-Josefsson, K. (2021). Why people failed to adhere to COVID-19 preventive behaviors? Perspectives from an integrated behavior change model. *Infection Control and Hospital Epidemiology, 42*, 375–376. https://doi.org/10.1017/ice.2020.245
52. Kleijnen, M., de Ruyter, K., & Wetzels, M. (2007). An assessment of value creation in mobile service delivery and the moderating role of time consciousness. *Journal of Retailing, 83*, 33–46. https://doi.org/10.1016/j.jretai.2006.10.004

Factors Influencing the Intention to Use Food Delivery Application (FDA): The Case Study of GoFood During COVID 19 Pandemic in Vietnam

Cuong Nguyen, Nhan Ha, and Nhan Nguyen

Abstract The study investigates the factors influencing customers' intention to use the GoFood application in Vietnam. The research model adopts the components of The Technology Acceptance Model (TAM) and Theory of Planned Behaviour (TPB). The sample size includes 295 respondents who are frequent customers of the GoFood application. The results show that 5 factors positively impact the intention to use the GoFood application: Subjective Norms (SN), Perceived Usefulness (PU), Perceived Ease of Use (PEU), Service Performance (SP) and Perceived Price Fairness (PPF). Subjective Norms (SN) are the most significant factor affecting the intention to use the GoFood application among Vietnamese consumers. The findings also provide some managerial implications for GoFood and other food delivery applications (FDAs) to serve customers efficiently in Vietnam.

Keywords Intention to use · GoFood · Food delivery applications · FDAs · Vietnam

1 Introduction

Online food delivery has been booming in Ho Chi Minh city and other urban areas in Vietnam. According to the Consumer Foodservice in Vietnam report, Vietnam's online food delivery market was forecasted to reach more than 38 million USD by 2020. However, there are many competitors in the online food delivery market. Some well-known applications are Now (Foody), Gojek and Grab Food in Ho Chi Minh

C. Nguyen (✉) · N. Ha
Industrial University of Ho Chi Minh City, 12 Nguyen Van Bao Street, Ward 4, Go Vap District, Ho Chi Minh City, Vietnam
e-mail: nguyenquoccuong@iuh.edu.vn

N. Ha
e-mail: Nhanntt2@fpt.edu.vn

N. Nguyen
FPT University, Block E2a-7, D1 Street Saigon Hi-tech Park, Long Thanh My Ward, District 9, Ho Chi Minh City, Vietnam

city. As a new entrant, GoFood was a new branch of Go Viet, and it was launched in Vietnam in November 2018 and Hanoi in March 2019. GoFood was developed by Gojek, which is the first Indonesian unicorn company. For consumers, GoFood can satisfy a variety of needs from consumers in terms of ordering food online. For Gojek's marketing strategy, GoFood can increase revenue with the number of orders that enter via GoFood [16]. GoFood has quickly gained a dominant position in the food delivery market. GoFood has many competitive advantages in operating online food delivery, and it has been recognised as one of the most popular apps among food delivery applications (FDAs) among customers in Vietnam. Alalwan [2] suggested that innovation channels have been applied to reach customers through mobile food ordering applications mobile and provide high-quality services to customers. Functionally, food delivery applications are used to order food from food-aggregator platforms [19]. Besides, Ray et al. [34] confirm that FDAs is an emerging online-to-offline mobile technology to help enterprises engage customers more efficiently. Sharma et al. [35] suggest that the FDA has become a popular source to order food during social distancing. Remarkably, as the Vietnamese government decided to implement social distancing in 2021, people are encouraged to stay at home, which promotes people's frequency to shop online, particularly in the big cities with a high population density. Vietnamese consumers began using FDAs to buy foods and other necessary goods online [28–30]. Furthermore, Nguyen et al. [28–30] showed that nearly 80% of the respondents in Hanoi decided to go shopping online more frequently than before the outbreak of COVID-19. The increasing use of FDAs necessitates the complexities of consumer behaviour toward them, particularly during a health crisis. As a result, this study aims to assess the factors that impact the intention to use GoFood among Vietnamese consumers during COVID-19 Pandemic.

2   Literature Review and Conceptual Framework

Tirtiroglu and Elbeck [38] defined the willingness of the customer to use the product or service as the intention to use that particular product or service. The sale of products or services can be predicted based on the intention to purchase those products or services. Ting et al. [37] insist that consumer behaviour reflects the decisions making of consumers over a while to acquire, consume, and dispose of goods. Consumer behaviour is described as individuals' reactions in the decision-making process to buy goods and services. The insight into consumer behaviour will help businesses make appropriate products, marketing, and sales strategies. According to Kotler et al., consumer behaviour is related to the consumption and disposal of goods and services, including before and after these actions. Moreover, customer behaviour studies investigate the factors influencing consumers' needs, preferences and habits.

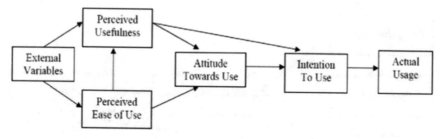

Fig. 1 TAM model [11]

2.1 Technology Acceptance Model and Theory of Planned Behavior

Davis [11] developed Technology Acceptance Model (TAM) to investigate the individuals' acceptance of new information technology (IT). His findings confirm that perceived usefulness and ease of use are essential constructs of personal acceptance (Fig. 1).

Developed from the Theory of Rational Action (TRA), the Technology Acceptance Model (TAM) was assumed that behaviour could be predicted or explained and preferred by behavioural tendencies to perform that behavior [1]. Behavioural propensity is a function that has got three factors. Firstly, depending on the outcome of performance evaluations, attitudes are conceptualized. The second component is social norms which refer to the perceived social pressure to perform or not to perform the behaviour. Finally, the perceived behavioural control factor was added to the TRA model to complete the Theory of Planned Behaviour (TPB). The perceived behavioural control describes the likelihood of performing a particular behaviour based on the availability of resources to perform that behaviour. Ajzen and Fishbein [1] confirms that behavioural control factors directly correlate with the tendency to perform the behaviour. As the perception of the degree of control is assured, perceived behavioural control also predicts the actual behavior (Fig. 2).

2.2 Hypothesis Development

Perceived Usefulness
Perceived Usefulness (PU) is derived from the TAM model. PU is widely applied to assess the intention of customers to use new services. Devis [11] defines PU as the extent to which a person believes that the intention to use a system will enhance his or her job performance. Unlike traditional services, online services are a significant motivator for consumers [17] because of their distinctive usefulness and new technology. Burke [5] confirmed that convenience was the most commonly cited factor for consumers' engagement in online services in the US. Online shoppers appreciate

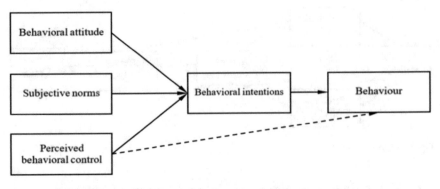

Fig. 2 TPB model [1]

the ability to access virtual stores at any convenient time, and they can perform other activities such as exercising, cooking, and taking care of the children during shopping transactions [5]. They can be used without transportation and avoid crowded parking lots or lousy weather. Online services eliminate driving and checkout time, and shoppers can access stores far away. Therefore, when consumers perceive the usefulness of new technological services, their intention to use them is more significant and vice versa. GoFood is a helpful FDA because it provides a service to the consumer, but not expected if the consumer's delivery is not met. Users can continue to use GoFood's services if they find them useful, regardless of not being satisfied with their previous intention to use them [4]. Lee et al. [23] argue that perceived usefulness affects attitude toward mobile apps in food delivery service. Choi [6] also confirms that perceived usefulness positive affects the intention to reuse food delivery applications. Besides, Dang et al. [20] insist that the most crucial factor influencing food purchases through the Internet among Vietnamese consumers is convenience. Thus, the first hypothesis is proposed:

H1: Perceived Usefulness positively affects the customers' intention to use GoFood apps.

Perceived Ease of Use
Perceived Ease of Use (PEU) refers to how an individual believes that the intention to use a specific system will be simple [11]. Hence, it dramatically affects consumers' intention to use a new technology service. When a computer user believes in performing a job on the Internet, it quickly depends on various computer interface designs, training programs, expression languages, and software installed on the computer. Potential users are more likely to accept and use innovative technology systems that are perceived as being less complicated [11]. Lee et al. [11, 23] confirm that perceived usefulness and ease of use relate to the attitudes toward mobile apps. Ray et al. [34] states that ease of use and listing were the significant antecedents of intentions to use the FDA. Choi [6] confirm that ease of use positive affects the intention to reuse food delivery application. Ease of use is regarded as a critical factor that directly impacts consumers' adoption to use new technologies. In the case

of GoFood, the company's goal is to cater to a wide range of customers. It creates an application with clear, easy-to-find interfaces, relevant content, useful functions, notifications, clear commands, and easy-to-understand commands at various income and level levels. Nguyen et al. [28–30] confirm that perceived ease of use for online food delivery positively impacts consumers' decision to use the service. Hence, the second hypothesis of this study is stated as follows:

H2: Perceived Ease of Use positively affects the customers' intention to use GoFood apps.

Subjective Norms

Smith and Carsky [36] state that the source of reference information that influences consumer intention can be classified into experienced consumers, followed by expert judgments about the product and decision purchase of consumer goods such as the company's support and consulting staff. Reference groups can help enhance consumers' intentions in choosing products and brands [9]. Subjective norms can also be described as the individual's perception of social pressures to perform or not perform a behaviour [1]. The subjective norm and behavioural decision are positively associated in both TRA and TPB models. Consumers are more willing to take advice from reference sources and adhere to a stronger subjective norm of the behaviour when they perceive a higher social expectation for a particular behaviour. The subjective norm is the most critical factor influencing the intention to engage in a particular behaviour [24, 26, 27]. Troise et al. [40] demonstrated that subjective norms significantly affect behavioural intentions. Belanche et al. [3] confirm that subjective norms positively affect the intention to use food delivery apps. Tran [39] confirmed that the subject norms positively affect the intention to use mobile apps to order foods online among Vietnamese consumers. The third hypothesis is stated as follows:

H3: Subjective Norms positively affect the customers' intention to use GoFood apps.

Perceived Price Fairness

Zeithaml [44] argues that its price concerning its quality determines the perceived value of a product or service. As the benefits of using technology outweigh the costs and positively influence the intention to use it, the price is considered positive. The manufacturer communicates the quality of the product or service to customers through the price. Manufacturers must optimize production and selling costs to lower prices, and prices must be reviewed and adjusted regularly. A product or service's price may also be quoted based on the average industry price for a comparable use and quality [24]. The price of the product or service is not required to be fixed but can be flexible according to consumer demand for the product provided by the business. Price fairness significantly impacts the intention to use the service [35]. For Vietnamese consumers, price impacts the purchasing behaviour of organic foods [26, 27]. According to Natarajan et al. [25], highly innovative users who intend to use mobile shopping applications are less price sensitive. Customers' willingness to use a service is influenced by their perception of price fairness [2, 31]. Dang et al. [20] confirm that price is one of the factors influencing food purchases through the Internet among Vietnamese consumers. Thus, the fourth hypothesis is stated as follows:

H4: Perceived Price Fairness positively affects the customers' intention to use GoFood apps.

Service Performance

Service performance is an essential factor contributing to the success of the business. However, many businesses are still struggling to improve their services and retain their customers. Negative experiences from service performance can impact customers for a long time. The majority of customers who will use the product or service always expect to fully meet their needs in many aspects of their daily life. Ray et al. [34] supports that customers experience the significant antecedents of intentions to use FDA. Alalwan [2] supports performance expectancy's role in using the FDA. Zhao and Bacao [46] also confirm that users' intention to continue using FDA is positively influenced by performance expectancy. Tran [39] confirms that food delivery hygiene positively influences mobile food delivery applications during the COVID 19 pandemic in the Vietnamese context. As a result, the final hypothesis in this study is as follows:

H5: Service Performance positively affects the customers' intention to use GoFood apps.

2.3 The Proposed Research Model

The proposed research model consists of five independent variables: perceived usefulness, Perceived ease of use, Subjective norm, perceived price fairness, and Service performance. The dependent variable is the intention to use the GoFood application (Fig. 3).

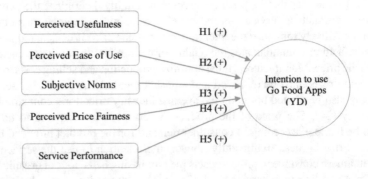

Fig. 3 Conceptual framework

3   Research Method

This study employs a quantitative research method called Exploratory Factor Analysis (EFA). The questionnaires were distributed via Google Form, and data were processed by SPSS 20.0 software. The data collection method is convenience sampling. The 5-point Likert scale measures the constructs. All items were measured by a 5-point Likert scale ranging from (1) strongly disagree to (5) strongly agree. Hair [14] suggests that the sample size for the EFA method is at least 5 times greater than the total number of observed variables. With 26 observed variables in the proposed research model, the required minimum sample size is 26 multiplied by 5 equals 130 observations. The formula to determine the minimum sample size for multivariable regression analysis is $n = 50 + 8*m$ [13]. Three hundred questionnaires were distributed in this study, but 295 valid responses were obtained. Cronbach's Alpha coefficient is used for the reliability testing of data collected. Multivariable linear regression analysis is used to assess the impact of each component on the intention to use GoFood apps among Vietnamese customers.

4   Results

4.1   Reliability Test

The Cronbach's alpha of all variables is more than 0.8, which means this study has high reliability [8] (Table 1).

The observed variables' factor loading coefficients all meet the conditions for factor analysis, which is that a factor loading coefficient of 0.55 ensures significance, so no variable is excluded. Furthermore, the KMO coefficient = 0.898 demonstrates that factor analysis is appropriate and trustworthy [15]. The significant coefficient of Bartlett's Test with sig. = 0.000 demonstrates that the results of factor analysis ensure statistical significance. The extracted total variance is 71.915 (>50%), indicating that the extracted factors explain 71.915% of the variation in the observed data, which is a

Table 1 Reliability test

Variables	Number of items	Cronbach's Alpha
Perceived ease of use	5	0.868
Perceived usefulness	4	0.843
Subjective norms	5	0.894
Perceived price fairness	3	0.805
Service performance	3	0.887
Intention to use GoFood apps	4	0.930

Table 2 Factor loading analysis

Items	Factors loading				
	1	2	3	4	5
SN4	0.800				
SN2	0.798				
SN5	0.771				
SN3	0.768				
SN1	0.737				
PEU 1		0.802			
PEU 2		0.795			
PEU 4		0.755			
PEU 5		0.695			
PEU 3		0.617			
PU 1			0.781		
PU 4			0.774		
PU 3			0.737		
PU 2			0.717		
SP3				0.810	
SP1				0.807	
SP2				0.781	
PPF1					0.853
PPF4					0.831
PPF2					0.799
Total variance explained (%)	40.711	50.947	59.927	66.596	71.915
Eigenvalues	8.142	2.047	1.796	1.334	1.064
KMO	0.898				
Sig coefficient of Bartlett's test (Sig.)	0.000				

fairly significant level. Thus, following exploratory factor analysis EFA, the observed variables retained were 20 (Table 2).

4.2 Correlation Analysis and Linear Regression

The received adjusted R^2 value is 0.599, representing the significance of seven independent variables explaining 59.9% of the change in the dependent variable. The remaining 40.1% is due to the effects of other variables not proposed in the model and the effects of random error. All variables have a linear correlation with the

Table 3 Summary of correlation analysis and linear regression

	t	β	Sig	VIF	Pearson
Constant	0.007		0.995		
Perceived usefulness (PU)	5.106	0.245	0.000	1.685	0.622
Subjective norms (SN)	5.685	0.278	0.000	1.748	0.640
Service performance (SP)	3.570	0.177	0.000	1.811	0.589
Perceived price fairness (PPF)	3.229	0.127	0.001	1.134	0.365
Perceived ease of use (PEU)	3.975	0.203	0.000	1.917	0.615
(ANOVA) sig $= 0.000$					
Adjusted $R^2 = 0.599$					
Note **$p < 0.01$					

dependent variable. The VIF values <2 satisfy the condition that there is no multi-collinearity phenomenon [15]. Variance ANOVA analysis showed that the F-value has a significance level of Sig. $= 0.000$ (<0.05). Hence, the regression model fits the collected data. All observed variables are statistically significant at a 5% significance level [14]. The following equation illustrates the relationship between independent variables and the dependent variable (Table 3):

$$YD = 0.203 * PEU + 0.245 * PU + 0.278 * SN + 0.177 * SP + 0.127 * PPF.$$

5 Conclusion

All of the hypotheses are confirmed by the findings. The results show that 5 factors positively impact the intention to use the GoFood application: Subjective Norms (SN), Perceived Usefulness (PU), Perceived Ease of Use (PEU), Service Performance (SP) and Perceived Price Fairness (PPF). Among these factors, the Subjective norm is the most decisive factor that affects the intention to use GoFood apps. Previous research has also found that subjective norms significantly impact the intention to use FDAs such as GoFood apps [3, 7, 18, 40]. In general, the COVID-19 Pandemic created a vast market space for food delivery service providers, and Vietnamese customers formed the habit to order foods online [39]. As a result, FDA has enormous potential in Vietnam even after the COVID-19 is over and consumers can resume their daily lives under the new normal. Many previous studies have found a link between perceived usefulness and intent to use FDAs [6, 7, 18, 23]. As an FDA, perceived ease of use influences the intention to use GoFood apps. This outcome is consistent with previous arguments [6, 12, 23, 43]. In Vietnam, the ease of payment for online shopping is the top priority to satisfy customers. The benefits of cashless payment have been demonstrated in cost savings and increased convenience for customers and businesses. Meanwhile, most Vietnamese consumers still prefer cash-on-delivery payments rather than online payment methods [28–30]. Furthermore, FDA developers must pay attention to service performance because it has been shown to impact the intention to use GoFood apps positively [46] . The findings align with previous studies [2, 32, 34, 46]. As a result, Perceived Price Fairness is the least important factor affecting the intention to use GoFood apps. According to Istanti et al. [16], price and promotion positively impact GoFood consumer satisfaction in Indonesia. As a result, GoFood should consider these factors when developing a marketing strategy for Vietnam. Moreover, numerous previous studies show that consumers value perceived price fairness when deciding whether or not to use FDAs such as GoFood apps [2, 25]. The findings contribute to the literature review on the intention to use food delivery apps in general and the GoFood app. Because this study used a convenient sampling method in Vietnam, it may not be highly representative of other Asian countries. To improve the generalizability, further studies should increase the scope of data collection, apply the probability sample method, and include factors influencing behavioural intentions such as attitude toward GoFood apps and perceived risk of using GoFood apps.

References

1. Ajzen, I., & Fishbein, M. (1977). Attitude-behaviour relations: A theoretical analysis and review of empirical research. *Psychological Bulletin, 84*(5), 888.
2. Alalwan, A. A. (2020). Mobile food ordering apps: An empirical study of the factors affecting customer e-satisfaction and continued intention to reuse. *International Journal of Information Management, 50*, 28–44.
3. Belanche, D., Flavián, M., & Pérez-Rueda, A. (2020). Mobile apps use and wom in the food delivery sector: The role of planned behavior, perceived security and customer lifestyle compatibility. *Sustainability, 12*(10), 4275.
4. Bhattacherjee, A. (2001). Understanding information systems continuance: An expectation-confirmation model. *MIS Quarterly*, 351–370.
5. Burke, R. R. (1997). Do you see what I see? The future of virtual shopping. *Journal of the Academy of marketing Science, 25*(4), 352–360.
6. Choi, J. C. (2020). User familiarity and satisfaction with food delivery mobile apps. *SAGE Open, 10*(4), 2158244020970563.
7. Chong, A. Y. L., Chan, F. T., & Ooi, K. B. (2012). Predicting consumer decisions to adopt mobile commerce: Cross country empirical examination between China and Malaysia. *Decision support systems, 53*(1), 34–43.
8. Cronbach, L. J. (1971). Test validation. *Educational measurement*.
9. Dai, H., & Palvi, P. C. (2009). Mobile commerce adoption in China and the United States: A cross-cultural study. *ACM SIGMIS Database: The DATABASE for Advances in Information Systems, 40*(4), 43–61.
10. Davis, F. D. (1985). *A technology acceptance model for empirically testing new end-user information systems: Theory and results* (Doctoral dissertation, Massachusetts Institute of Technology).
11. Davis, F. D. (1989). Perceived usefulness, perceived ease of use, and user acceptance of information technology. *MIS quarterly*, 319–340; Fishbein, M., & Ajzen, I. (1975). *Belief, attitude, intention and behavior: An introduction to theory and research*, Addison-Wesley.

12. Faziharudean, T. M., & Li-Ly, T. (2011). Consumers behavioral intentions to use mobile data services in Malaysia. *African Journal of Business Management, 5*(5), 1811–1821.
13. Green, S. B. (1991). How many subjects does it take to do a regression analysis. *Multivariate Behavioral Research, 26*(3), 499–510.
14. Hair, J. F. (2009). Multivariate data analysis.
15. Hoang, T., & Chu, N. (2008). Phân tích dữ liệu nghiên cứu với Spss, TP.HCM: NXB: Đại học Công Nghiệp TP.HCM.
16. Istanti, E., Sanusi, R., & Daengs, G. S. (2020). Impacts of price, promotion and go food consumer satisfaction in faculty of economic and business students of Bhayangkara University Surabaya. *Ekspektra: Jurnal Bisnis dan Manajemen, 4*(02), 104–120.
17. Jarvenpaa, S. L., & Todd, P. A. (1996). Consumer reactions to electronic shopping on the World Wide Web. *International Journal of electronic commerce, 1*(2), 59–88.
18. Kalinic, Z., & Marinkovic, V. (2016). Determinants of users' intention to adopt m-commerce: An empirical analysis. *Information Systems and e-Business Management, 14*(2), 367–387.
19. Kaur, P., Dhir, A., Talwar, S., & Ghuman, K. (2021). The value proposition of food delivery apps from the perspective of theory of consumption value. *International Journal of Contemporary Hospitality Management*.
20. Kim Dang, A., Xuan Tran, B., Tat Nguyen, C., Thi Le, H., Thi Do, H., Duc Nguyen, H., Hoang Nguyen, L., Huu Nguyen, T., Thi Mai, H., Dinh Tran, T., Ngo, C., Minh Vu, T. T., Latkin, C., Zhang, M., & Ho, R. (2018). Consumer preference and attitude regarding online food products in Hanoi, Vietnam. *International Journal of Environmental Research and Public Health, 15*(5), 981.
21. Kotler, P., & Lee, N. (2008). *Social marketing: Influencing behaviors for good*. Sage.
22. Krueger, N. F., & Carsrud, A. L. (1993). Entrepreneurial intentions: Applying the theory of planned behaviour. *Entrepreneurship & Regional Development, 5*(4), 315–330.
23. Lee, E. Y., Lee, S. B., & Jeon, Y. J. J. (2017). Factors influencing the behavioral intention to use food delivery apps. *Social Behavior and Personality: An International Journal, 45*(9), 1461–1473.
24. Michael, H. M, Malviya, S., Saluja, D., Singh, M., & Singh Thakur, A. (2013). A Study on the factors influencing consumer's purchase decision towards smartphones in Indore. *International Journal of ASPanced Research in Computer Science and Management Studies, 1*(6).
25. Natarajan, T., Balasubramanian, S. A., & Kasilingam, D. L. (2017). Understanding the intention to use mobile shopping applications and its influence on price sensitivity. *Journal of Retailing and Consumer Services, 37*, 8–22.
26. Nguyen, C. Q., Tran, P., & Nguyen, M. (2020). Factors that motivate young people's intention to undergo cosmetic surgery in Vietnam. *International Journal of Pharmaceutical and Healthcare Marketing*.
27. Nguyen, C., Nguyen, Y., & Quy, T. (2020). Organic foods: What are the driving factors of purchase intention? *Depression, 13*(11), 400–418.
28. Nguyen, C., Tran, D., Nguyen, A., & Nguyen, N. (2021). The effects of perceived risks on food purchase intention: The case study of online shopping channels during covid-19 pandemic in Vietnam. *Journal of Distribution Science, 19*(9).
29. Nguyen, M. H., Armoogum, J., & Nguyen Thi, B. (2021). Factors affecting the growth of e-shopping over the COVID-19 era in Hanoi, Vietnam. *Sustainability, 13*(16), 9205.
30. Nguyen, N. B. T., Lin, G. H., & Dang, T. T. (2021). Fuzzy multi-criteria decision-making approach for online food delivery (OFD) companies evaluation and selection: A case study in Vietnam. *Processes, 9*(8), 1274.
31. Nguyen, N. M., & Nguyen, H. T. (2019). How do product involvement and prestige sensitivity affect price acceptance on the mobile phone market in Vietnam?. *Journal of Asia Business Studies*.
32. Okumus, B., Ali, F., Bilgihan, A., & Ozturk, A. B. (2018). Psychological factors influencing customers' acceptance of smartphone diet apps when ordering food at restaurants. *International Journal of Hospitality Management, 72*, 67–77.

33. Peterson, R. A. (1994). A meta-analysis of Cronbach's coefficient alpha. *Journal of Consumer Research, 21*(2), 381–391.
34. Ray, A., Dhir, A., Bala, P. K., & Kaur, P. (2019). Why do people use food delivery apps (FDA)? A uses and gratification theory perspective. *Journal of Retailing and Consumer Services, 51*, 221–230.
35. Sharma, R., Dhir, A., Talwar, S., & Kaur, P. (2021). Over-ordering and food waste: The use of food delivery apps during a pandemic. *International Journal of Hospitality Management, 96*, 102977.
36. Smith, M. F., & Carsky, M. L. (1996). Grocery shopping behavior A comparison of involved and uninvolved consumers. *Journal of Retailing and Consumer Services, 3*(2), 73–80.
37. Ting, H., Thaichon, P., Chuah, F., & Tan, S. R. (2019). Consumer behaviour and disposition decisions: The why and how of smartphone disposition. *Journal of Retailing and Consumer Services, 51*, 212–220.
38. Tirtiroglu, E., & Elbeck, M. (2008). Qualifying purchase intentions using queueing theory. *Journal of applied quantitative methods, 3*(2), 167–178.
39. Tran, V. D. (2021). Using mobile food delivery applications during the COVID-19 pandemic: Applying the theory of planned behavior to examine continuance behavior. *Sustainability, 13*(21), 12066.
40. Troise, C., O'Driscoll, A., Tani, M., & Prisco, A. (2020). Online food delivery services and behavioural intention—A test of an integrated TAM and TPB framework. *British Food Journal*.
41. Wang, C. C., & Yang, H. W. (2006). Passion and dependency in online shopping activities. *CyberPsychology & Behavior, 10*(2), 296–298.
42. Wei, T. T., Marthandan, G., Chong, A. Y. L., Ooi, K. B., & Arumugam, S. (2009). What drives Malaysian m-commerce adoption? An empirical analysis. *Industrial Management & Data Systems*.
43. Zarmpou, T., Saprikis, V., Markos, A., & Vlachopoulou, M. (2012). Modeling users' acceptance of mobile services. *Electronic Commerce Research, 12*(2), 225–248.
44. Zeithaml, V. A. (1988). Consumer perceptions of price, quality, and value: A means-end model and synthesis of evidence. *Journal of Marketing, 52*(3), 2–22.
45. Zhang, J., & Breugelmans, E. (2012). The impact of an item-based loyalty program on consumer purchase behavior. *Journal of Marketing research, 49*(1), 50–65.
46. Zhao, Y., & Bacao, F. (2020). What factors determining customer continuingly using food delivery apps during 2019 novel coronavirus pandemic period? *International journal of hospitality management, 91*, 102683.

Digitization of Education in Vietnam in the Crisis of COVID-19 Pandemic

Tra My Nguyen

Abstract In dealing with the global pandemic, many sectors have extensive crisis management research to lean on but education has been virtually overlooked. With the recent global pandemic, the role of Internet of Things has been greater than ever before as most of economic activities have moved to online platforms. Education sector is one of the most heavily impacted where the immediate effect of lockdowns has been closure of schools, universities, colleges. Lockdowns sprung on everyone and everything, not just mode of studies, but also wellbeing, course effectiveness, student tuition, teacher's income. Despite the ever-presiding change resistance in academia, digitization of education took place almost instantaneously. The COVID-19 pandemic acted as an accelerator for education digital transformation utilizing a wide variety of digital solutions to facilitate classroom teaching and learning. Through a survey of 913 Vietnamese students, this study seeks to explore the digitization of education in Vietnam and its implications on Vietnamese students. The author expects to explore the students' readiness for digital transformation and their utilization of IoT in higher education through a quantitative regression analysis. Results show that students' readiness for digital transformation is positively correlated with all four independent factors and in the following respective order of importance: COVID-19, self-study ability, perceived ease of use, perceived usefulness and attitude.

Keywords COVID-19 pandemic · Higher education · Digitization · Internet of Things · Diffusion of innovations theory

1 Introduction

The establishment of the 'new normal' has integrated into all lives world-wide due to the COVID-19 global pandemic. The effects have been paramount and almost no area of the global economy has been left unaffected. This chapter aims to illustrate how

T. M. Nguyen (✉)
CMC University, 11 Duy Tan, Hanoi, Vietnam
e-mail: ngtramy79@gmail.com

© The Author(s), under exclusive license to Springer Nature Singapore Pte Ltd. 2023 145
N. H. Thuan et al. (eds.), *Information Systems Research in Vietnam*,
https://doi.org/10.1007/978-981-19-3804-7_10

students have coped with the transformed mode of studying in Vietnam and the role of Internet of Things (IoT) in facilitating online learning experience. In dealing with the global pandemic, many sectors have extensive crisis management research to lean on but education has been virtually overlooked. This chapter contributes to existing literature through insights into online education in a COVID-19 world. The pandemic has impacted many people and organizations across many countries around the world. The unfortunate reality of the outbreak, which has caused many losses and suffering, has acted almost as a catalyst for digitization of most areas in the global economy. It is hard to name a sector which stayed unaffected by the COVID-19 pandemic. All spheres of public life ranging from travelling, sports, entertainment, business and politics, religious gatherings, social events, education, research, networking, and many others have fallen in distress as a result of the worldwide challenging circumstances. As of October 2021, reports show almost 830 thousand cases of coronavirus patients in Vietnam, among which there have been over 20 thousand deaths and almost 760 thousand recoveries [9].

The IoT is widely defined as the vast connection network between all digital devices and the Internet. Users merely need an electronic device to be able to access infinite world of virtual resources. The benefits of IoT have been compared to a wave of change, opportunities, and possibilities [3]. Prior to the outbreak of COVID-19, IoT was already believed to be the future of education [1]. However, with the recent global pandemic, the role of IoT has been greater than ever before as most of economic activities have moved to online platforms. Education sector is one of the most heavily impacted where the immediate effect of lockdowns has been closure of schools, universities, colleges. Many campuses have been turned into field hospitals to aid the healthcare's capacity in dealing with the pandemic. Working remotely through the Internet has become the 'new norm' and the importance of making online learning one of the key pillar strategies of every university has been demonstrated by the stressful experience of most students and faculties who faced the transition to online teaching [8].

Researchers claim that the hardest-hit sector is the education sector [5] because of the significant and long-term nature of impact. Most economic activities had to move online including education. Excluding time periods of delay in education, whilst lessons continued to be conducted in line with rescheduled timetables and syllabi, the effectiveness of such activities was a major cause for concern. Using syllabi in Vietnamese schools and universities is an unreliable method of quality control as academics admit they do not always update and follow the syllabus very diligently. Márquez-Ramos [4] viewed the digitization of education as a tool to bridge the gap between academia and industry. Education trilemma has come into question specifically in light of the outbreak, that is, balancing teaching, research, and industry-oriented activities. It is important to note that digitization of education has always been a slow process due to the widely known change resistance of institutions as well as academics. April 2020 marked the start of social distancing and nationwide lock-downs in Vietnam due to the sudden spread of coronavirus from Wuhan (mainland China). Students had to remain home, schools were forced to close, majority of labor force was mandated to work from home. Institutions quickly realized that in order to stay afloat, they had to move digital. Digital education and remote work became the new norm. Despite the ever-presiding change resistance in academia, digitization of education took place almost instantaneously. The COVID-19 pandemic acted as an accelerator for education digital transformation utilizing a wide variety of digital solutions to facilitate classroom teaching and learning. This transformation impacts numerous stakeholders but the key players are students and teachers. They are the main contributors to the digital education implementation. Online learning is neither novel nor revolutionary strategy, nevertheless, education in Vietnam had never been forced to switch to online form overnight before, which presented considerable challenges. This study seeks to explore the digitization of education in Vietnam and its implications on Vietnamese students in terms of readiness and IoT utilization.

Similar to many other countries around the world, Vietnamese education faced a switch to online-only learning mode almost overnight. It is expected that students would encounter challenges and the quality of teaching and learning would be significantly reduced at the early stages of transition. This study explores students' readiness for digital transformation and their utilization of IoT in higher education. Lockdowns sprung on everyone and everything, not just mode of studies, but also wellbeing, course effectiveness, student tuition, teacher's income, and many more. Being an experimental study which replicates previous studies from other countries, this paper specifically looks at the readiness for digital transformation in light of COVID-19 pandemic in Vietnam.

Diffusion of Innovations theory [7], which first originated in 1962, has been adopted as theoretical framework in this study as it provides grounds for entry of a significant social change such as online higher education and examines its implications and effects on the members of society such as students. The version used for this paper is the fourth edition and revision of the original work which accounts for a broader foundation of diffusion, new concepts, new viewpoints. According to the theory, there are five adopter categories whose eagerness to adopt new ideas and innovation decline in the following order: innovators, early adopters, early majority, late majority, and laggards. In examining students' readiness for digital transformation of education in Vietnam, the ground understanding must be about the diffusion process when all education moved online and the ultimate characteristics of the key players in this social change—students.

2 Methodology

2.1 Research Objective

In light of transition from traditional face-to-face to unprecedented online classes, the aim of this study is to assess students' readiness for digital transformation through 6 dimensions: perceived usefulness, perceived ease of use, attitude, self-study ability, COVID-19, and students' readiness for digital transformation.

2.2 Research Method

Secondary Mendeley dataset has been used for this research: a survey administered to Vietnamese students [6] in Vietnam. The survey consisted of 28 questions divided into two parts. Part 1 aimed to assess students' readiness for digital transformation through 6 dimensions (perceived usefulness, perceived ease of use, attitude, self-study ability, COVID-19, and students' readiness for digital transformation), each containing between 3 and 5 items, and one dichotomous question about whether higher education should change towards digital transformation. Part 2 enquired participants' personal information such as sex, academic year, major, tuition, and living area to ensure no response duplication. The 6 dimensions (see Table 1) were presented as 5-point Likert scale statements where participants were required to indicate their level of agreement by choosing among 1 for Strongly Disagree through to 5 for Strongly Agree. The survey was distributed to students nationwide and 913 valid responses were collected. The survey data was processed and analyzed using SPSS.

2.3 Hypothesis Development

Each of the five independent variables are tested against the dependent variable (Student's readiness for digital transformation). The independent variables PU and ATT have been combined as per the EFA that follows in Sect. 3.2. The resulting hypotheses are as follows:

HO	There is no significant linear correlation
H1	Perceived usefulness and attitude is positively correlated with student's readiness for digital transformation
H2	Perceived ease of use is positively correlated with student's readiness for digital transformation
H3	COVID-19 is positively correlated with student's readiness for digital transformation
H4	Self-study ability is positively correlated with student's readiness for digital transformation

3 Data Analysis and Discussion

3.1 Demographic Data

Regarding gender of participants, the study includes 281 (30.8%) males, 631 (69.1%) females, and 1 (0.1%) other as self-identified. Among 913 surveyed students, the

Table 1 Survey dimensions

1. *Perceived usefulness*
The online learning system helps me absorb knowledge more effectively
The online learning system helps me improve my academic results
The online learning system makes me more proactive in learning
2. *Perceived ease of use*
I suppose that it is easy for me to learn how to use the online learning system
I suppose that the online learning system very easy to use
I believe that it is easy for me to competently use online learning systems
3. *Attitude*
I suppose that it is necessary to use an online learning system
I support the use of an online learning system
I suppose that using online learning is a good idea
I feel very excited when using an online learning system
4. *Self-study ability*
I always actively interact with the lecturers during class
I always actively participate in learning activities and do group exercises
I always actively arrange my own schedule
5. *COVID-19*
COVID-19 has helped me approach digital transformation in learning
COVID-19 has helped me adapt to the shift in learning methods
COVID-19 has helped me feel excited about the new learning method
COVID-19 has helped me more proactive and self-disciplined in studying
6. *Student's readiness for digital transformation*
I have been ready to acquire knowledge more proactively
I have proactively absorbed knowledge through digital platforms
I have proactively interacted with lecturers through digital platforms
I have proactively searched for learning materials through digital platforms
I have proficiently used digital platforms for learning and discussion

highest proportion are second-years constituting 38.9% (355 observations), then 240 (26.3%) freshmen, 239 (26.2%) third-years, 46 (5%) fourth-years, and 33 (3.6%) above the fourth year. In terms of tuition fee that the students are paying, the answers ranged from under 15 million VND per year to over 300 million VND per year, where the higher proportion (30.4%) belongs to those paying under 15 million VND, 27.7% pay from 15 to 30 million VND, 19.5% pay from 30 to 50 million VND, 3.9% pay from 100 to 300 million VND, and 3% pay over 300 million VND per year. In terms of living area, 716 (78.4%) come from urban areas where as 197 (21.6%) come from suburban areas.

3.2 Measurement Validity

The measurement scale is assessed and validated using the Cronbach's Alpha reliability coefficient to test the correlation coefficient and the relationship between variables. Exploratory Factor Analysis (EFA) is used to examine the interaction between measurement variables in each factor.

Cronbach's Alpha. The test of reliability shows the Cronbach's Alpha coefficients for Perceived Usefulness (PU), Perceived Ease of Use (PEOU), Attitude (ATT), Self-Study Ability (SSA), COVID-19 (COVID), and Students' Readiness for Digital Transformation (CHA) are above the threshold 0.6 (Table …), which imply that the measurement scales are reliable. Particularly in the PU scale, if PU3 is deleted, the Cronbach's Alpha is increased to 0.826, therefore this item is deleted from analysis. The measurement model includes 6 factors: Perceived Usefulness (PU), Perceived Ease of Use (PEOU), Attitude (ATT), Self-Study Ability (SSA), COVID-19 (COVID), and Students' Readiness for Digital Transformation (CHA). These factors are hereafter included in the EFA analysis (Table 2).

Exploratory Factor Analysis. The extraction method for this EFA analysis is Principal components method with Varimax rotation. The model includes 6 scales with 16 observed variables of 5 independent factors, and 5 observed variables of 1 dependent factor that meets the reliability requirements. Variables with a factor loading above 0.5 will be retained and the Cumulative Variance Explained must be greater than 50% [2]. The KMO measure of sampling adequacy must meet the conditions of $0.5 \leq KMO \leq 1$ and Bartlett's test of sphericity must show statistical significance with p-value less than 0.05 [10]. The EFA in this section is performed for each type of variables (dependent and independent) separately for clarity in presentation and for ease of discussion. However, to ensure that the variables are indeed distinct, a quick factor analysis had been performed prior and showed a distinct pattern mix presented in Fig. 1.

Factor analysis for independent variables. 16 observed variables represent 5 independent factors affecting Student's readiness for digital transformation that are reliable enough to conduct a factor analysis. Results show that all observed variables

Table 2 Cronbach's alpha coefficients

Variables	Scale mean if item deleted	Scale variance if item deleted	Corrected item-total correlation	Cronbach's alpha if item deleted
Perceived usefulness (PU), Cronbach's alpha = 0.826				
PU1	3.33	0.987	0.704	
PU2	3.33	0.929	0.704	
Perceived ease of use (PEOU), Cronbach's alpha = 0.887				
PEOU1	7.89	2.754	0.770	0.849
PEOU2	7.90	2.630	0.820	0.804
PEOU3	7.81	2.776	0.752	0.865
Attitude (ATT), Cronbach's alpha = 0.894				
ATT1	11.03	7.384	0.706	0.886
ATT2	11.09	6.637	0.815	0.846
ATT3	11.05	6.600	0.815	0.846
ATT4	11.38	6.357	0.743	0.877
Self-study ability (SSA), Cronbach's alpha = 0.788				
SSA1	7.54	2.744	0.591	0.756
SSA2	7.17	2.757	0.683	0.653
SSA3	7.09	2.934	0.615	0.726
COVID-19 (COVID), Cronbach's alpha = 0.848				
COVID1	11.04	6.839	0.652	0.822
COVID2	11.05	6.533	0.727	0.793
COVID3	11.55	5.915	0.715	0.794
COVID4	11.57	5.921	0.670	0.818
Student's readiness (CHA), Cronbach's alpha = 0.912				
CHA1	15.54	9.284	0.798	0.888
CHA2	15.57	9.320	0.828	0.882
CHA3	15.85	9.251	0.699	0.910
CHA4	15.55	9.283	0.786	0.890
CHA5	15.64	9.227	0.780	0.891

satisfy the factor loading threshold criteria and are above 0.5. The ATT (Attitude) and PU (Perceived Usefulness) variables loaded on the same factor, which is deemed reasonable and acceptable. Therefore, the measurement model now has 16 observed variables representing 4 independent factors to best explain the students' readiness for digital transformation. The KMO measure of sampling adequacy is at 0.903 which means that factor analysis is well suited with the actual data. Bartlett's test of sphericity has a p-value of 0.0000, which satisfies the threshold criteria, concluding that the observed variables are correlated within each factor. The Cumulative Variance Explained is 72.179% > 50% signifying that the observed variables explain

Fig. 1 Factor analysis
loaded together

Rotated Component Matrix^a

	Component				
	1	2	3	4	5
ATT4	.797				
PU1	.780				
PU2	.758				
ATT2	.688				
ATT3	.663				
ATT1	.580				
CHA2		.806			
CHA4		.778			
CHA5		.767			
CHA1		.749			
CHA3		.733			
PEOU2			.835		
PEOU1			.810		
PEOU3			.786		
COVID2				.814	
COVID1				.794	
COVID3				.627	
COVID4				.575	
SSA1					.787
SSA2					.766
SSA3					.686

Extraction Method: Principal Component Analysis.
Rotation Method: Varimax with Kaiser Normalization. ^a

a. Rotation converged in 7 iterations.

72.179% changes in factors. Pattern matrix as per Table 3 shows factor loadings of observed variables all satisfy the threshold criteria ≥ 0.5. The number of factors loaded is 4 with 16 observed variables.

Factor analysis for dependent variable. The KMO measure of sampling adequacy is at 0.876 satisfying the $0.5 \leq KMO \leq 1$ threshold criteria signifying that factor analysis is well suited with the actual data. Bartlett's test of sphericity has a p-value of $0.0000 < 0.05$, which satisfies the threshold criteria, concluding that the observed variables are correlated within the factor. Cumulative Variance Explained as per component row 1 in Table 4 is $74.387\% > 50\%$ signifying that 74.387% of factor changes are explained by observed variables. Exploratory factor analysis pattern mix showed that the factor loadings of observed variables all satisfy the threshold criteria of ≥ 0.5, producing a single factor with no excluded items (see Table 5).

Overall, the research model and measurement scales post-EFA include 4 independent factors affecting Students' Readiness for Digital Transformation and 1 dependent factor being the Student's Readiness. Figure 2 presents such model.

Table 3 Pattern matrix (independent variables)

	Component			
	1	2	3	4
ATT4	0.797			
PU1	0.794			
PU2	0.765			
ATT2	0.686			
ATT3	0.663			
ATT1	0.574			
PEOU2		0.849		
PEOU1		0.828		
PEOU3		0.820		
COVID2			0.841	
COVID1			0.795	
COVID3			0.674	
COVID4			0.632	
SSA2				0.804
SSA1				0.788
SSA3				0.754

Table 4 Cumulative variance explained (dependent variable)

Component	Initial eigenvalues			Extraction sums of squared loadings		
	Total	% of variance	Cumulative %	Total	% of variance	Cumulative %
1	3.719	74.387	74.387	3.719	74.387	74.387
2	0.438	8.754	83.142			
3	0.374	7.483	90.624			
4	0.273	5.468	96.092			
5	0.195	3.908	100.000			

Extraction method: principal component analysis

Table 5 Pattern mix (dependent variable)

	Component
	1
CHA2	0.898
CHA1	0.878
CHA4	0.869
CHA5	0.863
CHA3	0.801

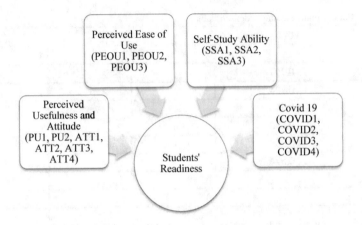

Fig. 2 Measurement model

3.3 Regression Model

Significance of Correlation Coefficient. After the reliability test of measurement scale, extracted factors are included in the model testing. The factor value is the average value of component variables in each factor. Prior to model testing, Pearson's correlation coefficient is used to measure the strength of a linear association between independent and dependent variables. Table 6 shows the correlation matrix between factors. Independent variables PUandATT, PEOU, COVID, SSA, and dependent variable Student's readiness are all statistically significant at 99% (sign < 0.001). The R value between dependent variable and independent variables ranges from 0.526 to 0.611. The four independent variables PUandATT, PEOU, COVID, and SSA are suitable for inclusion in the model to explain the dependent variable (Student's readiness for digital transformation).

Estimation of Regression Model. The independent variables are correlated with the dependent variable and are suitable for inclusion in the model to explain the dependent variable (Students' readiness for digital transformation). The following multivariate linear regression model is proposed:

$$CHA = \beta 1 + \beta 1 \, PUandATT + \beta 2 \, PEOU + \beta 3 \, COVID + \beta 4 \, SSA$$

where variables are derived by averaging method as follows:

CHA   (CHA1 + CHA2 + CHA3 + CHA4 + CHA5)/5
PUandATT (PU1 + PU2 + ATT1 + ATT2 + ATT3 + ATT4)/6
PEOU   (PEOU1 + PEOU2 + PEOU3)/3
SSA   (SSA1 + SSA2 + SSA3)/3
COVID   (COVID1 + COVID2 + COVID3 + COVID4)/4

Table 6 Correlations

		PUandATT	PEOU	COVID	SSA	CHA
PUandATT	Pearson correlation	1	0.530^{**}	0.627^{**}	0.496^{**}	0.562^{**}
	Sig. (2-tailed)		0.000	0.000	0.000	0.000
	N	913	913	913	913	913
PEOU	Pearson correlation	0.530^{**}	1	0.454^{**}	0.408^{**}	0.526^{**}
	Sig. (2-tailed)	0.000		0.000	0.000	0.000
	N	913	913	913	913	913
COVID	Pearson correlation	0.627^{**}	0.454^{**}	1	0.470^{**}	0.611^{**}
	Sig. (2-tailed)	0.000	0.000		0.000	0.000
	N	913	913	913	913	913
SSA	Pearson correlation	0.496^{**}	0.408^{**}	0.470^{**}	1	0.573^{**}
	Sig. (2-tailed)	0.000	0.000	0.000		0.000
	N	913	913	913	913	913
CHA	Pearson correlation	0.562^{**}	0.526^{**}	0.611^{**}	0.573^{**}	1
	Sig. (2-tailed)	0.000	0.000	0.000	0.000	
	N	913	913	913	913	913

** Correlation is significant at the 0.01 level (2-tailed)

Regression Model Discussion. Table 7 presents the regression coefficient results, where all variables are statistically significant with p-value ≤ 0.05. The regression results show a positive correlation of all four independent variables with the dependent variable (Students' readiness for digital transformation). The following regression model equation shows the correlation between the independent variables (with unstandardized beta regression coefficient):

$$CHA = 0.689 + 0.113 * PUandATT + 0.194 * PEOU$$
$$+ 0.285 * COVID + 0.269 * SSA$$

Table 7 Coefficients

Model		Unstandardized coefficients		Standardized coefficients	t	Sig	Collinearity statistics	
		B	Std. error	Beta			Tolerance	VIF
1	(Constant)	0.689	0.104		6.623	0.000		
	PUandATT	0.113	0.031	0.118	3.672	0.000	0.504	1.983
	PEOU	0.194	0.026	0.207	7.452	0.000	0.676	1.479
	COVID	0.285	0.028	0.309	10.153	0.000	0.562	1.780
	SSA	0.269	0.026	0.284	10.384	0.000	0.694	1.441

[a] Dependent variable: CHA

Table 8 Hypothesis testing

Hypothesis		Result
H0	There is no significant linear correlation	Rejected
H1	Perceived usefulness and attitude is positively correlated with student's readiness for digital transformation	Accepted
H2	Perceived ease of use is positively correlated with student's readiness for digital transformation	Accepted
H3	COVID 19 is positively correlated with Student's readiness for digital transformation	Accepted
H4	Self-study ability is positively correlated with Student's readiness for digital transformation	Accepted

Hypothesis Testing. Based on the regression results, Table 8 presents the hypothesis testing results of the research model.

Regression Model Fit. The R squared has been adjusted for the number of predictors in the research model and $R^2 = 0.525$ (sig < 0.001) means that 52.5% of the change in the dependent variable (Students' readiness for digital transformation) can be explained by the regression model with 4 independent variables (Table 9).

Variable Importance Order. The standardized regression coefficient and the variables' contribution to the model are presented in Table 10. The following conclusions regarding the variables' importance order can be drawn about how they affect the dependent variable (Students' readiness for digital transformation): COVID-19 has the biggest effect on Students' readiness for digital transformation. Self-Study Ability has the second biggest effect on Students' readiness for digital transformation. Perceived Ease of Use has the third biggest effect on Students' readiness for digital transformation. Perceived Usefulness and Attitude have the least effect on Students' readiness for digital transformation.

Table 9 Adjusted R^2

R	R^2	Adjusted R^2	Std. error of the estimate	Durbin-Watson
0.726[a]	0.527	0.525	0.51906	1.933

Table 10 Variable importance order

Code	Variable	Standardized beta	%	Order of importance
PUandATT	Perceived usefulness and attitude	0.118	12.85	4
PEOU	Perceived ease of use	0.207	22.52	3
COVID	COVID-19	0.309	33.66	1
SSA	Self-study ability	0.284	30.97	2
Total		0.919	100	

3.4 Discussion

Results show that students' readiness for digital transformation is positively corre-lated with all four independent factors and in the following respective order of importance: COVID-19, self-study ability, perceived ease of use, perceived useful-ness and attitude. These results align with the general understanding in Vietnamese culture where the importance of external factors (such as a pandemic) would precede internal factors such as abilities, skills, and attitude. Partly it reflects the collectivist culture of Vietnam and effectively the "late majority" adopter category in which Viet-namese students would fall into. The majority of social players tend to be skeptical of any drastic changes and would only justify changing once it has been tried by majority. The most effective strategy to motivate this type of society to successfully embrace change (such as digitization of education) is to publicly broadcast statistics of successful adoption of online learning, both domestically and internationally.

4 Conclusion and Recommendations

This study sheds light on the digitization of education in Vietnam in the crisis of COVID-19 pandemic from the perspective of university students, who are the most affected by the sudden shift to online learning. Quantitative data analysis shows that all factors namely COVID-19, Self-Study ability, Perceived ease of use, Perceived usefulness and attitude, in such order, impact how students cope with the transition. This study hints upon a strategic recommendation to aid a smooth and successful digital transformation of education, most important of all being to focus on providing information on how many countries, schools, students, households, etc. have tried and successfully adopted online learning. For "late majority" adopters, this type of information would most appeal and convince of the importance for change and innovation. Recommendations for further research include the exploration of estab-lishing hybrid campuses (online and offline) for times of crises such as the COVID-19 pandemic, whether COVID-19 pandemic can be seen as an accelerator for digitiza-tion of education as a whole, and investigating into ways in which COVID-19 and its challenges can actually help improve digitization of higher education in Vietnam.

References

1. Aldowah, H, Rehman, S. U., Ghazal, S., & Umar, I. N. (2017). Internet of Things in higher education: A study on future learning. 012017.
2. Anderson, J. C., & Gerbing, D. W. (1988). Structural equation modeling in practice: A review and recommended two-step approach. *Psychological Bulletin, 103*(3), 411.
3. Gul, S., Asif, M., Ahmad, S., Yasir, M., Majid, M., Malik, M. S. A., & Arshad, S. (2017). A survey on role of internet of things in education. *International Journal of Computer Science and Network Security, 17*(5), 159–165.

4. Márquez-Ramos, L. (2021). Does digitalization in higher education help to bridge the gap between academia and industry? An application to COVID-19. *Industry and Higher Education, 36*, 0950422221989190.
5. Onyema, E. M., Eucheria, N. C., Obafemi, F. A., Sen, S., Atonye, F. G., Sharma, A., & Alsayed, A. O. (2020). Impact of Coronavirus pandemic on education. *Journal of Education and Practice, 11*(13), 108–121.
6. Pham, H., Tran, Q. N., La, G. L., Doan, H. M., & Vu, T. D. (2021). Readiness for digital transformation of higher education in the Covid-19 context: The dataset of Vietnam's students.
7. Rogers, E. M. (2010). *Diffusion of innovations.* Simon and Schuster.
8. Sangster, A., Stoner, G., & Flood, B. (2020). Insights into accounting education in a COVID-19 world. *Accounting Education, 29*(5), 431–562.
9. Worldometers. (2021). https://www.worldometers.info/coronavirus/country/viet-nam/?ref=upstract.com&curator=upstract.com&utm_source=upstract.com. last accessed 01/11/2021.
10. Yong, A. G., & Pearce, S. (2013). A beginner's guide to factor analysis: Focusing on exploratory factor analysis. *Tutorials in Quantitative Methods for Psychology, 9*(2), 79–94.

Printed in the United States
by Baker & Taylor Publisher Services